Screenwriting
is Filmmaking

Brian Dunnigan offers a wealth of experience and knowledge in the field of screenwriting.

Robyn Slovo

In the beginning was The Word. Brian Dunnigan has brilliantly encapsulated the profound dependency all filmmaking has on the ideas that arise from a well written screenplay. *Screenwriting is Filmmaking* is an invaluable resource for anyone facing the task of making a film. I cannot commend it enough.

Iain Smith

Screenwriting is Filmmaking is the book I have been looking for! Uniquely tracing the origins of screenwriting up to present day, it gives an unsurpassed context for contemporary film writing. Whether a skilled professional or aspiring student, you will find this an invaluable tool in developing your script writing skills and turning your ideas into a screenplay.

Sandy Lieberson

Often a screenplay is thought of as an ends to a means. It is neither an image nor is it a piece of literature. Yet it is imperative to the success of a film. In *Screenwriting is Filmmaking*, Brian Dunnigan helps shed light on the symbiotic relationship between the two. Brian has a profound understanding of the craft, and his emphasis on story and character is essential reading for anyone wanting to uncover the beating heart of their own screenplay.

Gonzalo Maza

Screenwriting is Filmmaking

THE THEORY AND PRACTICE OF WRITING FOR THE SCREEN

Brian Dunnigan

THE CROWOOD PRESS

First published in 2019 by
The Crowood Press Ltd
Ramsbury, Marlborough
Wiltshire SN8 2HR

www.crowood.com

British Library Cataloguing-in-Publication Data
A catalogue record for this book is available from the British Library.

ISBN 978 1 78500 609 8

Typeset by Riverside Publishing Solutions

Printed and bound in India by Replika Press Pvt Ltd

CONTENTS

ACKNOWLEDGEMENTS

This book is based on my thirty years of writing, film-making, teaching and running workshops in the UK and internationally on screenwriting and what it means to be a screenwriter.

My first appreciation must go to the staff and students at the London Film School (LFS) for sharing their knowledge and passion for cinema, and in particular to Alan Bernstein, Ben Gibson, Barry Salt, Colin Tucker, Simon Louvish, Archie Tait, Les Blair and Howard Thompson for their specialist insights, and to Moshe Nitzani, Chi Yu, Umpha Koroma, Shirley Streete-Barath and Annette Streete for their unstinting support.

I also want to thank my colleagues on the MA Screenwriting programme at LFS. While I designed and launched the MA, it was the contribution of many, including Ellis Freeman, Philip Palmer, Roger Hyams, Margaret Glover, Jeremy Page, Jane Wittekind, Giles Borg, Katie Rae, John Sibley, Gillian Harrison, Amanda Schiff, Sue Austen, Richard Kwietniowski, Jon Gilbert, Jonathan Hourigan and Sophia Wellington, which made the course such a success and from whom I have learned so much.

Thanks also to the many professional friends and visiting tutors on the MA at LFS, all of whom so generously shared their insights on screenwriting and film-making with the students and myself; these have enriched the book, while all responsibility for any mistakes or faults rests with me.

Richard Raskin encouraged me to write on the short film and published my first work in the *Danish Journal of Film Studies*.

The Screenwriting Research Network gave me the opportunity to develop my ideas in a series of conference papers.

I am grateful to Jonathan Hourigan, Sophia Wellington and Jon Gilbert who read an early draft of the book and gave me useful comments.

Thank you to Caroline Penn for finding great film stills and illustrations at affordable prices!

My thanks to the staff of La Duchesse, the Yellow Warbler and the Green Room, the coffee houses in Stoke Newington, where much of the book was written. To my children, Madeleine and Pete, and especially to Louisa for several late nights of copy editing and collating. And, finally, to my wife Hetty Einzig, for her insightful comments and critical edits, without whom this book would not have been possible.

Brian Dunnigan

INTRODUCTION

The aim of this book is to illuminate the historical and theoretical context of current screenwriting practice and to emphasize the place of the screenplay in the process of film-making.

The book traces the development of the classical narrative and dramatic tradition from its roots in oral storytelling and early Greek theatre, through nineteenth-century theatrical forms to the emergence of a distinctive cinematic language. It discusses the principles, concepts and vocabulary of the practice of film-making in relation to case studies of specific screenplays and films.

Analyses are drawn from a wide range of classic and contemporary films, while the book also offers a wealth of practical insights, exercises and examples that you can apply to the writing of a short film or feature screenplay. The conceptual analysis is always linked back to the context of screenwriting and the development of the writer's personal voice.

At all times the book encourages the student to dig deeper into the background of conventional technique and its relationship to audience engagement, while highlighting alternative approaches and encouraging the reading and analysis of screenplays as complementary to the practical work.

Each chapter builds toward a conceptual framework that can be used as a basis for writing a short or feature film screenplay. The topics discussed are:

- **Stories and Narrative** The narrative impulse is linked to our need for order and meaning, empathy and cooperation, and our interest in risk and adventure, movement, action, information and knowledge. Simple narrative patterns are analysed with reference to fairy tales, detective stories and the short film. Exercises encourage the exploration of personal experience and memory as the basis for film stories.

- **Creativity** Writing is a creative act, a form of play, a powerful experience of something other within oneself. This chapter emphasizes exploration, discovery and making something new over rules and formulas, while finding originality in the personal. At the same time, it focuses on the importance of dialogue with other people, giving and taking feedback, listening and paying attention. Screenwriting is a collaborative process.

- **Language of Cinema** The origins of drama in ritual and early Greek theatre and Aristotle's Poetics as the foundation of the Western dramatic tradition are discussed, as well as the moral dilemma at the heart of dramatic narrative and the difference between narrative and drama. We chart the emergence of a distinctive, elliptical language of cinema through shot selection, editing and the use of close-up: telling the story in the cut.

- **Character** Character desire and networks, transformation and change are the topics of this chapter: the movement between the internal life of characters and the external actions of the plot. Sources of conflict, the importance of vulnerability and contradiction, reason and emotion, memory and imagination as the essence of the construction of character. Passive and flawed characters, the hero and heroine's journey and modernist alternatives to the classical model are discussed.

- **Structure** The classical three-act model of the goal-oriented character, rising action and sudden reversals, as well as alternative models where narrative drive and character arcs are replaced by a more observational or personal approach, is the focus of this chapter. We need to find the balance between screenwriting conventions and discovery, planning and improvisation. The importance of craft skills and techniques, the distinction between story and plot and key structural principles from causality to suspense and surprise are explored and defined.

- **The Feature Film** Drawing on Aristotelian ideas of drama, including the importance of dramatic unity and plot construction, this chapter outlines a variety of conventional and alternative approaches to writing the feature film screenplay. Theories of characterization and the full range of dramatic principles are analysed and applied to a range of classical and alternative strategies for developing a feature film screenplay.
- **Scene Writing and Dialogue** The focus here is the dramatic scene as a locus of change and conflict. Topics covered include: setting, action, dialogue and sub-text; scene structure; the importance of what is happening now, as well as what is happening next. Writing the scene – focus, choice, change, overwriting and editing; words on the page, flow and rhythm – are all addressed. Also: the writer as actor; dialogue and action; transitions, sequences and rewriting.
- **Development** The last chapter focuses on the development of a feature screenplay from script to screen and the importance of making it personal. The stages of development are discussed from ideas and research to the first-draft screenplay, including premise and logline, character networks, plotting and outlines, feedback and script notes, revision and rewriting.
- **The Collaborative Process** Screenwriting is film-making. The collaborative nature of film-making, working with the director, and the place of the screenplay and screenwriter in the process are addressed. A technical knowledge of film-making and editing is encouraged, as is gaining experience by working on short films. Pitching your ideas and how to approach an agent, as well as a range of options for continued development, are suggested.
- **Exercises** As well as case studies and analysis of short and feature film scripts there is a wide range of exercises at the end of each chapter, which encourage the practical exploration of theory and analysis through written work. In this way I encourage the development of craft skills that will make you a more skilful and, therefore, better writer.

Writing and film-making are ways of thinking about ourselves and in relation to others and the world we inhabit. It is a very human activity to reflect upon our actions and the consequences, the choices we constantly face, what is important or of value, how we deal with failure or the unexpected. Stories give shape to our hopes and fears, our dreams and nightmares, or they can reframe the trivial details of our lives, encouraging us to look at them afresh.

Screenwriting is a very particular kind of writing informed by the language of cinema, which uses images and sounds, time, sequences, dialogue and music to express thoughts that cannot be expressed any other way. A screenwriter needs to know what is required to write for this unique medium and she must know that what she writes will be taken up by others – the director, actors, Director of Photography (DoP) and editor – who will rework and reshape what she writes.

In this sense, the screenwriter is a film-maker and this book encourages the development of a personal voice allied to an understanding of dramatic principles and film-making technique acquired through careful study and constant practice. The development of any talent involves an element of craft but in the end there is no rule, technique or principle worthwhile unless you have discovered it for yourself and worked out your own way to play with – or against – convention.

All of the feature screenplays referenced in the book can be found on the websites listed under Further Resources. The short films can be viewed online either on YouTube or Vimeo.

1
STORY

Screenwriting is an elusive art form, but central to the development of most screenplays is a concern with story. The screenwriter is a storyteller in a tradition linked to the pre-literate world of oral tradition. As a writer, she may be a dreamer, playing with ideas and images. Thinking, remembering, rewriting, drawing on her sense memory, experience and observation, she develops a deeper relation with herself and the world, uncovering what is hidden in the shadows, and in this process discovering what she has to say. The writing has to be personal. This may be what it means to find your voice: you can only write it your way – including if you are adapting or translating a story from another medium. And the creative process is non-linear, more of a weaving back and forth – a search, a discovery – than anything mechanistic or formulaic.

Yet there are basic patterns and shapes to storytelling that can be studied and practised, or used as prompts or unconscious guides in the writing. For finally you, the writer, have to structure your idea or concept for an audience; you have to draw them in and keep their interest in what might happen next.

Ultimately, this may be the only rule: to be entertaining. For the path of exploration and reflection is leading to this point: having a dramatic story to tell to someone. And at a certain stage of development, this is what you might do. Try telling your story to a friend and learn from their reaction and questions where the gaps or problems are. From an outline of the story, you can then begin to develop a dramatic structure, as a basis for writing the screenplay.

At the heart of this structure will be your story; and at the heart of story will be character because your story will be about what happened to someone. Character *desire* will drive the story and shape the audience experience.

WHY STORY?

But why are we drawn to story – why do we find stories so compelling and seek them out? Why do we so often organize and communicate our experience in this narrative way?

Our first task, therefore, will be to explore some possible answers to these questions and thereby illuminate some key elements of storytelling itself.

Order and Meaning

It seems that storytelling is a basic human impulse. All societies create and consume stories. We all know how to tell and understand a story. Stories and narratives surround us in reality and fiction: news stories, gossip, conversation, religious stories, fairy tales, bedtime stories and jokes. We use the narrative form to summarize and communicate, to entertain and educate. Stories are a source of pleasure and insight, they locate us in time and space, they give our lives meaning and purpose. They create order from chaos and, through connecting the fragments and moments of our lives, humanize time. Stories create meaningful, purposeful time and, therefore, make life bearable, shareable and enjoyable.

Concentration and Pattern

The ordering and organizing energy of story that attracts our attention depends upon two principles found in many art forms: concentration and pattern.

We are drawn to patterned structures like narrative, because pattern reminds us of the regularities and symmetries in the world; that the world and nature are not random but ordered, connected and full of meaning; that all is not chance and chaos. And, even if it is, pattern concentrates and focuses the chaotic mind.

Storytelling is patterned in a way that attracts our attention. A story concentrates on what is important, while the relationships between the different elements intrigue us and alert us to the hidden patterns and connections in our own lives. We are encouraged to pay attention, to work out what is going on – like detectives.

We need to follow the clues offered by the narrative to work out the connections, to find out what is going on and what it all might mean. Stories make us curious, keep us focused – and, like Scheherazade's need to tell stories,[1] keep death and the dark at bay.

Empathy and Cooperation

Through sharing stories we come together around the fire, we tell others what happened to us and listen to what happened to them, we are given ideas about what to do the next time or what we might do if that happened to us – or perhaps give them reason to help us. Stories give us ideas about how to live, who or what to avoid, what makes people tick, what is of value to us, for example, why have you chosen to tell this story?

When we are involved in a story, we identify with the central character, developing skills of empathy and concern for others. We come to realize our own ignorance about events and, therefore, needful humility, rather than rushing to judgement. We are always surprised by how little we actually know about anyone – or ourselves. From folk and fairy tales to novels or television and what is reported in the news, we soon come to understand that life is a risky business. It requires strategies or friends or both to help us deal with the many problems that can arise, as well as to fill in the gaps in our knowledge.

Play

But whether helping us solve problems, think about how to get out of trouble or deal with what happens to us, by giving us a sense of our own agency or empathizing with another point of view, stories or fictions are not distractions from reality but ways of understanding, connecting and playing with that reality. Listening, watching or telling stories can make us more confident, more skilled in understanding other people and interacting with them. Stories offer alternative scenarios and help us think beyond the here and now. As a form of cognitive play, stories, therefore, encourage flexible and experimental thinking and help us to develop habits of imaginative exploration that we can use in our everyday lives.

Writing and storytelling are forms of play and creative exploration – hence the importance of writing exercises and free writing in the search for a story to tell.

WHAT IS A STORY?

There are several patterns, principles and dramatic devices that can help us clarify what a story is.

Time and Causality

Most stories are organized around a basic pattern, involving three linked events and two key principles of any narrative: time and causality:

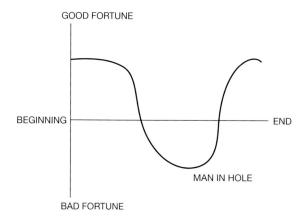

The oldest story in the world – someone getting in and out of trouble.

1. Stable situation.
2. Disturbance/action.
3. New situation.

This is story at its most basic, like the oldest story in the world: man falls into hole, man gets out of hole; this is the same as 'tick-tock' or change through time.

The briefest story tells us of something that happens to someone. The events are connected causally and happen in time: one event causes another. Because a man is not paying attention, he falls into a hole. He clambers out on to the pavement – now dirty, shaken and embarrassed. The everyday world is disturbed. As with a crisis: a character makes a mistake or gets into trouble and the world is changed forever.

Logic, Rising Action and Surprise

A story with more time to tell will build through a series of crises to a final, surprising, crisis or climax. A joke is often constructed in this way, with a protagonist and a series of linked events that take place in time – but with the addition of rising action and a twist in the tale that has been prepared for earlier:

A man seeking solitude and silence joins a monastery where he takes a vow of silence but is allowed to say two words every seven years.

After the first seven years, the man is called before the Abbot and when asked how he is doing, says: 'Bed hard'.

After the second seven years, he says: 'Food awful'.

And after the final seven years, he appears before the Abbot who asks him:

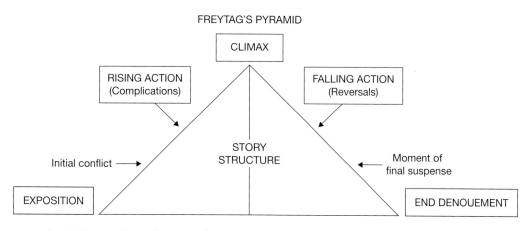

Many structural principles used by modern storytellers are to be found in Aristotle's *Poetics*. In this he stated that a tragedy should imitate a whole action, falling into two parts: the complication and the unraveling. In 1863, the German novelist Gustav Freytag modified Aristotle's basic triangle, breaking it into the five parts popular in nineteenth-century theatre and anticipating later screenwriting models.

'What do you have to say this time?'

The man says, 'I quit', turns around and walks out.

The Abbot turns to his colleague and says: 'I knew it. He's not stopped complaining since he got here!'

The opening and the events of the escalating action (the man's growing dissatisfaction) are part of a cause and effect chain. The pleasure and attraction of story lies in this patterned combination of logic and surprise. The through-line of character and action that provides clarity and coherence, the lines of dialogue that are repeated with variation, the information planted and paid-off, the surprise twist at the end, which, on reflection, seems inevitable – all are crucial to the meaning and pleasure of storytelling.

With the joke we are already elaborating a more complex narrative.

Exposition and Ellipsis

The main focus of concentration in a story is, of course, the principal character or protagonist (literally: the one who struggles). Character traits, supporting characters, backstory information, the selection and ordering of events and actions are designed by the screenwriter to keep the audience concentrated on, and involved in, the story.

Key information about character and plot is omitted or only hinted at. The balance between continuity and discontinuity, the gaps in our knowledge, the sub-text of thoughts and feelings, are all designed both to keep us on track and, therefore, understanding and apprehensive of what might follow, but also keep us uncertain of what may follow and in a state of recurring tension. The audience needs to be provided with enough information to understand what is going on but not so much that the story becomes boring and predictable. Finding a balance between exposition of both character and plot, while at the same time deciding on ellipses that intrigue and surprise, is another task of the screenwriter.

Desire and Contradiction

A character's desire is what the story is really about. As an audience, this is what we are following. In a sense, the story is about our own desire, our wishes and what happens to them, through our identification with the central character's desire. We want to know; we want what they want. Desire is what drives us, and the story, on – struggling through confusion, frustration, deception, but also moments of clarity, epiphany and delight, propelling us on into new worlds of encounter and experience, towards the unexpected discovery or realization.

The outcome of our desire is often unexpected because of the contradiction between what we want and what we need or deserve, between the world as we would like it to be and how it actually is. Many stories are about *not* getting what we want or getting it in a surprising way, or discovering that what we want is not what we need.

Reversal and Discovery

This moment of reversal and realization is what the story has been building to. In its vulgar form, this is referred to as the twist in the tale. But for the proper emotional connection with an audience to be made, this moment must emerge from the story material, from something that we saw earlier and whose significance we failed to understand – not be imposed from the outside as a *Deus ex machina* (L. 'god in a machine') – an unbelievable coincidence or contrivance – as this would weaken our belief in the story.

Obstacles and Conflict

Desire itself awakens opposition: the forces of antagonism that threaten the pursuit of the desired object but also make us think again, try harder or develop a new strategy to get what we want. But others put pressure on us by getting in the way of our desire – failing to understand our explanation or our jokes or running off with the one we love – not giving us what we want. The satisfaction we seek is often thwarted and how we deal with the frustration or defeat is what reveals character. It is also opposition to the protagonist's desire that keeps the story alive by delaying the end and creating uncertainty of outcome. This basic element of story structure – character, objective and obstacle – creates conflict for both protagonist and spectator.

Stakes

The uncertainty of outcome creates tension in the mind of the audience, giving rise to emotions of curiosity, suspense and anticipation. If there is also something at stake for the protagonist, this intensifies our interest.

Combining the simple formula of character desire and the obstacle to that desire with what

the protagonist stands to lose, the playwright and screenwriter David Mamet suggests a series of questions that might guide the writing of a screenplay.

STORY QUESTIONS

- Who is my main character? (Protagonist)
- What does s/he want? (Objective)
- Why can't s/he get it? (Obstacle)
- What happens if s/he doesn't get it? (What's at stake?)[2]

What the protagonist wants has to be important to her: there has to be something at stake (ambition, money, love, self-esteem) for the main character. If what she wants is not important to her, why should we care?

MASLOW'S MOTIVATION MODEL

Maslow's hierarchy of needs is a motivational theory in psychology comprising a five-tier model of human needs that is also suggestive of what might be at stake for your protagonist; what motivates them to action.

Journey

It should be remembered that there is internal movement of character, as well as the external action of plot events. How the character is moved, touched or gradually changed in interaction with the external plot is the point of many of the strongest screen stories: not the action itself but the consequences of the action on the soul of the character is often what moves us most.

If most stories can be said to involve a journey, then it is the internal psychological journey of the protagonist that we are following to the moment of change in their world, circumstances or even nature – and the catharsis of the feelings generated by the plot events. This relationship between the external and the internal also points up an important practical and inspiring element in storytelling: stories give us ideas about how we can make sense of the world and find our place in it.

Risk and Adventure

For, in a sense, every story that we tell mirrors our lives in some way – and raises some key questions: Who am I? Where do I come from? Where am I going? What does it mean? When Odysseus is trapped on an island with the beautiful enchantress Calypso, she offers him eternal life, a timeless life of bliss. But he chooses a human life, *his* life, a finite life, but one shaped by his choices and decisions: a life of risk and adventure and marriage to a woman who will age and die – as he will. Death focuses the mind on what is of importance, what makes life worth living.

Movement, Action and Emotion

But we also want Odysseus to set forth into a sea of troubles. As an audience, we want to experience the challenge and excitement of movement and action over stasis in a place where nothing of consequence happens. Stories play upon and nourish our emotions – fear, anticipation, grief, hope – which presuppose an active, resourceful but vulnerable protagonist. The emotions that are stirred by our identification with the hero or heroine's journey – hoping for success, fearing defeat or death – are part of our sense of human fragility and ignorance – as well as highlighting what is important to us – truth, loyalty, friendship, love, justice.

Our lives are finite but the knowledge that we are going to die intensifies and clarifies our experience and values. We don't know very much and we are not in control, and anything can happen at any time to damage us, but the possibilities excite us, and the courage and resolve of our protagonist move us and connect us to our own journey and the question central to Greek drama and philosophy: How should I live?

Motivation and Goal

The journey metaphor – human life and the adventure of being human conceived as a journey – assumes that characters are constantly faced with choices that define who they are and what is important to them: about what kind of life they want to live. They are constantly on the move, internally and externally; hence the importance of establishing a character's motivation and goal. This journey has a destination and a reason for setting out. Not only does this provide clarity and unity of focus but also a way for the audience to judge the significance of the events in relation to the protagonist's objective.

Rhythm and Pacing

On this journey, the writer must also attend to the organizing story beats – the rhythm of events and incidents that challenge the protagonist and hasten or delay the outcome. Both audience and protagonist need time to reflect upon and feel the consequences of actions and reactions externalized in the plot, conceived as a rite of passage for the main character.

Ritual and Transformation

For the image of story as journey is shadowed by ritual and pilgrimage. The need to leave home and seek out the sacred place of physical or spiritual healing, enlightenment or new knowledge – to go on a journey that you knew was going to be difficult and dangerous, with trials and tests to prove that you are worthy.

In a feature film, this is also a space of transformation and encounter, where you struggle to let go of the old way of life – your previous ideas about yourself and others – in order for your life to be renewed. The archetype here is death and rebirth. In Augustinian theology this was the moment when you escaped time and entered another reality – eternity. Hence the reminder of a basic narrative pattern in the lyrics of the song *Amazing Grace* – I once was lost but now am found.[3]

Lost and Found

What is lost or desired, what one lacks, is often the underlying or unconscious reason why the hero or heroine has set out on the journey in the first place – the feeling or realization that something important is missing or unresolved. Or the protagonist – and we – may only become conscious of this lack as the story develops. This is another way of considering a deeper level of story – the internal journey of the protagonist, as opposed to the pursuit of an external objective.

For example, in *Silence of the Lambs* Clarice is haunted by her failure in the past to save the lambs from slaughter and this gives her the impetus to confront the serial killer and, this time, save the innocent victim. Her successful capture of the killer allows her to realize her ambition to move from being an apprentice to a professional FBI agent. Before she could achieve this desire, she had to confront her failure in the past. This is also a classic plot pattern, where what a character wants is not what they need, or this inner lack needs to be addressed before they get what they want. Sometimes this lack is defined as a character flaw or wound – an element of denial that is blocking the protagonist's way to a more fully human life, where they are aligned – rather than in conflict – with their essential selves.

This idea of the journey through a narrowing passage of increasing threat or a journey in and out of darkness, offers both pattern and meaning that connects to the narrative meanings embedded in ritual and religion, and in the earliest forms of storytelling.

STORY ARCHETYPES

The Oral Tradition

Sing in me and tell the story.[4]

The screenwriter is part of an older storytelling tradition that pre-dates literacy and has its roots in the Homeric epic. In old Welsh, 'story' came from the stem '*arwydd*' – a sign, a symbol, a manifestation or miracle from the root meaning 'to see'. Story implied guidance, wisdom and knowledge. The storyteller of the tribe was a seer who guided the souls of his listeners though a world of mystery. It was a form of improvisation and performance, like the development of a film story.

The screenwriter too is a storyteller and, therefore, also a director, an actor, an editor – as he imagines and improvises his screen story – rewriting and revising in interaction with others: what to show and when, what to reveal, what to conceal, what to emphasize. The story is alive and present in the moment and comes from within the storyteller. He has made the story his own and is alive and responsive to his own and others' reactions – which help shape the order, the pacing, rhythm and delivery of incidents, events and meaning. These qualities of the storytelling have to be just right to keep the audience involved.

There are many kinds of narrative in the oral tradition – myth, saga, legend, epic, romance, parable, anecdote, history, folktale – but I want to focus on two: the ballad and the fairy tale.

Ballad

A ballad is a folk song that tells a cathartic and dramatic story – of love, murder, revenge, romance, or of encounters with magic and the marvellous. The ballad singer, like the oral storyteller, did not work with a text but with his auditory memory, a simple story line, a ritualized form of repetition and variation and the vivid imagery of the ballad to guide him.

His world was an imagined aristocratic one, where characters set out into a wide world of adventure and possibility, offering an imaginative escape from the demands of rural life. And, crucially relevant to screenwriting, this was a world with an emphasis on action – of people doing things. Ballad language is a language of act and event – descriptive not prescriptive. This is what gives ballads their power and distinguishes them from more literary poetic forms, as we can see in this verse from the old Scottish ballad *Burd Ellen*:

> He's pitten on his cork-heeled shoone, [shoes]
> An fast awa rade he;
> She's clade herself in page aray,
> And after him ran she.

Most ballads have at their base two people in relationship with each other who are threatened by a third person. The central pair's reaction to this new threat (a parent, another lover, a rival) forms the development core of the simple story.

Thus we have another version of a familiar storytelling pattern that recurs in many film stories: initial situation, threat, complication, development and resolution; where the development relates to the efforts to promote or combat the threat and the resolution deals with the happy or tragic outcome.

To think of screenwriting as a performance or a practice where stories are not memorized but spun out of variant verses and formulaic phrases, reimagined and reformulated in new combinations, leads us to the most pervasive of literary forms with its roots in the oral tradition: the folk or fairy tale. This is the Ur-tale, the original story, at the heart of our globalized film culture. Folk tales contain the origins of the detective story, romance, horror, sci-fi and action-adventure.

Fairy Tale

Folk or fairy tales are stories that have been in circulation for centuries. Oral tales improvised around a series of dramatic situations, they offer pattern and provocation for our own storytelling. Relayed to them by matrons and nurses and written down by Charles Perrault and the Brothers Grimm in the eighteenth and nineteenth centuries (for different audiences), the tales became more polished, amplified, stylized – literary. Along with the French translation of *Tales of a Thousand and One Nights*, they created a sea of stories from which writers and screenwriters, poets, composers and dramatists have drawn ever since; a source of inspiration for literature and mass entertainment. Originally retold to an adult audience as entertainment at the end of a working day, fairy tales' otherworldly settings, the enchantments and the magic objects, made them seem stories more appropriate for children than for rational adults in a post-Enlightenment age.

THEMES

But for the Romantics, they were a powerful reminder of the primitive, imaginative world of the past, a world of powerful emotions. Mysterious and wondrous settings and happenings engendered feelings of wonder and awe in the face of implacable yet redemptive Nature. Stories like *Hansel and Gretel*, *Snow White* or *Little Red Riding Hood*, reconnect us with the fears and anxieties of childhood and the utopian hopes of the human spirit repressed by an over-rational culture. Underlying and troubling themes of sexuality and violence, sibling rivalry and moral obligations, all gave these stories a continuing relevance for adult readers.

ACTION

The tales themselves have a compelling, stark quality, with the teller offering no comment or judgement on the often brutal facts of the story: a woman dancing to death in red hot shoes or a little girl raped and eaten by a wolf. There is an emphasis on action but also a mystery here, a lack of explanation that provokes further thought. Angela Carter is just one of many modern authors who have rewritten and provided an inner life to these tales, exploring and revealing the seduction, the repressed sexuality and extreme violence, the guilt and fantasy that still trap and entrance more adult audiences.[5]

PROTAGONISTS

The protagonists in fairy tales lack inner lives – they have no self-doubt, they are simple and naive; fairy tale protagonists are single-minded and one-dimensional, struggling under a curse or lost in the forest, finding help and hate in equal measure as they experience trials, tests and horrors; they are us or at least that narcissistic, naive self-searching for a new home in the world.

STORY WORLD

Part of the power of the fairy tale is the world it evokes: a black and white world of simple polarizations and happy endings; good and bad, enemies and helpers, debasement and recognition; restoration of the moral order and justice. The locked rooms, dark caves and impenetrable forests remind us of the dominant dramatic form of melodrama in cinema and television – where some hidden truth is dramatically brought into the light and evil is defeated. It is sometimes said that there is only one story: the struggle of light against dark.

NARRATIVE PATTERN

In *Morphology of the Folktale*, the Russian formalist Vladimir Propp analysed and summarized this basic narrative pattern.

FAIRY TALE STRUCTURE

1. The story begins with a violation or prohibition – a spell or a curse.
2. Banishment or leaving home – assignment of a task that defines the identity or destiny of the protagonist and gives them a goal.
3. Encounters – with deceitful villain, helpers, a magic gift.
4. The protagonist is tested.
5. Reversal of fortune/set-back.
6. The protagonist makes use of their gift to achieve their goal.
7. Final battle with villain/breaking of the spell.
8. Marriage, wealth, knowledge or simple survival.

You can see in the structuralist analysis of story, the roots of later models and paradigms referred to in screenwriting books and many contemporary films from *Star Wars* to *Wonder Woman*. And while it may be useful to consider these patterns as a guide, what this formal approach fails to catch is what continues to draw us to these stories.

WONDER AND CHANGE

The fairy tale world is a world of possibility, of hope, of wonder. But also of fear – fear of darkness, of sexual intimacy, of growing-up; fear of not being loved or not being worthy of love; powerful existential emotions that go to the heart of the human predicament and the enchantment of story for both storyteller and listener.

The tasks, obstacles and gifts marking the change and growth; the struggle to survive against enemies and bullies and those with power over you; the forming of alliances, the discovery of friendship and kindness; the crisis that leads to breakthrough and a movement out of isolation into affection and companionship, to change and breaking of the curse. The possibility of wondrous change is what has kept these tales alive, a change that can happen at any time – a change of status, or perception or of fortune, a breakthrough and movement out of isolation and powerlessness into affection, companionship and independence.

In this sense, fairy tales are wish fulfilments: they nurture our imagination and give hope that, although there is no guarantee, we will find our place in the world – a place where we are recognized and loved. You can see in this kind of interpretation the connection between the fairy tale as a reflection of the psyche with initiation rites and religious ritual: dark interiors full of secrets that seek the light of revelation, community and transformation. Another link is with the detective story.

The Detective Story

KNOWLEDGE

For Sergei Eisenstein, one of the earliest film theorists and practitioners, the detective story provided the ideal model of film structure. The central quest of the detective story is the search for knowledge and the journey, therefore, from the darkness of ignorance to the light of truth. And this knowledge is not only of the outside world but knowledge of the self.

INITIATION

The detective story is also a story of initiation; a rite of passage where the protagonist moves from one state of being to another. This is the deep structure underlying most stories – how new knowledge transforms the protagonist's view of himself and the world. He is no longer the same person and the world has also changed for him – happily or tragically. Like Gittes, the private detective in *Chinatown* who thinks he knows what is going on – but doesn't – and tragically fails to save the woman he loves. Most detective fiction is organized around this failure to read the world around us.

LOOKING FOR CLUES

As viewers we are trying to get to the bottom of the mystery – like Gittes or Holly Martins in *The Third Man* who wants to find out how his best friend Harry Lime died – we watch the screen closely for clues, we try to figure out who to trust, what has happened, what that action or line of dialogue means. The word 'clue' comes from the Anglo-Saxon meaning ball of yarn. We can lose the thread of the plot, so we try to remember what happened earlier, to understand what is happening now and consider what might happen next.

SPINNING A YARN

Both the writing of a screenplay and the experience of viewing involve a moving back and forth more like weaving than anything more linear. Like the spinners and weavers of Greek myth – the three Moirai, the Fates – the screenwriter is spinning the yarn, teasing out the thread of the story and cutting between the narrative elements – creating a patterned plot that requires memory and intelligence to spin and weave together and to understand – and to begin the unravelling of the plot.

We understand stories in general and we like to play the detective because the skills required are a heightening and focusing of skills we bring to understand everyday life; working out what other people want, what their intentions and objectives are, what they are concealing. We draw on past experience to make judgements and decisions.

The study of classical structure in general and the detective story in particular reveals the ways in which an audience makes sense of story information and how they interpret dramatic patterns. These insights offer screenwriters clues about how to structure their screenplay for an audience, but should not distract from the essential humanity of their story.

THE SHORT FILM

Personal Storytelling

Stories are ways of making sense, forms of cognitive play and explanation that are also attempts to grasp a mystery: the mystery and contradictions of human desire in a contingent universe. Who we are and what we are not, what we want and need, what has happened to us, what is going to happen to us and how to survive and flourish in an unpredictable world are constant human concerns given shape by story and drama.

Stories are more powerful than facts or reason because they stir our emotions through vivid imagery and selected events; we have an emotional response to the dilemmas of the suffering and struggling humans in stories because they raise questions of value, of what we believe is important in human life. An emotional response is also a rational response. Stories encourage us to think and reflect on how we deal with the challenges and problems of our own lives.

As a screenwriter, what is of most value is your personal view of the world. Screenwriting is a process of working out what you have to say, what you feel strongly about – more a process of discovery than working from a fixed plan. Developing a story outline can be part of the process but the point is to work from the inside out, from the idea or situation to a story shape, rather than imposing a structure on your material. For the novice screenwriter, a good place to begin is with the short film.

Writing a short screenplay and making or working on a short film are ways to learn and practise the craft of film-making before developing a feature screenplay. In the writing and collaboration you will learn more not only about your own creative process, but also about structure and the visual language of cinema. Making a short film provides an excellent training ground and place to meet other writers and film-makers, demonstrate your skills and perfect your craft. Short films can range from one to thirty or forty minutes in length but many festivals place a twelve- to fifteen-minute limit for short submissions. These limitations are a good discipline for learning the craft.

Focus

Short films demand economical and focused storytelling, with every shot and line important and every scene having a clear purpose. Short, simple ideas work best: a focus on a single character and no sub-plots create a concentration and intensity but also a space for the viewer to enter into the world of the story. In a good short film, there is as much emotional impact as in a feature film but without the distractions of competing storylines or several other characters.

Drama

One scene flows into the next and everything is in the present tense of performance as the story is dramatized. Drama involves people interacting and in conflict with each other and reacting to the actions of others. It demands audience participation in working out what is going on, what each character knows about the other, what they want, what they are concealing. The dramatic narrative of a good short film allows time and space for reflection.

Image and Sound

You are writing for actors who have to fashion a character from your text but you are also writing for the camera, which can pick up small gestures and actions that reveal the emotional sub-text of the scene: the thoughts and feelings of your characters conveyed through action and reaction, image and sound. This is the distinctive language of cinema that will be discussed in more detail in Chapter 3.

Internal Journey

In the screenplay, you are discovering the nature of your character and theme, the spine of your story. The screenplay and film are acts of perception and revelation, a selection of moments and scenes showing the internal journey of your protagonists and their relationship to the plot through the choices they make, and the decisions taken that reveal who they are.

Beginnings and Endings

Endings are important: the consequences of the protagonists' actions, how they feel after the event, the recognition of what has happened or what they have achieved or failed to achieve. Audiences are profoundly affected by how things work out in the end and how this relates to the beginning. The emotional progression in every story springs from the inciting incident that helps define the aim and purpose of the protagonist and leads through rising action to the climax and denouement of the end.

In the denouement, we often witness a symbolic or reflective moment that locates the story in the ongoing flow of life, in a way that clarifies and reframes the meaning of the story events: and how the ending was embedded in the beginning.

Surprise

Any good drama takes us deeper and deeper toward a conclusion that is both surprising and inevitable: the realization that what seemed insignificant at the beginning is the most important thing at the end. This can be achieved by holding back key information about a character or situation until the end. But because we have so little time with them, characters in short films are always unpredictable and surprising.

Character

Character is the focus and driver of the short film. Each character has to decide how to resolve the problem of the plot, and through his or her choice of action reveal the theme, what the story has been about, what the writer has chosen to say about life. Characters are not static but come alive through encounter and interaction, illuminating each other by contrast and conflict. These moments push the story forward.

Plot

The actions and interactions of the protagonist become the incidents and events of the plot, including the moments of reaction and reflection. The writer selects and orders these story beats in a way that engages audience attention and builds through turning points to the final crisis of revelation and recognition.

Setting

Where the story is set, the time, place, weather, are integral to character and theme, and, therefore, to the overall meaning of the story. The interplay of character and setting grounds the action in a physical reality. The narrow alley full of shadows that the boy has to navigate in *The Bread and Alley* (1970) and the claustrophobic darkness of a dying woman's bedroom in *Alumbramiento* (2007) add texture and meaning to the action.

Storytelling Strategies

There is a range of storytelling strategies that can be used in developing a short script from plot-driven to character-driven, image- or dialogue-based, sharp clear narratives of rising action or a more enigmatic, poetic style full of atmosphere and ambiguity.

But whatever strategy you select, you will always have to consider where to begin and how to end, and what links these two moments. Reading and viewing a broad selection of short scripts and films should be part of your study and preparation for deciding your own approach. There is a list of recommended shorts to view in the Filmography at the end of the book and a number of case studies relating to these films below and at the end of Chapter 3

Case Study 1: *The Bread and Alley* (1970) Abbas Kiarostami

This is an early short film, written by the Iranian film-maker Abbas Kiarostami, drawing on his memories of a childhood experience when a large dog frightened him and he ran away. It is a simple story of a young boy trying to get home from the bakery, but who first has to pass a difficult test.

We meet the boy on a summer's morning, heading home with a loaf of bread under his arm, happy and carefree, kicking a ball of paper down the road.

The story shifts tone as the boy turns off the wide-open street of sunlight into a narrow, darkened alley. A dog suddenly appears from the shadows, snarling and barking, and the boy runs away back to the top of the alley. Here the boy stops and stares into the shadows where the dog is lurking.

A man astride a donkey appears from behind him and clatters down the alley whipping his team of donkeys along without any problem from the dog. He is shortly followed by a cyclist, his bell ringing all the way down the alley, until he too disappears around the corner.

The boy watches them go. He looks around, desperate. This is the only route he can take to get home but he is frightened to go into the alley. There is no one to help him. He begins to cry. Then he sees an old man approach and turn into the alley. The boy wipes away his tears and quickly steps in behind the old man, keeping close as they go deeper into the alley.

Then the old man abruptly turns off the alley into a side street leaving the boy suddenly exposed as the dog races out of the shadows in an explosion of loud barks. The boy has to face the dog alone.

At first the boy runs, then stops and crouches on the ground clutching the flat bread he has been carrying. In a moment of decision he throws a piece of the bread to the dog, who gobbles it up happily.

In this moment their relationship changes: the dog stops barking and follows the boy as he now heads home. We see them both walking down the alley together like two old friends, the dog wagging his tail, the boy no longer frightened.

Music on the soundtrack signals a return to the carefree mood of the opening sequence. The boy has passed this test of character, overcome his fear and found his way home.

In the denouement, the boy arrives home, leaving the dog outside in the alley. As the dog settles down outside we can see another young boy approaching.

ANALYSIS

This is a simple story about a boy facing his fear, learning how to compromise and replacing antagonism with friendship. It is shaped like a fairy tale, a rite of passage where the boy is forced to find a solution to a difficult problem on his own. He solves the problem with ingenuity and in the process reveals qualities of tenacity and courage. His reward is the fulfilment of his desire, the completion of his task and a new bond of friendship. This is a distillation of the kind of story central to mainstream cinema, in features as well as short films.

The story is simply structured around the boy's objective to get home and the obstacle to that objective. The protagonist needs to work out a way to deal with the problem that reveals his inner struggle, while the uncertainty of outcome creates suspense. The solving of the problem releases the tension and the successful outcome is cathartic for both boy and spectator. His inner journey from despair to happiness is expressed in the external actions of the plot.

The ending, where another boy appears, suggests there is no formula to dealing with life's difficulties; each has to find their own solution.

Case Study 2: *Alumbramiento* (2007) Eduardo Chapero-Jackson

This Spanish short film takes place late at night, in the bedroom of an elderly woman who is dying.

The conflict lies between the doctor-son's desire to keep her alive and his wife's recognition that it is time to help her die rather than prolong her suffering.

The film begins with a tiny flashing light in the dark that is revealed to be a mobile phone buzzing on a bedside table. A table lamp is switched on illuminating a middle-aged man (Rafa) who sits on the edge of the bed downcast and thoughtful. He replies to the call, 'We're coming'. Another bedside light is switched on. A woman (Sara) sits up and asks, 'How is she?'

Now they are driving together through the night. Sara looks concerned and scrutinizes her husband's face. She reaches out and touches his hand. 'What else can I do?' he says resignedly, then pulls his hand away.

We are in a darkened apartment. An old woman (Maria) lies in bed in obvious distress. A nurse reports that Maria has been restless and in a lot of pain. She is close to the end. But another woman, Rafa's sister, intervenes, 'She will make it, she always does'. Sara looks troubled. Rafa expertly fills a syringe with morphine to calm her suffering. Sara looks on, increasingly disturbed by what is happening.

Time passes. Maria is waking up but in a delirium, in real distress and panic, struggling to breathe, crying for her mother. Sara suddenly steps forward and sits by the side of Maria's bed. She cradles Maria's head and strokes her hair. Then gently tells Maria that she is going to die.

We see the uncertain reactions of Rafa and his sister but they seem to realize that Sara is doing what they are unable to do. It is time. Sara tells Maria to be calm; that she will not suffer any more. She eases the respirator from Maria's face and talks to her about her long life, her children, how they laughed at her jokes and how she sang to them when they were frightened at night. Maria is calm now and drifting away, the hint of a smile on her face.

Rafa is sitting on the other side of the bed and starts to sing quietly: a children's lullaby that Maria may have sung to him as a child.

'That's it.' Maria has stopped breathing. Sara and Rafa look at each other.

Sara reaches out and puts her hand over Rafa's. This time he does not take his hand away.

ANALYSIS

Sara is the focus and protagonist of the story but a relatively passive one, whose internal journey of concern for her husband, but more especially the suffering of her mother-in-law, finally breaks out into her intervention. The camera captures her thoughts and through her eyes we gradually realize what is happening and what is at stake: the suffering of Maria and the doctor-son trying to prolong the life of his mother beyond reason.

The tension caused by the rising concern of Sara, the increasing distress of Maria and the impotence of Rafa is released by Sara's decision to intervene and ease Maria's passing. Other themes circulate: the medicalization of death, the difficulty of letting go and working out what the right thing is to do.

The set-up is delivered in short lines of dialogue that are also lines of action, pushing the story on; the dramatic questions that the audience will also seek answers to: 'How is she?' and 'What else can I do?'.

The inciting incident is the phone call, and the move from Rafa and Sara's house the turning point that takes us into the middle of the film; the moment of final crisis, when Maria is in extremis, turns the story to its climax. The structure of short films is often like this: a short, sharp set-up, a long middle with a reversal and realization leading to a sudden end.

CONCLUSION

While acknowledging the centrality of story and storytelling in our culture and cinema, we should remain alert to other approaches: story can be secondary to mood, atmosphere, theme or to a poetic evocation of place or the enigma of character. Story can become lost in the episodic spectacle of

Hollywood blockbusters or in films that are more interested in moments and fragments than in a coherent narrative. But the storytelling principles of mainstream cinema, inheriting a long tradition of dramatic theory and practice, are an important source of options in structuring your screenplay for an audience.

The following chapters will continue to review and analyse these principles with reference to the short film but especially to the feature film screenplay. However, prior to any conceptual or historical analysis is the discovery and development of story ideas. It is to the nature of creativity and the creative process that we now turn.

EXERCISES

1. Write down three brief summaries (half a page each) of stories that you want to develop.
2. The worlds of home and school are sources of continuous conflict for most of us. Write down an incident, period, encounter that brings this conflict into sharper focus. What happened? Why? How did it change you?
3. Who in the family has had most influence on you? A sister, brother, mother, father, aunt, uncle, grandparent? Write about this, exploring any crucial events that show that precise influence.
4. For the writer P.D. James, it always starts with place. Write down a list of places that you find interesting or atmospheric. Or that have been important to you in the past. Choose one and write down the associations you have with the place, describe the atmosphere, who lives there and the daily activities. Write a story set in this place.
5. A couple goes into town on some sort of expedition – pleasure, shopping, a doctor's appointment. They may be married, lovers, mother/daughter, father/son or friends. But there is trouble between them and they have to make an important decision. While they are in town, they are marginally drawn into some sort of event that strikes them, shocks them, disturbs them or that they even just observe. Somehow out of that encounter, the decision becomes easier to make. Write down what happens.
6. Select a folk or fairy tale and analyse it using some of the narrative examples in this chapter. Who are the protagonists? What do they want? What are the obstacles to their desire? Why is this objective important to them? What are the main turning points of the story? What is the climax and the moment of reversal and recognition?
7. Write down what you find intriguing about the fairy tale. Now use the fairy tale you have selected as the basis for writing a story set in the present day.
8. Think of an experience that changed you in some way. It could be an experience of betrayal or death or recognition. Bring the incident into focus and decide where to begin, how the story will develop and how it will end. Remember the changing emotions you felt. Run through the sequence of events in your mind. Notice what you want to emphasize, how you might even exaggerate to improve the story. What will you leave out? Sketch an outline of the main story beats. Tell it to someone else. Later, having told the story a few times, you may wish to write it down.
9. Imagine a tree. A storyteller sits underneath. What stories would you like him or her to tell? He/she tells you a story. What is it?

2
CREATIVITY

Screenwriting and film-making require not only storytelling skills, but also an understanding of the creative process. Creativity has been reduced to a slogan in our consumer society but remains an essential human quality available to all: an ability that can be developed through practice and the play of imagination. Practising an art like screenwriting is a way of living more creatively, more consciously; of connecting with something important – the playful child, the mysterious self, the yearning to articulate half-formed thoughts and ideas; to find out what you think or who you might become. Writing is a creative act and is itself a form of play, an experience of something other within oneself. Good writing demands something of the honesty and vulnerability of the child.

We are all born with this ability to play with ideas, to strategize, to discover new and more productive ways of thinking and doing; and this begins in our earliest years. Picasso said that all children are artists. He added that the problem was how to remain an artist once we grow up: how to reconnect with the creative imagination and energy of childhood play.

Creative in modern English implies innovation, originality, with the Latin root meaning to make or produce. To be creative is to produce something new, to see the world in a different way, to imagine new possibilities but also to bring them into reality. The emphasis here is on exploration, discovery and making, rather than on rules or formulas.

Being creative can start with small things like writing down a few words every day, collecting images or learning to cook, dance, sing, draw; a step-by-step process that requires patience and practice and the development of new skills. Becoming skilful at anything makes us feel worthy – but we risk ourselves in the process. To be creative demands a kind of courage because the risk is that what we have to say or show will be mocked or ridiculed: our internal critic reminds us constantly that what we are doing is not worthy and that we are not good enough.

Dealing with our internal critic and a sceptical world is part of the creative process that also promises moments of deep satisfaction and pleasure in making new connections, finding unexpected solutions to problems, being acknowledged and doing good work. There will be friends and colleagues who will help you to bring your idea to fruition, and sudden insights that result from weeks or months of writing and rewriting.

This chapter will look in detail at some of the ideas and ideals that lie behind our contemporary notions of creativity. It will include a set of exercises to stimulate your creative imagination and provide a context to the art and craft of storytelling for the screen. But first we will look at some of the different aspects of the creative process.

ELEMENTS OF CREATIVITY

Play

Storytelling, like the other arts, is a form of cognitive play – a playground for the mind that also contributes to our survival by giving us more options and the ability to link past and future. Both play and storytelling engage our attention but, crucially, also improve our capacity to think strategically and beyond the here and now: to place ourselves imaginatively in the minds of others and, therefore, to see the world from different perspectives. Storytelling and play develop our minds and give us more options in dealing with the challenges and conflicts of life.

Originality/Voice

The idea that we each have a unique way of being human, *my* way, *my* life – and that I miss something important if I do not discover and articulate this – became central to the romantic credo of self-expression through artistic creation. We can also see how these ideas form a background not only to contemporary ideas around creativity, but also to the modern ideals of authenticity, self-realization and self-fulfilment, and their vulgarized forms such as 'do your own thing' or 'follow your star'.

But what an exclusive focus on self-development fails to account for is that in life, as in art, we might want to consider values and demands beyond ourselves, as well as our ties to others. Human life is fundamentally dialogic: we understand who we are only in relation to others, especially those who matter to us. Even in solitary reflection, their voices form the background to our thoughts.

The creative screenwriter too must take account of significant others in their process, while working out how to keep in touch with their original impulses in the face of scepticism and challenge, as well as encouragement. For while the exploration and discovery of an original voice is central to the creative process, an understanding of the tradition they are working within and the collaborative nature of film-making are important considerations for the screenwriter and crucial elements in the making of work that has a personal signature, whether it is commercial or art-house. For this is what you have to offer that no one else has – yourself and how you see the world.

Encounter

Creativity involves an assertion of the self: we express our being by creating. For this we require courage to move ahead despite our doubts and anxieties, including our fears about our relationships with others. We need to confront the fears that grow from the struggle with oneself but also with others; both solitude and solidarity are required.

In the creative act we need to be fully committed, while being aware that we could be wrong. This is where real learning and development begin: in uncertainty, an awareness that the truth always goes beyond anything that can be said or done at any moment, and in encounter with something new that absorbs our attention like a child at play – an idea, a place, an image, or a character.

Receptivity

This in turn requires that we be comfortable in silence, while remaining open and attentive to what is happening, actively listening and waiting; receptive to what we might glimpse and alert to possible new meanings. The creative process includes periods of waiting and reflection; a lightness of touch, a sensitivity, to what is emerging in its own organic time, and dealing with the feelings of anxiety that arise in the gap between our ideas and their realization. For this is also a process of understanding, of finding the shape, of discovering meaning; it takes time and constant reworking to bring ideas into the light.

Insight

The hard and disciplined work that is part of the creative process prepares the ground for breakthrough. Creativity is not just what goes on inside the artist, but is also a process, an interaction between the writer and her world. The intensity of this encounter can give rise to a kind of ecstasy, an opening of unconscious thoughts and feelings, the heightened consciousness of being 'in the zone', the moment of insight, the breakthrough that only comes after a long period of preparation, hard work and commitment.

Limits

In this struggle, the spontaneity and freedom of imaginative play must work within certain limits. Creativity itself grows out of that which limits us – not only our own limitations, but the qualities of the medium that we are working in; whether a song lyric, a short film script or a feature screenplay, there are formal limitations that challenge our free-flowing ideas and provide them with direction and purpose. Confronting these limits, and the tension between them, is what leads to expansiveness and growth. Childhood play is just a stage in the process of finding your story and the best way to tell it.

Imagination

Finding your story, a subject that passionately interests you or a compelling idea, is the work of our imagination. This is the faculty of the mind that reaches out beyond the self, that dreams of other worlds and possibilities, that plays with ideas and impulses and ventures into the unknown. Our imaginative, dreaming self is an essential part of our humanity and our reality. It is also the source of our creativity – creating new forms and relationships, new perspectives on our lives and worlds.

Attention

This takes time, as well as periods of silence and solitude. The creative process cannot be hurried and requires a particular kind of attention: some kinds of insight only come after periods of contemplation. This may require a suspension of judgement or interpretation, a focus on what is happening now rather than what has happened or might happen.

Too often what we know obscures what we don't know and prevents learning or understanding something new. Attention of this kind requires questions rather than answers, invites us to stay with the experience of the unknown, to be present not only to the other outside of ourselves, but also within ourselves. A stage of the creative process where remaining open and waiting, rather than reacting, will allow new thoughts and ideas to arise.

David Lynch suggests that 'Ideas are like fish. If you want to catch little fish, you can stay in the shallow water. But if you want to catch the big fish, you've got to go deeper.'[6] For Lynch, practising meditation is a way to go deep, but all creativity requires the right space to work and some kind of mindfulness or suspended attention that takes us away from the habitual and the distractions of the everyday.

Attention opens a space in our minds and comes from the Latin *tendre*, meaning to stretch or extend, and the implication of two forces pulling against each other like the ebb and flow of the tide, the tendons of animals that link muscle power with action or the tension between the known and the unknown. There is a clear distinction between a suspended attention that means to listen, to take notice of, to be mindful; and focused attention, to select, judge or revise.

Opportunity

The psychoanalyst Carl Jung refers to the Trickster figure in folk tales and myth as an archetype of the creative, disruptive imagination. Trickster figures from myth and folk tale – Hermes, Mercury and Prometheus – are the mythic embodiment of uncertainty and the opportunities this space offers to the creative mind.

Tricksters are boundary figures, lords of liminal space, wandering aimlessly between places. Messengers, thieves, masters of deceit, they cross

Looking both ways – an image of mischief, disorder and uncertainty but also a reminder of opportunity and new possibilities for the creative mind. PETER HORREE/ALAMY STOCK

the boundary between heaven and earth, the living and the dead – like Prometheus stealing fire from the gods. They are the spirits of mischief and disorder but also of new possibilities. Opportunity comes from the Latin *porta* meaning entrance. Trickster figures remind us to remain open to new possibilities, their very aimlessness the embodiment of learning and the creative imagination. A trickster wandering aimlessly encounters the unexpected but, like any good artist, has developed the intelligence to make use of happenstance.

THE CREATIVE PROCESS

Planning vs Chance

Most writers will have a plan before they sit down to work; they know what they want to accomplish.

But they will also be careful not to over-plan – to leave a space for the accidental or unexpected. Good planning alone will not make the work successful. Transforming your ideas rarely goes to plan. We cannot control and order our lives absolutely, nor would we want to.

The 'good life' requires that we remain open to the new and the unexpected. The art of living and writing require us to find a balance between order and disorder, control and vulnerability: too much regulation and we atrophy; too much risk and we might lose everything. Yet we sometimes need to traverse the line between the two in order to keep life fruitful and renewed. We need to develop the skill to work with the accidental, to find ways to weave whatever happens into the design of our lives and art.

Artists learn how to treat coincidence seriously; how to respond creatively to whatever arises or happens. The screenwriter too must develop skills of creative perception and seek what is outside of ego's controlling knowledge, to pursue the darting, gleaming fish of inspiration in the uncertain depths: to take a chance. In the creative play of necessity and chance, certainty and uncertainty, the accidental, the found or discovered is at the root of all creativity. There is happiness in this freedom from what we already know, from established patterns – a release of creative energy in the play of fate and uncertainty.

Then our creative imagination can work with what is glimpsed, the darting ideas and disparate elements – and bring them into coherent relationship with each other. This requires analytical and logical skills. We need openness, receptivity, flexibility and presence of mind, but also a responsive, organizing intelligence

Left- and Right-Brain Thinking

The creative process involves both imaginative, intuitive work and a more analytical, organizing approach. The first requires what Edward de Bono calls lateral thinking – random, intuitive,

LEFT BRAIN

Logic
Rules
Analysis
Rationality
Knowledge
Language
Craft skills
Problem solving
Objectivity
Conscious

RIGHT BRAIN

Creativity
Intuition
Curiosity
Chaos
Uncertainty
Imagery
Original voice
Ideas
Belief
Unconcious

We need openness, receptivity, flexibility and presence of mind, but also a responsive, organizing intelligence to catch the fish.

emotional – occurring in the right side of the brain, where we find the personal, subjective, original ideas that then need shaping for an audience.

The selection and organizing of these ideas require a type of vertical thinking that draws on the logical or left side of the brain, which makes judgements and finds the connections between often disparate elements and motifs. These two types of thinking are involved in all good writing and all the way through the creative process are in interaction with each other. Both have their place. They can be summarized as:

- Left brain: logic, rules, analysis, rationality, knowledge, language, craft skills, problem-solving, objectivity, conscious.
- Right brain: creativity, intuition, curiosity, chaos, uncertainty, imagery, original voice, ideas, belief, unconscious.

Being over-analytical or pre-planned can stifle the original or unusual and lead to the formulaic. Without some technique, ideas remain unformed and unavailable to an audience, but it is important to remember that technical skills are always at the service of something more essential – an image, a feeling, a vision. This comes from a transaction between your internal and external worlds. Everything is raw material and feeds into your creativity: your observations, your lived experience, your memories are all potential sources of tension and inspiration.

Finding Ideas

The original tension is the fragment of an idea that might lead to another thought or feeling – the one pulling against the other or suggesting hidden secrets or powerful emotion. You bait the hook, wait patiently and pay attention to what arises, to what catches your interest.

It is in the nature of being creative to go fishing, to indulge your childlike and playful self, to follow your impulses and intuition, not to rush too quickly to judgement – you are searching for feelings or fragments that slowly or suddenly connect to each other; or, like Ariadne in the labyrinth, for the thread that will lead you out into the light.

This ideas-generating stage can be liberating and empowering – you give yourself permission to daydream. Only afterwards do you need to find the links or patterns that can be the basis of a story. At the very least you will have a range of ideas and situations from which to select.

David Lynch describes his process this way: 'An idea is a thought. It's a thought that holds more than you think it does when you receive it. But in that first moment there is a spark. In a comic strip, if someone gets an idea, a light bulb goes on. It happens in an instant, just as in life.' He goes on to say that it would be great if the whole film came in this way, but, for him, it appears in fragments, like a puzzle that he has to work out. In *Blue Velvet* (1986) 'It was red lips, green lawns and the song – Bobby Vinton's version of *Blue Velvet*. The next thing was an ear lying in a field. And that was it.' And he adds: 'You fall in love with the first idea, that little tiny piece. And once you have got it, the rest will come.'[7]

For Callie Khourie the original idea for *Thelma and Louise* (1991) was two women going on a crime spree. For George Lucas the inspiration for *Star Wars* (1977) came from wanting to make a contemporary action fantasy in space, like the Flash Gordon films of his childhood. Graham Greene found the idea for *The Third Man* (1949) when he saw an old friend, whom he had thought dead, walking along the Strand.

A good idea is one that opens you up and generates new characters, themes and situations; a bad idea closes you down, confines, restricts. Often a good idea is the combination of two small ideas. *Toy Story* (1995) began with a group of toys and the boy who loved them – told from the toys' point of view. But four writers and two years of story development were involved in the final screenplay, with the plot eventually coming to revolve around a cowboy named Woody whose place as Andy's favourite toy was challenged by a new rival – Buzz Lightyear.

Preparation

Finding new ideas, being creative, comes from developing good habits that prepare you for creative

work: routines and patterns of work that avoid distractions and provide context and focus for the writing time.

WHAT KIND OF WRITER ARE YOU?

- Where do you like to work?
- Do you write best in a quiet room or a busy café?
- Are you a morning or an evening person?
- Do you prefer to write longhand before working on a computer?
- What kind of notebook and pen do you like to work with?

Find out what kind of writer you are, the place you work best, the tools of your craft and what approach works best for you. You will find this out by trying out different routines and writing regularly.

Most writers establish routines, such as starting early or working late in the evening when everyone else is sleeping or aiming to write a certain number of words each day. Creativity is 90 per cent perspiration and requires hard work and discipline to create the grounds for the 10 per cent of creative inspiration.

The real secret is to do it every day, even if you only have a couple of hours before or after you go to your day job. Creativity is a habit and you should develop good work habits. Good habits and regular practice will develop your writing skills and also help you to work through any blocks or fears that you may have about writing. This way you make your own luck and encounter happy accidents along the way.

The exercises at the end of this chapter are designed to encourage this daily practice of writing.

Premise

As you write and research and sift through ideas, you begin to narrow your focus and move into the next stage of preparation – developing the premise. This involves working out the underlying themes, what you want to say, what you intend to explore in the story, how it might begin and end. What is the dramatic question that the screenplay will explore?

At first these will be notes to yourself and not for any other audience – though as you progress you might want to try your ideas on a friend and use their questions or responses to clarify your intent. You are still searching for a coherent through-line, the narrative arc or spine, and this usually comes from your characters and their relationship with each other.

As you work with character, plot and theme, the dramatic focus will become clearer. Decide on the world of the story, the protagonist and her objective, and what the central conflict will be. Write this down in a paragraph and then in one sentence. This will become a starting point and a guide to future development. It may change but it is a statement of intent that you can return to when you get lost in the details of the screenplay; it will help ground and guide your creativity.

Craft Skills

Clarifying the premise takes skill. Creativity itself is not just dreaming and imagining or free-writing, but requires a developing understanding of the craft skills necessary to communicate an idea and engage an audience. The more skilful you are, the more you will be able to express your talent and your ideas. Skill gives you the ability and the confidence to execute your ideas. Without skill there is no confidence – you can't fake it.

Developing craft ability involves entering that zone where rules and resistance encounter each other: it is exploratory work. It takes time to discover what you want to say and how to say it – to test and explore all the difficulties of constructing an engaging screenplay. You acquire an understanding of dramatic principles step by step in working through your idea – and by making

mistakes. You learn by creating problems for yourself and working out how to solve them.

You have to find your own way – no rule or teacher can do this for you, but a good mentor or friend will be a first audience and will ask the questions that provoke a deeper understanding of the problem. Beginning to understand that this is the right thing to do is what it means to develop craft skills: knowledge that you have made your own and can make use of in the future.

Technical mastery is not a block to creativity but a means to being truly creative. In other words, when technique is no longer mechanical but instinctive it allows the writer to think and feel more deeply about what they are trying to do. As you will discover, as you practise the exercises and develop your screenplays in discussion with others, improving your technique is never a routine, mechanical process but involves a good deal of questioning and experimenting, of opening up problems that will lead to good work. This is available to us all: we all have the ability through study and practice to be more skilful and better at what we do.

Theory and Practice

Screenwriters develop these technical skills through practice and reflection on that practice, rather than through a strictly rational or theoretical approach. Theory may offer guidelines and tools to problem solve but will not help you find your voice or the exciting idea that will absorb your attention for weeks or months.

Theoretical models and technical skills cannot be applied in an instrumental way. Each project is unique and exploratory – there is no one rule that applies. You need to improvise and try and test different strategies to solve script problems rather than follow some strict rules.

Writers learn how to do this through practice: they learn by doing and by being initiated into the traditions of their practice by experienced practitioners – either in an apprenticeship or in workshops.

TACIT KNOWLEDGE

In daily life we are all required to live in uncertainty: we are not always sure of what is going on, what is going to happen or what we might do in certain circumstances. Although we have our theories about life and our past experience to guide us, we often have to make decisions and take action spontaneously without thinking about rules or correct procedures; like when riding a bicycle or catching a ball, interacting with colleagues at work or writing a screenplay. In these situations we need a kind of tacit knowledge that is fluid and dynamic. By contrast, rules and theories are static, lacking the spirit of life.

EXPLICIT KNOWLEDGE

If something goes wrong, if we fall off the bike or fail to catch the ball or our story lacks dramatic energy, we wonder why. We reflect upon our earlier reflection-in-action and thereby make explicit our knowledge of why we failed to get it right. This gives rise to experimentation, trying new actions. Like jazz musicians or participants in an open-ended conversation, we pay attention and learn to respond, to reframe, to rethink our actions and go beyond the rules and conventions.

CONCLUSION

Reflection during and after the writing of a draft screenplay will develop an ability to analyse your story problems in the future and a vocabulary to discuss them with others. A film school or evening workshop, or a good screenwriting course, is a place where you are initiated into the conventions and tradition of writing for the screen and where you learn through practice and by making mistakes, and where you are required to make explicit your understanding of what you might do the next time. You are also working with the paradox that every time is the first time: every story and screenplay has its own particular challenges and unexpected problems.

For even as you approach a state of technical mastery, you need to find the balance between knowing and not-knowing that allows original ideas to appear and flourish and your personal voice to shine through.

In the following chapters you will find the kind of screenwriting techniques and craft skills, as well as an understanding of dramatic tradition, that will free up your creative imagination to develop the stories close you your own heart.

EXERCISES

1. Develop creative habits: (a) keep a notebook, (b) collect images, (c) try to write every day and (d) keep a reflective journal.
2. A useful daily exercise is to complete three pages every day. Write about how you are feeling now, physically, emotionally, psychologically – be adventurous, follow your thoughts, feelings, associations. Don't edit or judge. Write continuously. At the end of the week, go back through the writing journal and highlight images and ideas that seem promising for further development.
3. How did you become the person you are? Select five words that summarize key elements of your development, e.g. mother, school, music, friends, town, and write about them.
4. List five things you like about yourself.
5. List five things that you have done that you are proud of.
6. Make a list of ten things that you love. Describe and explain what they mean to you.
7. Why write? Why screenwriting? What are your aims and goals as a screenwriter? What are you trying to achieve? Reflect on these questions in your journal.
8. What are your fears about writing? List and reflect on how you can acknowledge these fears and still continue to write.
9. Analyse your skillset – what are your strengths and weaknesses as a screenwriter? What do you need to practise to improve your skillset?

10. Broaden your range of skills – attend an evening class or join a writers' group. Attend free lectures, museums and art galleries. What can you take from a broader range of interests back to your writing?

11. The right brain is stimulated by rhythm, e.g. walking, dancing, swimming. These activities stimulate creativity and are a good way to solve writing problems.

12. Set yourself a question or task and take your notebook along for a walk. Notice any strategies or ideas that come up. On return write up your experience.

13. Go to a part of town or a place where you have never been – an aquarium, a market, a building. Write about what you find there. Use the location for the start of a story.

14. Write down five subjects you would like to write about. Choose one. What would you write about and why?

15. Think about your most traumatic experience, joyful incident or most persistent daydream. How would you turn this into a story? How would you dramatize it? Focus especially on the beginning. What other ways could the story begin?

16. Go through a newspaper or go online and select three news stories that attract your attention. Write a story based on one of the cuttings.

17. Write about an incident or situation that marked your shift from childhood to adolescence. An encounter or initiation – something that *changed* you.

3
LANGUAGE OF CINEMA

Drama is an intensification of the everyday – a way of drawing attention to events that we have witnessed or have been involved in. We want to tell someone what happened – to amaze, entertain or just clarify for ourselves what we saw and how it made us feel – and have that feeling recognized.

As a highly social species we are strongly attracted to sharing information and attention, especially in the form of a vivid story or the mini-dramas of our daily lives. It is in our nature to dramatize – to exaggerate, to enhance the emotional importance of everything from the weather to everyday encounters: 'You will never guess who I saw!' We create drama, just as Aristotle discussed, for our own pleasure but also to amuse or entertain others. For this we use the skills of a dramatist.

When we dramatize an incident we use dramatic techniques – point of view, exaggeration, irony, juxtaposition, ellipsis – we compress the events, cut out the boring bits, refer to something early on that will become a surprising pay-off later. We are careful to draw on dramatic principles of probability (the listener has to suspend their disbelief) and cause and effect (this happened because that happened). Our lives are full of little dramas and tragic conflicts that become the over-arching plot of our lives. We are, after all, protagonists in our own dramas as we strut and fret our hour upon the stage.

In our daily lives we are grappling with the strangeness of our experience and the implacable, mysterious nature of other people, their vindictiveness, kindness, sudden changes of mood,

unexpected behaviour – just as a dramatist does. We are confused and surprised and, finally, like Oedipus, we may come to recognize our own part in the drama. In the end, a dramatic account of our day soothes and satisfies our capacity for rational synthesis and understanding. It is difficult not to see life as a drama.

Story and drama stir our emotions through vivid imagery and selected events. In mainstream cinema, a dramatic narrative compels our attention because we identify with the protagonist on the screen. Their struggle becomes our struggle: we too want to solve the problem, destroy our enemies, discover love or find redemption. Knowing our protagonist's objective we want to know if they will succeed in their endeavour.

In the mythic dark of the cinema, a distinctive visual language makes the drama feel real, immediate and personal. It is this specifically cinematic language that the writer needs to study and understand to become an effective screenwriter.

NARRATIVE AND DRAMA

A story or narrative is not the same as a drama. A narrative is an account of something that happened in the past: a story told. A drama is more immediate, a conflict in the present: a story enacted, dramatized, constructed and complete. Film dramatizes what has happened and makes the story seem real and present to an audience through selection and ordering of incident, but also through shot selection and the editing within and between scenes. In this sense the screenwriter is writing for the camera: showing us what is significant from moment to moment. But showing is not the same as dramatizing: dramatic involvement requires making the story seem present before our eyes and editing is the cinematic means. The screenwriter is also a film-maker and the more she understands how film creates meaning, the better a screenwriter she will be.

Telling a story is like counting: ordering events and putting them in sequence. There is something arbitrary and artificial about this process; one thing does not always follow another in time. A sequence is always an open-ended arrangement: there is always more to tell. A painting is the opposite of narrative in that everything is there at the same time: it may tell a story of love or retell a myth but the form is simultaneous. A narrative, however, is incomplete, you cannot recount everything that happened, and this makes us curious; we wonder what is missing or what might happen next.

A photograph also has this quality: we know it is only a partial view and what we are seeing would look different from another angle or at another time. A photograph is not a sequence but it invites the thought that it is only a fragment of a larger reality. Narrative makes life into a sequence that is coherent and meaningful but not necessarily how life is experienced or lived. It is an artifice, a construction that links the teller with her audience.

A movie camera automatically creates a sequence but not necessarily a narrative one. In the first movie (1895), the Lumière brothers placed their camera in front of factory gates and recorded the gates opening and the workers streaming out for lunch. Their interest seems more in trying to achieve the completeness of a painting rather than creating the curiosity and suspense of a narrative. For this, they would have had to hold the camera frame on the gate before it opened and make us wonder what would happen next, or go in closer with the camera to emphasize a puzzling detail or stay on the gate after the workers have left to suggest there is more to come.

The Lumières' interest seemed to be in achieving the completeness of a painting, rather than creating the curiosity and suspense of a narrative. RGA

A camera is an observer: it sees but it also directs our seeing, just as the screenwriter directs our attention on the page like someone telling a story; playing upon our expectations that there is more to reveal and surprising us by what we were not expecting to find. In this way, story showing through the camera is a way of storytelling, a structure of discovery, a gradual revelation through sound and image. Many screenwriters and film-makers believe that for this showing to engage an audience, the narrative sequence of what happened needs to be dramatized.

There are, of course, film-makers who work more in a narrative mode, such as Robert Bresson whose films like *Pickpocket* (1959) are deliberately anti-dramatic: scenes and fragments taken out of dramatic context, rigorously ordered one after the other to create a narrative not a dramatic sequence. The sequence of shots is like a carefully composed sentence; the camera a narrator.

We can see also the narrative use of camera in the films of Renoir, e.g. *Boudu Saved from Drowning* (1932) or Antonioni, e.g. *L'Eclisse* (1962), where the camera often keeps us at a distance from the drama or conveys the feeling that what we are seeing is not enough or not what is really important. The narrative camera has its own point of view that conflicts with what is happening before it. It modifies our response and de-dramatizes the intensity of the action.

As with the narrative mode of Bertolt Brecht's epic theatre, we are prevented from becoming too involved. Brecht's aim was to break with the dramatic principles laid down by Aristotle, to make the audience aware that it is only a story that we are watching, one of many possible stories and open to revision or reinvention. His influence can be seen in the work of many modern film-makers from Godard, e.g. *Vivre Sa Vie* (1962) and Fassbinder, e.g. *Fear Eats the Soul* (1974) to Hal Hartley, e.g. *Simple Men* (1992) and Michael Haneke, e.g. *Code Unknown* (2000). For Brecht 'all the world' was not a stage, and the stage was not reality. In this sense Brecht was a dramatist who wanted to be a narrator; he wanted to reveal the conventions and ideology that lay behind the drama, to wake us up from the enchantment of drama and bring us back to the real world.

For in enacting a story, the drama becomes the whole world, and every action, gesture and line of dialogue is there for a reason: to enchant us, draw us in to the action and to keep us involved to the end. A play is like a painting. While the narrative camera of Renoir and Antonioni wanders and enquires (there is always more to tell, more to see), the dramatic camera knows exactly what to show us. The dramatic film is complete and self-contained.

In his early silent films, DW Griffiths developed editing techniques that laid down the basic grammar for dramatizing film narrative, for making an intense drama out of showing and thereby engrossing the audience. Through editing techniques, like crosscutting, point of view shot and close-up, he made visual narrative into dramatic action; a showing turned into drama that made the movie-viewing experience feel so real. The coming of sound only added emphasis to the dramatic presence created through cutting. The screenwriter as film-maker is also an editor, creating a drama out of his story through selecting what we see and hear, when we see and hear it and from whose point of view. To think like an editor is to consider what you cut from and to, and what you cut out, in order to make the story dramatically interesting.

In a dramatic film we feel we are seeing everything we need to see; each shot is as self-contained as a theatre play with a perfect fit between action and picture. Most mainstream films do not simply tell a story but dramatize it, which means dramatizing the action – people doing things with actions and their consequences knitted together through a tight, causal structure. This is the root meaning of drama from the Greek 'to do.' As Aristotle saw it, tragic theatre was the imitation of an action, not of narrative, of a doing not a telling, and therefore immediately present, unlike the past of narrative.

It is to his defining text on drama that we will shortly turn. First we will look at the origin of drama in ritual.

THE ORIGINS OF DRAMA

Ritual

Ritual is something we are all involved in, even if only at the level of a wedding, funeral or birthday. Rituals are part of our imaginative lives, like art, music or film. Like the repetitions and rhythms, the patterning and stylizations of narrative and drama, ritual expresses an idea about life, about what is considered important. In a contained and focused way, ritual is concerned with both change and continuity – but also offers a promise of revelation, clarification or new knowledge. Repetition or action or gesture reminds us what it is important to know or experience – in drama as in ritual.

In Werner Herzog's documentary *Cave of Forgotten Dreams* (2010), we are shown the wonders of the Chauvet caves in the south of France: drawings of lions, panthers, rhinos, bears, horses in action – in rhythmic movement across the scorched walls of the cave. Sketched more than 30,000 years ago, the network of underground passageways and caverns contains some of the world's earliest known art. There are also traces of human and animal tracks, a bone flute, the remains of fires and the skull of a huge bear resting on a rock. The atmosphere in the cave and the

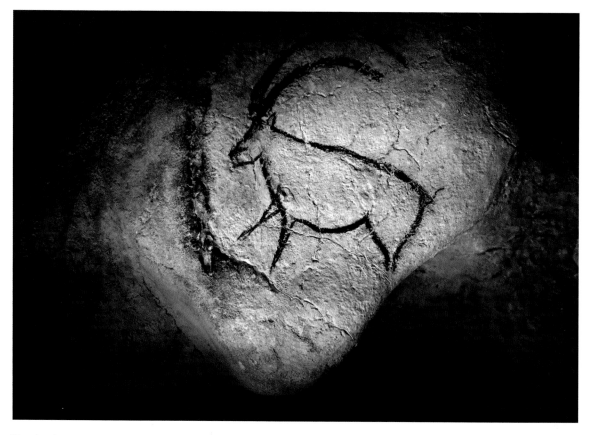

The drawings on the cave walls had a practical purpose but also gave aesthetic expression to visionary experience and were connected to ritual practice and performance that pre-figures the emergence of drama. ANDIA/ALAMY STOCK

emotional power of the images suggest a place of importance to the people who lived in the area; this was clearly some kind of ritual site, a place of shamanistic practice.

While shamanistic rites had very practical concerns – hunting and healing or ferrying the dead – the chief characteristic would have been a ritually induced trance, an altered state of consciousness, a vision. It is now thought the work on the cave walls, rather than being simply decorative or expressive, is related to these visionary experiences; profoundly human experiences given aesthetic form, not unlike the kind of theatre where the end of drama is the creation of a higher consciousness.

Ritual and performance are both liminal and reflexive; they involve a crossing of boundaries and

what is discovered when we cross over. Ritual and drama, while rooted in tradition, are both crucially concerned with change and transformation, resistance and conflict, recognition and catharsis.

Greek Theatre

If ritual practice and earlier art forms, such as music and painting, song and dance, can be traced back millennia, the basic conventions of Western drama began with the Greek theatre of fifth-century Athens. The words we use to describe modern theatre, for example, are largely Greek in origin – theatre, drama, scene and chorus. Drama comes from the Greek *dran*, meaning to do or act, while theatre was a place for watching

The roots of Western drama can be found in early Greek theatre, a place of insight, ritual and reflection for the entire community.
CHARLES STIRLING/ALAMY STOCK

and reflecting upon these human actions. It was a place where we bear witness to, and become emotionally involved in, dreadful and exemplary acts performed on stage. A performance was not mere entertainment but closely related to the political life of the city. Attending the theatre was a means of instruction on what it meant to be a virtuous member of the *polis* – a responsible and reflective citizen.

The theatre was also an important part of the religious life of the community, a sacramental area where divine forces were invoked and where the performance for both actors and spectators was part of a ritual, a form of worship that at times might involve ecstatic possession. For the drama emerged from a celebration of Dionysus, the god of wine and laughter, of the wild and untamed countryside.

Tragedy

In contrast to bawdy songs, playful dance or celebration, this new tragic art grappled with the most challenging events that humans had to face – loss, death, injustice, thwarted passion, madness, despair, trauma. Tragic drama developed out of a culture seeking to understand and confront the human condition: the causes of suffering, the indifference of the gods, the limits of human reasoning.

The rules and conventions, the pattern and order of this new aesthetic form were itself a way of testing the limits of order and rationality constantly threatened by chance events, human passions, the fickle ambiguity of the gods. *Oedipus Rex*, the story of a man who tried to avoid the prophecy of Apollo, only to find out that he had already fulfilled it, was a subject of contemporary relevance

Oedipus was a man who tried to avoid his fate but discovered that he had already fulfilled it. Through him the audience were made to confront their own suffering and lack of agency in a mysterious universe. GRANGER HISTORICAL PICTURE ARCHIVE/ALAMY STOCK

in the Athens of Sophocles. Oedipus is both an active human who kills his father and sleeps with his mother and a passive victim of fate: his life already prefigured by the gods. In this the audience were made to confront their own suffering and lack of real agency and freedom, in a mysterious universe beyond rational understanding and control.

Aristotle thought *Oedipus Rex* an exemplary model of dramatic writing and refers to it frequently in the *Poetics* to which we now turn.

The *Poetics*

Aristotle's analysis of Greek tragedy, while condensed, allusive and incomplete, still offers a clear outline of the dramatic principles that have been so influential in the Western theatrical tradition. The *Poetics* is a series of Aristotle's lecture notes and not meant to be a guide to writing drama so much as a description of how the tragic dramatist engages the audience and the importance of this dramatic engagement for human emotional and cognitive development. The analysis of drama was an aspect of Aristotle's ethical philosophy and part of a wider exploration into the human and natural world. It is worth reading for the acuity and insight of his conceptual analysis.

Later interpreters from the Renaissance on made a dogma of certain of these Aristotelian principles, while at the same time having a profound influence on the development of playwriting in the West. The *Poetics* is important reading if you want to understand not only modern drama, but also current screenwriting techniques. Even if you remain sceptical about the usefulness of any rules or principles, you will have understood more about the underlying rationale of drama.

POETS VS PHILOSOPHERS

For Aristotle, tragic drama was not just an entertainment, it was part of a process of enquiry, reflection and feeling about what it was to be human. Though he was a philosopher, rather than a poet or dramatist, he shared the fifth-century Greek playwright's concern with the ethical significance of how chance events, conflicting obligations and the passions can disturb the ambition to lead a good human life. Tragedy addressed these issues.

The central question of both philosophy and drama in ancient Greece was: what is the good life or what is the right thing to do? How do we know what the right thing is, given how easily we can take a wrong turn or are blown off course through ignorance, greed or poor judgement? At the heart of most compelling modern drama this remains the underlying moral dilemma that powers the narrative and engages the audience's emotions.

Drama, like philosophy, was rooted in this basic human instinct to know and understand more about the world and our place in it. We took pleasure in watching the imitation of humans in action because it satisfied our curiosity, our desire to know, and added to our range of options when it came to deciding on what we might do when faced with the same problems. Animals act out of instinct or habit, but humans are capable of acting from understanding. This is what Aristotle calls *tekhne* – craft, skill, art.

For Aristotle, dramatic writing is a kind of *tekhne*, an activity with its own intrinsic rationale that is better if it has a structured plot and if the action is presented directly rather than mediated by a narrator. By identifying with the action on stage, the spectator will take pleasure and insight from the experience. The *Poetics* reveals the techniques used by the skilful playwright in creating a dynamic, engaging drama.

KEY CONCEPTS

For Aristotle, the plot, 'a combination of the things done or the incidents in the story', was the most important element in drama. It structured the action, engaged the emotions of the audience and provided a gradual revelation of meaning. The plot was also, in itself, a form of investigation and understanding: part of a rational enquiry into man and nature. Character was important but secondary: character traits and qualities were revealed through the action of the plot. But plot and action were logically prior to the other parts of the drama because, Aristotle argued, it was through our actions that we were happy or otherwise and, therefore, 'the end is everywhere the chief thing'.

The action of the plot must be complete, with a proper beginning and end, and a coherent relationship with the middle through a causal chain of linked events. A plot is unified by the characters but also because it is constructed around a single action, for example Thelma and Louise attempting to escape from the pursuing police, the servant becoming the master, a toy cowboy finding his place with the other toys. The drama is not only a representation of a single, complete action but also of incidents that awaken the emotions of pity and fear. These effects are heightened when things happen unexpectedly, as well as logically.

For Aristotle, the most important of those plot devices are reversal (*peripeteia*) and recognition (*anagnorisis*). Both are still central to modern dramatic construction. Reversal refers to a change of fortune for the protagonist, an inversion of the expected outcome, while recognition is described as a move from ignorance to knowledge. The concept of discovery or recognition is something essential to the plot: it is the moment the protagonist realizes the consequences of their action, what they have done or who they have become. The final discovery is also a moment of clarification and, therefore, catharsis. Aristotle thought the most effective form also involved reversals, such as when the messenger comes to relieve Oedipus of his fears, only to inadvertently confirm them.

In a simple plot, the change of fortune for the protagonist comes about without either a reversal or a discovery, while a complex plot requires both. This is the kind of plot Aristotle advocates as the strongest and most likely to excite the interest of an audience. Complex plots, with their sudden reversals and discoveries, appeal to our humanity, awaken feelings of pity and fear, and enhance the audience's sense of astonishment and enjoyment. They enhance the emotional impact of the drama.

These surprising events, however, must be prepared for, and essential to, the plot: a probable not just possible consequence of what has come before. There is also an intimate connection between the integrity of the plot and the emotional impact. This requires the protagonist to act in ignorance and to gradually discover or realize what he has done: hence the importance of the end where the final recognition gives meaning to all the previous actions and events. Aristotle thought that often the strongest plots were what had seemed insignificant at the beginning becomes crucial to the emotional impact of the end. In Pinter and Losey's *The Servant* (1963), the master's reply to the prospective servant that he required 'everything' turns out to be the most important thing at the end, where the servant now has total control over the master's life.

SUMMARY

Aristotle in his *Poetics* is primarily interested in what people do and is only interested in what they think or who they are in relation to what is revealed through their actions. The action is not simply an aspect of the play's construction – it is the construction itself. In this sense, Aristotle's description of plot took the first step toward an organic theory of drama that underlies contemporary screenwriting theory.

Dramatic Construction from Stage to Film

The *Poetics* offered not only an analysis of Greek tragedy, but detailed the key techniques required in turning a story into a drama; how to catch and keep an audience's attention and to communicate the underlying meaning through action and dialogue. These ideas continued to inform playwriting

from the Renaissance up to the end of the nineteenth century and the birth of cinema.

As film production and exhibition became standardized in the first decade of the twentieth century, theories of how the film screenplay should be structured were all variants of the 'well-made' play and other theories of dramatic conflict and unity taken from Aristotle.

THEATRE AND CINEMA

As film historian Barry Salt[8] has shown, from the beginning, the model of dramatic construction for American films was theatrical. As writers and directors from the theatre gravitated to Hollywood, many early films were adaptations of successful stage plays. And, of course, early silent films began as photographed theatre with a fixed camera acting as the proscenium arch.

But with DW Griffiths, Edwin Porter and Sergei Eisenstein, a new language and practice emerged that seemed to emancipate cinema from its theatrical roots: a new art form with incredible potential for both spectacle and intimacy. The moving camera, different angles and perspectives, the close-up and the unique power of montage, all spoke of an exciting, dynamic medium with its own way of representing reality. Theatre appeared static and artificial compared to the fluid and immersive realism of the cinematic image.

For Susan Sontag[9] this is too simple a distinction. Cinema is still shaped by, and can incorporate, all the performing arts, including theatre. The apparent realism of film, for example, conceals the artifice and aesthetic control involved in the organized setting, staged action and the framing of a shot. While many films are simply filmed versions of stage plays, what was distinctive about film was not photography itself nor the image but the connection between the images: what came before and after, the relationship between shots – in other words *editing.* Where theatre was trapped in a limited continuous space ('all the world's a stage'), the cutting together of different perspectives allowed cinema to play with a space that was discontinuous and fragmented. Editing also meant you could manipulate time as well as space. This gave cinema enormous potential for disorientation, complexity and excitement.

The British playwright and screenwriter Sir Ronald Harwood is clear about where he believes the difference between theatre and cinema lies: 'The place where you sit to watch a play is called the auditorium, which literally means a place where you listen. Theatre is about language, the cinema about imagery.'[10] In the theatre, characters talk, discuss and argue, revealing their thoughts and feelings and what they have tried to conceal through words. In cinema, one look between characters may take the place of two pages of dialogue.

The use of close-up was the beginning of a new way of telling stories: silent cinema had invented a language that could enter the world of the mind. The secret thoughts and dreams of the protagonist became ours. BRIAN DUNNIGAN

THE SECRET LANGUAGE OF FILM

The French screenwriter Jean-Claude Carrière in his book of the same name reminds us that in the beginning cinema was based on a sequence of static shots derived from theatre. The development of a distinctive film language began with the breakdown of action into a series of juxtaposed shots: the second cancelling out the first. He gives the following example: a man looks out of a window, then we cut to the street below where a woman is talking to another man. Now we are curious. Who are they and what is his relation to them? If we cut back to the man's face in close-up and see that he is enraged, we may suspect that the man is witnessing his wife and her lover. We cannot be sure but the unfolding of a story through the conflict between shots and the use of close-up was the beginning of a new way of telling, or more precisely showing, stories: a visual medium where both lighting and setting would add nuance to character and plot.

From the way characters act and react, we could infer emotional states and anticipate future action: we could feel their pain. The lack of direct exposition through dialogue meant the audience

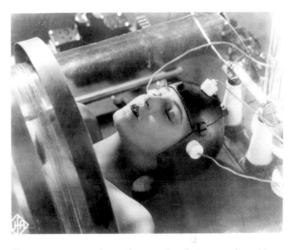

Cinema was a new form of expression that came closest to the life of the unconscious mind during sleep. RGA

had to work out what was going on and in this way are drawn in. Silent cinema had developed a language that could enter the world of the mind: the secret thoughts and imaginings, the hopes and dreams of the protagonist became ours. Audiences very quickly learned this new primitive code, which had all the qualities of some ancient dream.

In the early days of cinema everything was shown in clear, broad actions and simple movements. Actors drew on theatrical styles of expressive emotion and exaggerated gesture. But with the close-up, performances could be more nuanced and internalized. As cinema developed its own techniques, film-makers soon realized that they did not need to show everything: mystery and uncertainty was more intriguing, complex and dramatically interesting than crystal clear exposition. This new kind of visual storytelling was a more visceral, intuitive experience playing like music on our imagination in a language of looks and glances, images and sounds, movements and gestures. Photography made it all seem real but it was a reality constructed by the shot selection and the relationship between the shots created in the cutting room. A visual reality created through linkages and dislocation of imagery that gave new form to feelings: a sensual art form like painting.

The camera could photograph thought and for the film-makers this introduced new possibilities and complexities to their storytelling. For the audience, their imagined life became real or as real as a dream. Cinema was a new form of expression that came closest to the life of the unconscious mind during sleep: the sudden leaps and connections, images appearing and disappearing, time and space contracting and expanding. Editing was the secret heart of this new language, playing with time as an organic component of the new vocabulary.

Screenwriting and Editing

Walter Murch, the American editor of films such as *Apocalypse Now* (1979) and the *English Patient* (1996), suggests that the work of the editor and the screenwriter have much in common. Knowledge of editing is also a prerequisite for a director. They are all concerned with telling the story: deciding on the focus of interest, the pacing and linkage of scenes and sequences, the emotional beats that best reveal character and theme, the moral tone.

Murch is also alert to the dreamlike qualities of film, referring to the 'invisible specifics', the subliminal connections that surface as the editor cuts the shots together: the looks and glances between characters that suggest hidden feelings; the importance of sub-text, silence and sound; how visual cuts can be foreshadowed by a sound cut, for example the rasping sound of sandpaper on stone before we cut to an archaeological dig or the sound of a bell that prepares us for a move back in time.

THE QUESTIONS EDITORS AND WRITERS ASK ARE SIMILAR

- How essential is this scene?
- What can I cut or save for later?
- Where is the audience looking?
- What are they thinking?
- What do you want them to feel?
- Do I reveal she has a gun before she gets into the car or is it something we learn after she drives away?

These are all questions of focus, ellipsis and orchestration that concern the screenwriter as much as an editor.

Exposition cannot be too obvious or the audience will become bored and if the story is too fragmented, they will become confused. For Murch, the editor's principal task is to organize the images and sounds and the flow of information in such a way as to provoke the audience's creative participation. Each person makes the film their own, but this is only possible if there is enough ambiguity for the audience to draw on their own experience in making sense of the scene.

Film narrative is elliptical. You do not show the audience everything, but clarity in the storytelling is important. Murch cites a scene from the *Seven Samurai* (1954) where a thief is holding a little girl hostage. We see the head samurai enter but we remain outside waiting in silence, then 'the film cuts to the doorway and, in slow motion, the thief with a bewildered expression on his face comes out clawing at the air'.[11] We realize that the head samurai has sliced him.

Music

When putting together a film, Murch is searching for resonant links between sound and image – visual harmonies, thematic harmonies that are not apparent on the surface. Finding these associations and emotional connections is also what a screenwriter is doing in the drafting process. Murch compares these patterns to musical motifs and themes that are orchestrated in a symphony. Like film, music gives expressive form to feeling through rhythm and repetition; like film, it is a visceral art form. Murch believes the revolutionary music of Beethoven is a prime inspiration for cinema and the language of film.

If you listen to Beethoven 'the sudden shifts in tonality, rhythm and musical focus, it is as though you can hear the grammar of film – cuts, dissolves, fades, long shots, close shots – being worked out in musical terms'. Compared to the more orderly architectural compositions of the eighteenth century, Beethoven's music is 'wild, natural, sometimes supernatural'.[12] Murch believes that the dynamism of this new musical language, combined with a fascination for the everyday, was what gave birth to cinema.

Realism

Realism was the name given to the late nineteenth-century reaction to romanticism in the arts, which found meaning not in some ideal, but in the close observation of everyday reality. The camera's ability to move and to record movement of everyday events, and the editing techniques, which cut quickly between shots, gave cinema the quality of a dynamic lived reality that fascinated the growing urban audiences of the industrialized cities. But if the technology behind this new attraction was complex, the new visual language of film had to be clear and simple – a universal language of pictures (and later sound) that everyone could understand.

Screenwriters and editors at the beginning and end of the film-making process had to find ways to bring clarity and coherence to this fragmentary and dynamic language in order to engage the emotions of an audience. What developed was a way of storytelling through suggestion, rather than through exposition.

Tell the Story in the Cut

The playwright and screenwriter David Mamet sees the invention of the close-up as the revolutionary essence of cinema. It touches on the essential nature of film as pre-verbal and intimate, like the story around the campfire. Film narrative is closer to oral storytelling than theatre. His conception of story and film owes something to Hemingway's attitude of cutting out any ornamentation or elaboration in the writing, leaving only the simple unfolding of the story. Hemingway advised: 'Write the best story that you can and write it as straight as you can, one true sentence after the other'. Mamet sees screenwriting and film-making like this: 'A good writer gets better only by learning to cut, to remove the ornamental, the descriptive, the narrative, the deeply felt. What remains? The story remains.'[13]

A film is much closer to simple storytelling than a play. If you listen to how people tell a story, they jump from one image and sound to another: 'I was walking down the street, a child ran across the road, a screech of brakes, someone screamed, it began to snow'. This is like a shot list, with the shots eliding and erasing what came before but in the process creating new feelings and meanings, and building emotion. Here, Mamet's guide is the Russian film-maker and teacher Sergei Eisenstein.

Eisenstein discovered in the 1920s that 'two film pieces of any kind placed together inevitably combine into a new concept, a new quality arising out of the juxtaposition'.[14] This juxtaposition of partial details creates a new image and emotion that resonates in the feelings and minds of an audience. Any work of art is precisely this dynamic process of arranging images that draw an audience in to complete the meaning. A perfect example is the Japanese haiku, a three line poetic form developed in the seventeenth century. Each haiku is a visually expressive meditation based on a close observation of nature that crystallizes a moment of realization. The one below is by one of the great masters of the form, Matsuo Bashō.

> ### THE JUXTAPOSITION OF PARTIAL DETAILS CREATES A NEW IMAGE
>
> - The old pond.
> - A frog leaps.
> - The sound of water.[15]

The details are juxtaposed to create the unfolding meaning and emotion of the narrative and the unifying image that binds these details together in the minds of the audience. In this way 'feelings arise, develop, grow into other feelings to live before the spectator'. Eisenstein thought that all film-makers needed to study playwriting and the actor's craft but also 'the subtleties of montage creation'.[16] His ideas remain central to contemporary film language.

For Mamet it is the contrast between juxtaposed images that moves the story forward for an audience. Simple, uninflected images: a tree, a stream, a body – without elaboration – is what will move and involve an audience. 'Let the cut tell the story' he advocates; let the drama emerge in the conflict between the images. In this way, the audience will be surprised. In Mamet's ideal of film-making, what the audience wants is drama, not narration. We keep the audience's attention by withholding information, showing only what makes the story clear and understandable. For Mamet this is simply tracking the progress of the heroine in pursuit of her objective. What does she want? That is the question that will trick the audience into paying attention: they will want to know whether she will succeed in finding out or not.

Her character will also be uninflected, like a character in a fairy tale. The less she is described, the more we will identify with her and ascribe to her meanings of our own. We will discover who she is through the simple action of the story: the juxtaposed shots. The most interesting thing is what happens next in the story. This is the job of the film director – to make us wonder where we are going through the juxtaposition of uninflected shots. Mamet's perfect movie does not have any dialogue: you should be striving to make a silent movie.

Poetry

For the Russian film-maker Andrey Tarkovsky, cinema has the potential to be the most truthful and poetic of art forms. Instead of theatrical writing, character arcs and narrative logic, he favoured the logic of poetry and passion; images and dramatic action linked by the logic of a character's thought, rather than the logic of traditional drama. Poetic connections heighten feeling and require the audience to be active participants in the process of discovery. This is a method of writing and film-making that is associative, cumulative and affective. It expresses the complex inner life of the protagonist in a series of intense images, where narrative causality is increasingly replaced by poetic articulations and the poetry of the dream.

Ivan's thoughts shaped by the poetry of dream and nightmare, are not abstract but precise images of reality. RGA

In Tarkovsky's first feature, *Ivan's Childhood* (1960), the protagonist is a young orphan boy who is already a brutalized and experienced reconnaissance scout for the Red Army during the Second World War. The film, however, is less interested in military heroism than the hyper-tense atmosphere of war and the single-minded passion for revenge that has replaced Ivan's childhood. The landscape is a blasted land of mud, dead bodies and burning buildings.

The simple plot focuses on Ivan being ordered away from the front line, his refusal to go and his preparation for a final mission. But instead of the turns and twists of plot, the film focuses on Ivan: his thoughts and feelings; on the waiting and preparation; the growing sense of foreboding and death – contrasted with dreams of love and light and home. An understanding of all that has been lost, a sense of imminent tragedy, shaped by the poetry of dream and nightmare linked by repetition and a mingling of image and sound. These images are not abstract but precise observations of reality, each self-contained and filled with time like the haiku by Bashō.

PRECISE OBSERVATIONS OF REALITY

- Reeds cut for thatching.
- The stumps now stand forgotten.
- Sprinkled with soft snow.

Image

Kaneto Shindo, a Japanese screenwriter who worked with Akira Kurosawa and Kenji Mizoguchi, thinks of cinematic storytelling in a similar way. His film the *Naked Island* (1960) is a sound feature with no dialogue: 'You can only hear the wind, the sea, the indistinct sound of voices'.[17] The drama is developed through images and external action, and the conflict between images rather than through character psychology. It is the story of a Japanese farmer and his family as they struggle to survive on an island without fresh water, requiring constant trips to the mainland and endless backbreaking climbs to water their crops.

We follow the rituals of the day, family meals, school, grinding corn, rowing back and forth from the mainland, the tension as the adults carry their buckets of precious water up the hill. Their arduous life broken only by brief moments of respite: a hot tub as the sun goes down, bursts of ritual song and dance, fireworks over the bay.

The turning points of the plot – the husband striking the wife for spilling the water, a happy family day out on the mainland, the sudden illness and death of their oldest child – punctuate the otherwise relentless struggle for survival. Shindo's aim was to show the reality of farming life 'in a kind of visual poem'. As he wrote the script 'it became an experiment in how to create drama and conflict without dialogue'.[18]

The shots and scenes become the narrator, clashing with each other, developing conflict and creating the drama. We catch glimpses of the emotional life of the characters, their fears, despair, joy and resignation. This is a film where the family itself is the protagonist and we remain outside as distant empathic observers. Shindo believes 'that screenwriters write to create images. Film is all about images. Dialogue is not the primary force in cinema. Although they write text the ultimate product is not text.'[19] Screenwriters write for the camera.

SHORT FILM EXAMPLE: *GASMAN* (1998)

Gasman (1998), a Cannes prize-winning short film written and directed by Lynne Ramsay, makes full use of this cinematic language. Elliptical and poetic, but also grounded in reality and a clear narrative line driven by the images.

In the opening sequence we begin with a close-up of shoes being polished, a young girl (Lynne) running excitedly through frame, the exasperated voice of a mother, a boy playing with a toy car and crashing it through the imagined snow of spilled

The child's growing realization is shaped and conveyed by action and imagery, the use of sound and silence and sub-text, setting and atmosphere: the story told in fragments, in the cut. LYNNE RAMSEY

sugar. The father smokes and drinks tea in his vest, a recently dry-cleaned suit is taken from a hanger, while Christmas music plays in the background.

A series of elliptical and surreal images, sounds and actions demand our involvement. The children are going to a Christmas party with their father but the boy doesn't want to go with 'him' and there is unspoken tension between the father and mother, and the mother and daughter. The girl runs after the father. The mother stares bleakly after them from the window as the father spins his daughter round against the skyline. She is daddy's little girl and the earlier scene, where she clicks her shiny shoes together in the style of Judy Garland in *The Wizard of Oz* and chants the famous line 'there's no place like home', ironically highlights the family tensions. It also foreshadows leaving a home that will not be the same when she returns.

On the way to the party, along an abandoned railway line, they meet another family group: a mother and two children, a boy and a girl. From their posture this meeting has clearly been

arranged. The father gives the woman some money but not as much as she was expecting. He tries to touch her hair and she pulls away. The little girl asks her brother, 'Who are they?' He doesn't know but teasingly points to the other little girl, 'She looks like you'. They continue to the party where Lynne discovers that the other girl is her sister – daddy had another little girl.

The sparse lines of dialogue certainly add to our understanding of character and relationships, of what is happening, of what has happened (the backstory). The dialogue is also a structuring element, creating story beats, turning points, moments of revelation that help build tension to the reversal and climax:

You are hurting me.
I don't want you to help me.
Coming daddy!
Who are they?
She looks like you.
They look like tramps.

Is that all you've got?
Your dress is lovely.
He's my daddy.
She says you're her daddy.
She's hurting me.

These lines also add emphasis to the discoveries and the emotional reactions of the protagonist.

But we do not depend on the dialogue to understand most of the action. The adult's shame and the child's sense of betrayal are carried by what characters do, by the way they look or turn away – the small gestures that carry meaning, the sub-text of emotions that lie behind any speech. When they do speak, it feels they must, from the need to know or act, rather than a need to explain something to the audience. The dialogue is prompted by anger and joy and confusion, expressing puzzlement or pleasure.

The child's growing realization is shaped and conveyed by the action and imagery, the use of sound and silence and sub-text, setting and atmosphere: the story told in the cut. The audience is required to make the connections for themselves. Repetitions and variation of imagery: the father spinning one girl and then two; the girls holding hands in affection and later in violent anger; the girl hurt by the mother at the beginning and hurting Lisa at the end because she herself has been hurt by the discovery that her father has another family.

In the end, this is a rite of passage film about the loss of innocence. It is the story of a child who encounters a complex adult reality of guilt and deception against the fantasy of consumer Christmas. It is also a world of possibility and strange excitement, of powerful feelings stirred by the discovery of a sister she didn't know she had. In its rhythm, its use of light and dark, close-up and fragment, it is a story shown in the language of cinema.

CONCLUSION

Writing screenplays requires storytelling and dramatic skills drawn from a narrative and theatrical tradition: an understanding of character development, plot structure, scene writing and how to write dialogue that combines with the other elements to characterize, convey information, suggest sub-text and expose the lines of conflict. These skills need to be aligned with a grasp of a specific visual and cinematic language that most directly engages the emotions of an audience. You are writing for the camera and for performance, where actions and reactions of the actors, their gestures, movements and facial expressions, reveal intentions, changing moods and turning points in the story.

Setting and locale are chosen to set up the story world, create atmosphere and contrast (abandoned railway tracks, a small town in the mid-west or a deserted alien spaceship in deep space), as well as providing important visual information about character, plot and dramatic possibilities – a bathroom is a confined space with water, mirror, pills; a forest dark and full of hidden secrets and primal fears. Props and objects can characterize or animate the plot: a stolen bicycle, a gun, a special dress. While sounds have a life and importance of their own – footsteps, a moving car, the sound of love-making – they imply specific actions and by suggesting more than we can see, add complexity to character and theme, and suspense and dramatic irony to the plot events.

The film unfolds through this interaction of sound, image and action, edited fragments of time and space, carefully crafted dialogue scenes and thematic motifs orchestrated like music – all to one end. The task of the screenwriter as filmmaker is to dramatize the internal story of the protagonist's persistence in a strange and challenging world.

British screenwriter Tony Grisoni describes the process this way:

> When you write the film you see in your mind, you hear the music cues, you visualize the camera moves. Be playful. Be light on your feet. Pretend the characters can't speak. Write a silent movie without exposition. Tell the story in pictures.[20]

EXERCISES

1. Select three films and summarize each story. Then analyse how each story has been dramatized, i.e. how the initial conflict has been set up, developed and resolved for the screen.

2. A drama most often focuses on two elements in conflict. Use the contrasting images of light and dark, or order and chaos to write the opening sequence of a possible feature.

3. A father and daughter are preparing a meal and the daughter is strangely silent. Decide who they are and why the daughter is silent. The father tries to make her talk but in an indirect way. Write the scene focusing on the characters' objectives and the build to a moment of crisis and reversal.

4. Write about a situation or relationship at home or at work that you are finding difficult. How did it arise? What part did you play in creating the situation and what strategies could you use to resolve it? Write a scene based on this conflict.

5. Write about a key moment of conflict in your past – an incident that involved acceptance or rejection, e.g. the disillusionment with an admired older person, the betrayal of a friend, being excluded from the group. How did it begin and how was it resolved? What were the key moments?

6. Choose a favourite folk tale or myth. Analyse the source of dramatic conflict. Use it as a basis for writing a contemporary short film script, e.g. how would you dramatize *Little Red Riding Hood* in a contemporary setting?

7. Write a short drama based on one of the following words: brother, sister, mother, father.

8. 'Most drama is about betrayal' (David Mamet). Write an outline for a short film script based on the theme of betrayal.

9. List four films that are based around a lie or a secret. What part do they play in creating the drama? Outline a story idea based on a lie or a secret, then dramatize it using only image and sound.

10. One of the best ways to understand the language of cinema is to break down a film into shots.
    (a) Select a film you like and watch it through at normal speed to feel the emotional shape and flow.
    (b) Then play the film back slowly and analyse it in depth, noting the cuts from image to image. List all the shots and describe the size of the shot, camera movement, sounds and action.
    (c) Read through your notes, which should now cover several pages and give you a detailed understanding of how a film narrative is dramatized through the cut.

11. Select three films that have inspired you and read the screenplays. Try to find early drafts online. How has the screenplay been translated to the screen? What are the differences between the screenplay and the filmed version? Note how the screenplay uses image and sound, setting and atmosphere to reveal character and tell the story. Give examples. What image or images best capture the meaning and atmosphere of the film story?

12. Write a short film on the theme of betrayal, using only images and sounds. It should be understandable without the use of dialogue. When you are satisfied with that draft, write a second version using dialogue. Compare the two versions and discuss with a partner. What have you learned about the place of dialogue in cinematic storytelling?

13. Write an opening sequence from a feature film using only image and sound. It should be both clear and elliptical. Will the audience understand what has happened and want to know what happens next?

14. Select a feature screenplay to read and choose scenes with examples of elliptical dialogue and sub-text. How has the reader been made aware of thoughts and feelings not directly expressed by the characters? What do you think the characters themselves are thinking and feeling and on what basis?

15. Collect or cut out images, postcards and photographs. Select three that have a powerful resonance for you. Sketch out a story inspired by each image.

16. Write a short script that you could direct or could be directed by a friend. Work as a crew-member on a student film. Try to get into the cutting room and see how the film is cut together.

17. Find a location that inspires you. Spend time there making notes and, if possible, taking photos. What attracts you to this place? What memories or feeling does it trigger? Use the photos and notes to write a short script.

18. List five objects that have some emotional meaning for you. Describe each object and the reasons for its emotional relevance.

19. Look at the following sequence of images:

Character A is walking down a street.
Character B watches from a building across the street, then pulls an object from their bag.
A turns the corner of the street.
B follows A.
A is standing outside a house, waiting.
B catches up with A.

Using these images as a basis, develop them into a short screenplay, describing characters, setting and action. Once B catches up with A, allow yourself no more than twenty lines of dialogue.

4
CHARACTER

Character is central to the storytelling experience, both as a motivator of action and a mystery to be revealed. In mainstream cinema, the central character is a point of engagement and identification for the audience, while the actions of the protagonist create the incidents and events of the plot. We should be drawn in to characters' lives by their compelling but contradictory and changing natures, concerned about what happens to them, clear about their objectives and how they will deal with the dramatic question of the narrative.

For this to happen, the screenwriter needs to develop skills in characterization, including how to create character backstory and networks, how to build both external and internal conflicts, and find subtle and visual ways of integrating character and plot to the point of crisis and revelation. This chapter will look at theoretical approaches and techniques for developing character, as well as exercises for reflecting on your own experience as a character in the world.

Any writing must build out from an understanding of your own nature: an understanding of life and character that cannot be reduced to tick boxes or paradigms. Research and imagination, along with a deepening understanding of craft, are important tools in developing a screenplay, but the roots lie in your experience and observations. Writing a screenplay is a way of finding out who you are and how you see the world, what you think is important and of value, what you think it is to be a human being: what we want and need from each other. Our fictions are ways of exploring these questions and working out what matters to

us. Stories are driven by the desire of readers to understand (more) and by the desire of characters who struggle through disappointment and failure to some kind of enlightenment or understanding. Good character writing must come from within your characters: understanding what they want and fear.

Our desires inspire, confuse and distract us, often conflicting with each other and forcing us to change direction and strategies if we are to get what we want in a world that is full of difficult and sometimes dangerous obstacles to that desire. In a mainstream screenplay, therefore, conflict is central and continuous across scenes and sequences, both externally with other people and internally as characters are torn by competing values and loyalties.

SOURCES OF CONFLICT

Individual vs Society

We live in society with many of our individual needs and desires bound up and dependent on others, yet we have been encouraged, since the Enlightenment, to see ourselves as individuals – free and autonomous, independent and original; struggling against the demands of others, yet wanting to make demands on them; wanting to be free but not wanting to find ourselves isolated or lonely; wondering what others want from us or what we can get from them or how we can help them as they once helped us.

Once our material needs are met, the real difficulties in our lives come from personal relations and the internal conflicts that arise between our self-interest and our attachment and responsibility to others, our wish to be a unique individual and the pressures to conform. These conflicts are basic to our human nature and to the stories we tell. The trouble we have in choosing between different loyalties or satisfying competing desires is at the heart of dramatic characterization.

Morality

The intelligence to resolve these conflicts is crucial to our social survival, as well as to characterization, and it is this need to arbitrate that gave rise to our moral sense or conscience. We are social animals with natural feelings that bind us together: loves and hates, fears and desires, affections and dependencies that often conflict with each other and require arbitration if we are not to tear ourselves apart. Our conscience is what distinguishes us from other animals and is a primary source of human action; a way of thinking and feeling that shapes our actions and helps us sort out our difficulties with each other and decide a course of action.

Every story, too, has a moral or amoral core, expressed through the premise and the clash of characters. As in *The Third Man* (1949), where the protagonist Holly Martins seeks to find out the truth about his old friend, only to discover the depths of Harry Lime's moral corruption and its effect on those around him. Holly has his own struggle to decide on what the right thing is to do – whether to save his friend or betray him to the police as justice demands.

The action of the plot reveals his moral purpose to be a good one. In mainstream cinema, the protagonist, as Aristotle reminds us, though imperfect, should be on the side of good. She can have mixed motives and contradictory qualities but she should tend to the good – this is why we relate to her. The hero or heroine should be on the dividing line between good and bad against which the other characters can be measured and around which their characters develop. This is the moral orchestration that gives tone and depth to the screenplay.

Memory and Imagination

We are also creatures who remember and make promises: we have a past that has shaped us and the ability to plan for, and imagine, future actions and outcomes. Our large brains allow us perspective on where we have come from and to plan or plot where we might go and who we might go with. Stories themselves rely on a reader recognizing the significance of what has happened earlier in the plot, just as characters reflect upon, or deny, a past that is important to their present.

Unlike other animals, we experience remorse for past actions and carry traumatic memories that can prevent us flourishing in the present. Certain kinds of film stories are constructed around a protagonist's need to heal a past trauma before they can achieve an important goal or move into the future.

Clarice's memory of the lambs she could not save in *Silence of the Lambs* (1991), Louise's experience of what happened in Texas in *Thelma and Louise* (1991) and Olivier's terrible loss in *The Son* (2003) are crucial experiences in the past that have shaped their character and motivation in the present. It gives them more depth and as the audience come to understand the nature of their traumatic past, they become more involved in the story.

Guilt and Shame

Our ability to remember gives us not only perspective and an awareness of different points of view, but also a sense of responsibility for the decisions and choices we make or have made. These can be the cause of feelings of guilt or shame, feelings that become a source of tension for the audience and for the central character. We can feel remorseful and seek redemption or find ways to conceal a shameful, often impulsive action. In certain films, regret is itself the story, the motivating force, the source of a character's internal conflict and plot tension.

The feature film *What Richard Did* (2012) establishes the fine qualities and promising life of a young protagonist who then struggles with admitting to his critical involvement in the death of a school friend, which could bring that good life to an end. The main character at the beginning of *Force Majeure* (2015) impulsively abandons his wife and children in the face of an apparent avalanche at a ski resort, and is brought face to face with a cowardly, shameful self that threatens to fracture his family and shatter his sense of self. In *The Square* (2017) a middle-class art-curator's regret at inadvertently damaging the life of a young working-class Arab boy becomes an important frame story as he tries to redeem himself in the eyes of his children.

In fact, the witness to shameful behaviour of adults and, therefore, the moral centre of many films is often a child. The son taking the hand of his father after the father's failed attempt to steal a bicycle at the end of *The Bicycle Thieves* (1948) and the daughter asking her father if he was telling the truth at the end of *A Separation* (2011) are both examples of a parent made to feel ashamed in the light of a child's innocent love or scrutiny. They feel ashamed but also frightened that they may have lost something important – the respect of their children – and, therefore, their self-respect. This is because the bonds with their children are of real value and matter to them.

Internalizing the gaze of significant others can be the final moment of recognition and realization of what has happened to the protagonist, of what they have lost through their actions. Susan's confused look of hurt and anger at Tony's final drug-addled collapse in *The Servant* (1963) or Holly Martins watching the woman he loves walk away from him after his betrayal of Harry Lime in *The Third Man* (1949) are examples of a look or a glance that resolves both the internal and external journeys of the protagonist in this cinematic way.

Reason and Emotion

As Mary Midgley[21] points out, our affections are deeper and longer lasting than our impulses; they are how we perceive those whom we love and the otherness of others. They remind us we are not alone and also our need for each other. We think about our feelings as a way of deciding our values and guiding our behaviour.

In this sense, our rational and emotional lives are aspects of our whole person and not separate elements in opposition to each other. Our emotions – fear, pity, longing, delight – and, as viewers, our anxious concern for the protagonist, are related to judgements of value, of what or who is important to us. Emotions have an important cognitive dimension in life and fiction – they help to organize the way we see the world and guide our actions. They are able to pull us back to the centre, as well as distract or destroy us.

Yet as stories reveal, our motivations are complex, our dependencies risky and our passions overwhelming. We do not always act in our own best interests nor consider others – even those closest to us. Caught in a web of connectedness and between our kindness and our cruelty, our yearning to be free and our responsibility to others, our knowledge and our ignorance, we are the stuff that stories are made of: the drama of our lives playing out in the gap between our infinite desire and our finite lives.

Lack

This idea that there is something missing or a better or truer version of ourselves waiting to be discovered often drives our ambition in life and art. Characters in film are often striving, searching, exploring for something that might complete them, might solve the puzzle of their lives or make them whole. But frustration is inevitable. The world will not always deliver what we want: ego wants more than it deserves.

We cannot make others do what we want, as Woody in *Toy Story* (1995) realizes: he cannot make Andy love him better than Buzz; he has to accept that painful realization and live in harmony with Buzz and the other toys. For we are not self-sufficient, we are dependent on others for many of our needs and desires, including our sense of self. Our very identity is formed in dialogue with others in agreement or struggle. This goes to the heart of many stories.

This fight for recognition or respect, for self-discovery or confirmation, so central to story-telling, primarily takes place in relationship with others who help or hinder the character's struggle for enlightenment. The selection and placing of secondary characters is of particular importance in story and character development.

The protagonist of *Precious* (2009) is an African-American teenager with multiple problems at home and school who has been betrayed and abused by her parents, her sense of self crushed. But she finds redemption through a new teacher and circle of friends who give her the love and support she needs to complete her education and become a confident young mother in her own right.

This need for autonomy and loving respect is also a central motivating force in driving Jo's character in *Midnight Cowboy* (1969) and provides an internal goal that complements, and then replaces, his external objective of becoming a male prostitute in New York. At his lowest point, with no money and no clients, he begins a loving relationship with another man who makes him feel valued

Odysseus chooses all the risks and difficulties of the human adventure. INTERFOTO/ALAMY STOCK

for the first time in his life. At the end, when he dumps his cowboy outfit in the garbage, he is signalling that he no longer needs the false persona of machismo and has found a self he can live with.

Vulnerability

Jo is a small town guy seemingly lacking the intelligence, friends or social skills to survive in the tough world of 1960s New York. He is naive and vulnerable, and we feel for him. What he wants and needs seems out of reach and, certainly, out of his control. Like Jo, we are dependent on what is outside of us and outside of our control. This makes us anxious, vulnerable, defensive: yet it is this very incompleteness and vulnerability that makes us human, and our emotions that offer insight into that humanity.

Understanding your characters' source of vulnerability is important in any characterization. It is a way of making an emotional connection between your character and the audience, while opening up the possibility of growth and plot development.

As the philosopher Martha Nussbaum[22] observes, a completely self-sufficient person would have no need to grieve over the loss of a friend or be angry at an injustice or fear what could hurt him. Cool or ironical characters risk losing this emotional connection with themselves and an audience, unless this is the beginning of their story, as with Ryan the self-sufficient corporate downsizer in *Up in the Air* (2009), who comes to realize the emptiness of a life lived in isolation from others.

This is why Odysseus chooses all the risks and difficulties of the human adventure, over an eternity of bliss with Calypso (she who conceals). For the eternal gods there might be never-ending pleasure and kindness, but there would be nothing at stake and nothing of any consequence would ever happen. There would be no possibility of learning or growing, of experiencing love and achievement, as well as the failure and suffering from which future success might spring. There would be nothing to struggle or suffer for, no good or evil – only beige.

DRAMATIZING THE CONFLICT

The Protagonist

In mainstream cinema, the protagonist is the character central to the story and the one with whom we identify. We have to care about them and their problem or predicament. For this to happen, their intentions, according to Aristotle, may be mixed but should tend to the good. This will help build the necessary emotional bond with an audience. But for characters to be interesting, good characters also need to be contradictory and vulnerable, active and reflective: they should excite us; make us curious about our lives and our objectives. They have secrets and, therefore, surprise us. They dramatize the limits and possibilities of our humanity in a contingent world where things that matter to us are out of our control and where chance events can shatter our happiness. We identify with their struggles and this nourishes and develops our emotions, our hopes and fears, our feelings of grief and joy.

They have something at stake – a goal or objective – that is of high importance to them. The audience will be clear about what the protagonist is aiming for and, therefore, engaged in the outcome. However, they also begin to understand the character's limitations and weakness, which make the outcome uncertain. In pursuit of their objective, the protagonist will learn, and have to change, tactics or attitude to get what he wants.

In a feature screenplay, a well-developed character will be constructed around these all too human limitations, their neediness and ignorance, but also the possibilities of their flourishing and succeeding: their resourcefulness and creativity; the support and inspiration of those who love them. Characters are embedded in a network of other characters, selected to put them under pressure with their conflicting demands. This makes the final resolution uncertain and reveals their true nature.

Characters in a mainstream feature screenplay persevere, they are determined; they push through all difficulties, including the risk of loss and the danger of conflict, to reveal what was hidden, to

9   I want! I want!.

Pub. by WBlake 17 May 1793.

Our desires inspire, confuse and distract us, often conflicting with each other and forcing us to change direction and strategies if we are to get what we want. Stories reveal the gap between our infinite ambition and our finite lives. THE FITZWILLIAM MUSEUM, CAMBRIDGE

heal the wound or trauma, to make whole what was lost.

Anti-Psychology

Some writers are more sceptical about this type of checklist; they are not interested in the kind of crisp, clear characterization or delineation of desire that you find in Hollywood screenplays. Drawing on a long literary and philosophical tradition, screenwriters and film-makers as diverse as Roberto Rossellini, Harold Pinter, Michael Haneke or Claire Denis refuse to offer easy psychological accounts of character. They point to the mysterious nature

of the self and question the certainty of knowing another human being. For these film-makers, human life is more elusive and people more enigmatic than conventional cinema represents. For Chekov, we are always on the surface: with other people, there is always a mysterious secret kernel beyond our reach; it is capitalism and its emphasis on competitive individualism that has given rise to the goal-oriented protagonist. According to Chekov, we have to work hard at being human; human nature does not have a goal, whereas everything in capitalism has to have a point and a purpose.

Character Types

If you follow this argument, then a certain degree of flattening or stereotyping is inevitable in characterization, as in life. Here the use of character types becomes relevant: the strong, silent hero, the bully, the rebel, the cheat, the nerd, the stud, the evil child, the worm that turns, the prostitute with the heart of gold. Character types can be inflected and synthesized to suggest human complexity, as well as our essentially enigmatic natures. Typology is a way of thinking about how to create complex characters, while acknowledging their artifice; there are alternative ways of representing character in film.

In modernist fiction and art-house cinema, characters are often less clearly defined or knowable, they lack definable traits or definite goals, and there are gaps in the causal link between their actions and the incidents of the plot. They may seem passive or the film-maker may resist any effort to offer a psychological interpretation of their character. The point of view is more objective and elliptical, the film seemingly uninterested or unable to offer explanations.

The classical Hollywood approach to character is quite different.

Desire and Causality

According to contemporary film theory, narrative causality is at the centre of the Hollywood system, with character as the prime causal agent. A character's psychological motivation, their drive toward their goals and the overcoming of obstacles become the tight interweaving of cause and effect, action and reaction that creates the movie plot. Character and plot are intertwined.

Drawing on the stock characters and types of melodrama (the villainous lawyer, the old maid, the innocent beauty) and the more complex characterizations of the nineteenth-century novel, characters in early Hollywood films were clearly defined by specific qualities and traits that gave rise to key actions that drove the plot. Basic character was defined by age, occupation and gender. Individualized traits provided a close causal connection with the plot action, and character action became an outward expression of inner feelings.

Character desire was central to causality and the drama. Hollywood took from the well-made play of nineteenth-century theatre the idea that the central law of drama was the conflict arising from the obstacle to a character's desire. Each action provoking a reaction, a step-by-step progression with each step an effect that becomes a new cause, keeping the audience engaged in the turns and twists of the plot.

In art-house or certain kinds of realist cinema, causal connections between characters and events are often looser, more ambiguous and mysterious. Causality is more impersonal, objective or elliptical with coincidence, chance or the oppressiveness of society, fate or a transcendent reality more important than any personal action of the characters. In these films, the story world is opaque and determines, constrains or limits any individual actions, making any real change difficult or impossible.

Mainstream cinema, however, remains grounded in the psychological causality established by Hollywood and the possibility of change. For this we require characters who are incomplete, flawed and at the point where they need to change in order to survive.

Character Flaw and Change

Where early screenwriting manuals emphasized character plausibility and consistency, today a key focus in characterization is on the protagonist's vulnerability, their 'flaws' or psychological weaknesses. This becomes the source of inner conflict and links the protagonist's inner motivation to the external goal of the plot. The protagonist has to deal with their inner demons, unresolved past or cynical present in order to progress. They come to realize that to get what they want, or to act decisively, they need to change.

This internal struggle provides underlying motivation and acts as a counterpoint to the hero's pursuit of an external goal and in some stories becomes the moment of recognition and reversal, where the protagonist realizes that what they thought they wanted is not what they need. As with Jo in *Midnight Cowboy* (1969), Holly in *The Third Man* (1949) or Ryan Bingham in *Up In the Air* (2009), where the protagonists finally realize that their original objective in the world is less important than an intimate, loving relationship with another human. Only the loss of the desired object wakens them up to their isolation and the true nature of their existence.

The flaw should appear early in the story and become a point of departure for character development. As, for example, in *Sideways* (2005) when we first meet middle-aged Miles telling his friend on the phone that he is 'on his way', then we cut to him sitting reading on the toilet obviously lying and literally not moving forward in his life. Miles is a struggling writer and wine enthusiast who feels like a failure in love and life. Drinking and depressed, desperate to get his book published but still hoping to get back with his ex-wife, he is unhappy and unable to let go of his past and move on. The drinking, pill-popping and drunken phone calls to his ex-wife become a measure for the audience of what needs to change for Miles to find happiness.

In *Thelma and Louise* (1991), Thelma is a child-woman who needs to break with her abusive husband, grow up and take responsibility for her life, while Louise's organized, over-controlling persona conceals a dark secret, whose revelation might allow her to let go for the first time. In *A Short Film About Love* (1988), Magda has a cynical view of love that has led her into a lonely and promiscuous cul-de-sac of self-loathing and unhappiness.

Early in the screenplay, the reader is shown how all of these characters need to change if they want to flourish – a realization they must come to themselves through the action of the plot. The screenwriter's task is to plan the conflicts that will challenge the protagonist to grow and develop. These will be the confrontations and encounters that incrementally shift the protagonist's thinking and feeling to a point of recognition. As, for example, the low point at the end of the trials and tribulations of the second act, where the protagonist gains insight into their predicament, an understanding that prepares them for the final confrontation in the third act climax.

Thelma has a new calm and confidence, Magda a new sincerity and openness to love, while Miles lets go of his obsessions, his ex-wife and fine wine and his fear of failure, before climbing the stairs to a new life, inspired by an encounter with a woman who has recognized and valued his true qualities. Moments like these become the turning points and revelations of the plot that surprise and give pleasure to the viewer.

In these films, characters have debilitating flaws that require them to change in order to achieve their objective. This involves them going on both an internal and an external journey, where the discovery of their true self releases the insight or knowledge that helps them solve the problem in the external world. The nature of the protagonist's change is referred to in contemporary screenwriting theory as the character arc.

Character Arc

A range of Hollywood films are premised on this redemptive idea that characters can, and must, change, hence the character arc – the internal journey of the protagonist to a reconciling of inner doubt with worldly ambition; the acquiring of self-knowledge, self-understanding, self-love. Characters change incrementally through interaction with the plot and other characters; they arrive at new understandings of themselves and the world. The change a character undergoes is usually also directly related to the theme, such as Holly's journey from naive innocence to the bitter knowledge of experience in *The Third Man* (1949).

Any character change requires the screenplay to establish the protagonist's need for transformation and then track the steps taken to deal with their internal problem and its connection to their external objective. By the end, in a redemptive narrative, the truth has been revealed, the emotional wound healed, the internal and external conflicts reconciled.

Miles stops his self-destructive behaviour and moves forward into a promising new relationship; Thelma leaves her husband behind and becomes a more proactive agent of her own life; Magda begins to question her cynical stance and is made to think what a true loving relationship with another human might be like.

These modern narratives are clearly shadowed by earlier ritual dramas of death and rebirth – the protagonist dying to an old way of life and born into a new – that has been formalized in the hero or heroine's journey. The journey from dark to light can, of course, go in the other direction: as in the award-winning TV series *Breaking Bad* (2008–2013) where mild-mannered chemistry teacher Walter White becomes a ruthless drug king or in the feature film *The Godfather* (1972) where Michael gradually changes from an idealistic young lawyer into the murderous Mafia leader of the film's title. In other films the resolution and realization may be more ambiguous and open-ended.

The underlying thought is that life is about change – about how to deal with it or try to avoid it. Mainstream cinema regularly has character change as the motivating force and through-line of the plot action. The idea that we need to let go of the past to make way for the future, that there is a truer, more authentic self to be discovered or a wound to be healed, a ghost to be exorcised, is what sustains the dream world of Hollywood. For a story to be dramatically or thematically interesting, we should enter it at a point where the protagonist is at the point of change: a point where external pressures demand an internal change if she is to flourish.

But, as we will see, there are other approaches to character in film, where character change is ignored, denied or rejected; where the very idea of a 'character arc', with characters going through a form of moral metamorphosis is seen as a formulaic Hollywood idea unrelated to real life. Or it could be that the film is more concerned with the objective conflicts and simply what happens, than in offering a psychological account of a character's journey.

This is more often the case in genre films than in character-based dramas, but even comic book heroes now go through transformative arcs, revealing their vulnerable side as a catalyst to change. *Thelma and Louise* certainly have simple and clear character arcs, as does *Precious* and Clarice in *Silence of the Lambs*, but their stories are precisely predicated on a premise that demands change if they are going to survive, with the plot events linked to their internal transformation.

While Ree Dolly, the protagonist of *Winter's Bone* (2010), or Llewelyn Moss, the hunter who becomes the hunted in *No Country for Old Men* (2008), experience life-threatening challenges, their characters are fully formed and undergo no essential change by the end – other than a renewed appetite for life or the final transformation of death. As Homer Simpson replies, to Bart's question about whether people ever really changed or not: 'Yes sometime people change – but they change back again almost immediately'; or as situationist graffiti on a wall in Paris (1968) scrawled: 'People do not change they only stand more revealed'.

Internal Conflict and Sub-Text

The idea that the solving of internal and external problems were linked to the through-line or character change, also owed much to a theory of acting brought to the States in the 1920s by the Russian director Konstantin Stanislavski. His ideas were developed further in the Actor's Studio during the 1950s in New York and had a significant impact on American cinema.

His method required actors to access their memories and emotions in building a character from the 'given circumstances' of the play. As he had discovered in working with Chekov, an apparently languid surface could be charged with emotion and tension if there were hints of deep inner conflicts, passions and desires drawn from the actor's own experience. His actors were, therefore, encouraged to develop rich inner lives for their roles that would become the source of 'a through-line of action'; the unarticulated emotion becoming a motivating force driving the external action. Even minor characters were encouraged to have a backstory, motivations and psychological depth that aligned with the characters' desire in the scene.

Stanislavski's linking of sub-text with external action harmonized with Hollywood's emphasis on goal-oriented characters. Characters were in process, continually working through their conflicted thoughts and feelings, deciding what to do, how to act and react to external circumstances, but they also had clear objectives in any given scene, as well as a super-objective for the play as a whole. It was action in pursuit of these objectives that revealed their intentions and true nature. This kind of imaginative work is also required of the writer.

Screenwriters, as well as directors and editors of their own screenplays, should be actors, inhabiting each of their characters, knowing their backstory, their current situation and understanding their competing desires, knowing how they will act and react, what they will say and what they will conceal in scenes with other characters.

For it is in the clash of wills, the struggle and interaction with others that reveal protagonists' affections and antagonisms, their sense of morality, who they really are. Every character is caught in a web of connections and competing demands that allow the screenwriter to externalize the internal world of the protagonist.

Character Network

In a novel, the omniscient narrator can explore the soul of a character but the screenwriter does not have this privilege. Story and character ideas have to be expressed through the action and reaction of characters, through what they do and say, for an audience to have access to their inner life. They may offer glimpses of their internal process in intimate exchanges with friends or lovers but it is primarily through action that we have access to the truth.

In this sense, character in art as in life, is not a static quality but is constantly emerging and changing through encounters with others. In a well-told story, characters operate within a complex web of tensions and relationships that make vivid their qualities and intentions. It is also through dramatic conflict and rising tension that the underlying ideas and themes are clarified and made less abstract.

Rather than thinking of individual characters, it is more useful for the screenwriter to consider the dynamic and interactive nature of character in relationship: in action and reaction to others, such as in *The Third Man* (1949), where the writer Graham Greene describes his characters not only through given qualities, such as age, sex, personality and occupation, but specifically in terms of how they are connected to, and affected by, their transactions with each other, the clash of their differing needs and wants. In these descriptions we can see also how character contradictions and secrets will create tensions and pressures that become turning points of the plot.

The main characters are connected through a web of tensions creating patterns of conflict, especially for the protagonist Holly Martins, torn between his love of a woman and the betrayal of a friend, his sense of natural justice and his loyalty to a man who helped him in the past. These triangular patterns appear in most stories where character A is caught between his relationship with B and C, while B has a different relationship with C and A, and C with A and B.

In the Netflix series *The Last Kingdom* (2015) set in ninth-century England, the desires and contradictions of the central character, Uhtred, are in constant tension. Competing loyalties involving his Saxon birth and his Viking upbringing, his oath of fealty to King Alfred and his warrior's need to settle a blood feud, his love of wife and children but also of battle, are constant sources of plot tension and character revelation.

In this sense, the writer has to plan not only the over-arching antagonisms of the plot, but to think through every scene from the point of view of each character, to work out the dynamics and conflicts: who knows what about whom, what each character wants from each other, what they are hiding, what debts are owed and revenge due. These internal and external conflicts build in intensity, creating ironies and contrasts, reversals and surprises leading up to the final crisis and climax where the narrative lines are finally resolved.

THE PASSIVE CHARACTER

In this hyperactive world of goal-driven protagonists, what is the place of the more reflective, inner-directed character? Screenwriting manuals often advise not to put anything in a script that the camera cannot photograph in action because passivity in a character threatens the dramatic power of the story. It is acceptable in a novel to digress on whales or have a character reflect on the meaning of life, but the narrative feature film requires clear, dramatic progression; this means a protagonist who relentlessly drives the action forward toward crisis.

It is possible, however, that dramatic tension can be the consequence of some aspect of character or a character's inner, rather than external, goal, and that in certain situations an apparently inactive character is liable to create tensions around them. One technique is to create a strongly aggressive foil character – a confidant or antagonist – who questions the protagonist and brings the internal conflicts out into the open, increasing the audience's understanding of him or her.

Short Film Example: *Natan* (2003)

This is the structure of the short film *Natan* (2003) written by Jonas Bergergard and Jonas Holmstrom, where the action is driven by a secondary character against which the central character struggles to assert himself. The protagonist Natan is a temporary worker in a burger bar, sacked by his boss Viggo who then takes pity on him and tries to help him sort his life out. When Viggo discovers that what Natan really wants is a dog, Viggo quickly checks the small ads and drives him out of town to a woman (Sabina) with a dog to sell. Overwhelmed by Viggo's assertive take-over of his life, the nervous and inarticulate Natan runs away and hides in the nearby woods. It is only when Viggo drives off in frustration that we see Natan emerge under the gentle and sympathetic attention of Sabina to bond with the dog and accept an invitation to stay over.

Although physically and emotionally awkward and passive for much of the film, Natan displays a stubborn integrity that gives him a presence at once vulnerable and unpredictable. Despite making snap decisions, barking into his mobile and organizing the lesser mortals around him, the businessman Viggo is a secondary figure; a catalyst, an antagonist, a foil character.

Natan is the still centre of the film around which our thoughts flow. Sabina has what the busy Viggo lacks – spiritual qualities of patience and empathy. She treats Natan with respect and speaks to him in a way that evokes his trust. He is a fellow human to be listened to and taken care of, to be allowed to discover his own way rather than to conform to someone else's fantasy of what he needs. You feel that Sabina is not in a hurry to know or control this person who is a mystery to her.

In this sense, the character of Natan is only superficially passive. His vulnerability and integrity, like the characters in Dostoevsky's novels, give Natan an intensely dramatic quality. They offer an alternative way of thinking about how to create a dramatic character, where the internal life becomes the source of tension for an audience.

Feature Film Example: *Poetry* (2010)

Lee Chang-Dong, who won best screenplay at Cannes for his feature *Poetry* (2010), has this ability to create dramatic tension from unspoken thoughts and feelings, and create dramatic interest in interior worlds.

Mija, the main character of *Poetry*, is one of those characters. For most of the film she observes the world around her, struggling to find words of poetic expression, while coping with the discovery that her teenage grandson has been involved in a brutal rape and suicide of a fellow pupil. Her poetic search for beauty in the everyday, mixed with the horror of her grandson's action and lack of remorse, as well as her growing identification with the dead girl, take her into a strange realm where her own lost youth, repressed sexuality and sense of morality find expression in her rejection of a violent patriarchy.

Carefully woven sub-plots involving a libidinous policeman and a stroke victim challenge and illuminate her character development. At the end, her final decisive act of resistance and justice becomes a gesture of transcendence and opens her up to a deeper sense of her place in a corrupt world, where money and male power crush all other values.

Mija does have an external goal that we can follow – to raise the blood money to pay for a cover-up organized by the fathers of the other boys involved in the rape – but the interest of the film is more with Mija's internal journey: her observations of nature and the men in her world, her memories of childhood, her identification with the dead girl. The screenplay builds up the emotional turmoil of her inner life and the gradual formation of her moral character, which leads her to break free of the plot and the patriarchy. Mija's internal journey is anything but passive. It is full of uncertainty and conflict. It is also carries the tension between the requirements of plot and the nature of character. The internal work, the invisible sub-text, is the source of a character's unpredictability, the moment of reversal where they break out of the confines of the plot. By creating active antagonism and externalizing the conflicts, the apparently passive character becomes active in the minds of the audience.

The dominant model in classical cinema, however, remains the active protagonist whose desire, ambition and objective drives mainstream movies, as exemplified by the model of the hero's journey.

THE HERO'S JOURNEY

A popular paradigm that combines the energetic goal-oriented character with an internal world of transformation is the 'hero's journey' based on *The Hero With a Thousand Faces* (1949) written by Joseph Campbell and turned into a screenwriting manual by Christopher Vogler in his book *The Writer's Journey*.

Campbell's book is a distillation of Jungian ideas of personal growth that he reads into world mythology, interpreting myth psychologically with the external adventure of the hero being symbolic of an internal journey. Influential in the 1950s amongst other anti-modernist works on mythology, it subsequently inspired George Lucas and his film *Star Wars – A New Hope* (1977), as well as a feminist counter in Maureen Murdock's *The Heroine's Journey* (1990).

Campbell's model and Vogler's reinterpretation presents a hero who crosses a threshold into a special world of tests and trials, allies and enemies that threaten him, as well as offering magical aid. Finally, he approaches the 'inmost cave', where he undergoes a supreme ordeal and, after emerging victorious, the hero returns to everyday life transformed by his experience and ready to improve the life of his community.

In outline this is no different from a conventional narrative or folk tale structure, but it was Campbell's distinctive psychological interpretation of myth and his claim for the deep meaning and universality of the journey metaphor that attracted the interest of a Hollywood that had noted the growing market for quest narratives, fantasy and comic book franchises.

The hero's journey model linking external conflicts with internal archetypes, like the Shadow (the dark side) and the Trickster, also meshes neatly with New Age spirituality, where everyone is on a psychic journey from birth to death and death to rebirth. Recent screenwriting books, such as John Yorke's *Into the Woods* (2013), integrate Campbell's work with a Jungian language of individuation, where all stories are, at some level, a quest to find a missing part of ourselves, our life partner or even God. In the adventure, we are made whole through assimilating opposites, discovering the truth and resolving our internal and external conflicts.

The simplicity and universality of this model allowed for Vogler and other admirers of Campbell to state that Campbell had revealed the secret code and underlying pattern of storytelling.

You can see the appeal – a model that connects to people's everyday lives and concerns, both individual and spiritual, a pattern at once universal and particular that offers hope and meaning, and ideas about how to plan a film story, as well as think about one's own life – a template that has since been used by screenwriters as the basis for fantasy and action-adventure films ranging from the original *Mad Max* (1979) through *Raiders of the Lost Ark* (1981) to *Lord of the Rings* (2001) and *Black Panther* (2018).

Professional folklorists and anthropologists, however, dismiss Campbell's account of myth as speculative, vague and generalized, abstracted from the cultures and societies where these stories were told, in order to fit a very American story type of individual heroism and personal transformation. But it is a story model that continues to resonate and influence screenwriting theory, Hollywood movies and the wider culture. For some it also offers a useful guide and plot outline of their main character's adventure. It should also stimulate the writer to read the classic myths for themselves and find their own meaning and inspiration in the imagery and archetypes of the journey metaphor.

THE HEROINE'S JOURNEY

For the feminist writer Maureen Murdock, Campbell's heroic model, with its emphasis on ambition, achievement and male power, misses something crucial to woman's experience, both in life and art. For her, the heroine's journey is a quest for empowerment, for women to fully embrace their feminine nature, to value themselves as women and to heal what she referred to as 'the deep wound of the feminine'; the mother/daughter split provoked by a rejection of feminine values. These values are not exclusive to women but form part of the Jungian definition of the feminine archetype in both men and women: the sensuous and passionate, the intuitive, cooperative, nurturing aspects of the self, undervalued in a culture that valorizes intellect, physical courage and individual success.

The Heroine's Journey may share structural elements of the heroic model, such as withdrawal from the world, the encounter with helpers and enemies, and the movement through the dark night of the soul toward autonomy and independence. The focus is on a woman's inner journey, the internal conflicts of self-doubt, self-hate and paralysing fear, and the healing that comes from reclaiming her sexuality and creativity, and in enjoying the company of other women.

This is the inner-directed journey toward self-assertion noted by Peter Brooks[23] and found in the nineteenth-century novels of the Brontës, Jane Austen and George Eliot, and also in films written by women, like Thelma and Louise, The Girl with a Pearl Earring and Precious. In these films, the female protagonists break with an abusive and controlling patriarchy to find other women or responsive men to bring them to a new balance and freedom.

In the heroine's journey model, the Jungian concept of uniting the masculine and feminine principle in each individual remains an ideal, an awareness of interdependence between men and women that tempers the heroic drive to dominance and success.

Little Miss Sunshine (2006) is a comedy drama that embodies these values, with a woman at the moral centre, and a range of male egos letting go of their personal individual ambition to act cooperatively for the sake of the common good.

THE MODERNIST ALTERNATIVE

With the Hollywood model, the implication is that the world is coherent, comprehensible and continuous, but this is not everyone's experience. The modernist revolt in the arts early in the last century rejected the romantic world-view of cosmic harmony and Aristotelian unity inherited by American cinema. Artists explored new ways of representing reality, and in literature and cinema this meant avoiding straightforward causality and chronology, playing with point of view and introducing characters who lack clear-cut objectives, motives and traits – the interest being more in theme or mood, rather than character and conflict.

The influence of these writers and artists continues to shape the many alternative ways of writing and making films that can be found around the world. Mainstream film-makers have absorbed techniques and ideas from what was once the preserve of art cinema, while modernist tropes and obsessions continue to influence contemporary art and cinema.

The French film-maker Claire Denis and her regular co-writer Jean-Pol Fargeau, for example, are less interested in the kinds of narrative and dramatic approaches discussed elsewhere in this chapter; their films pay little attention to character flaws and arcs, the hero's journey or the goal-driven protagonist. In fact, character itself is problematic, the protagonists often fragmentary and enigmatic with no necessary causal connection between their personality and actions, and no psychological explanation of their behaviour.

Emancipated from character and plot conventions, Denis's films are free-floating, non-linear, dream-like and sensuous; a cinematic language, where meaning is often conveyed by image and sound, rather than plotline. Her interest lies in the strangeness and impenetrability of the Other – how other people make us curious, and generate the confusion of fear and desire: cinema as a way of exploring the sources of desire and sexual awakening. Combining aspects of modernist fiction and the time-cinema of Deleuze, Denis makes time and vision part of the texture of the film itself.

Feature Film Example: *Chocolat* (1988)

Chocolat (1988) was Denis's first feature, set in colonial French Africa in the 1950s. The main characters are a young girl, France, her mother, Aimie, and their black servant, Protee. Aimee's husband is the local administrator, often away from home, leaving his young wife trapped in the heat and slow-moving inertia of colonial life. The film is observational rather than psychological, focusing on

The writer has chosen not to reveal the inner lives and thoughts of the characters. AKG-IMAGES/MONDADORI PORTFOLIO

the daily rituals and banalities of everyday life as seen through the eyes of the child.

Instead of the markers of plot, the focus is on specific details and atmospheres that slowly reveal the latent tensions and absurdities of the colonial presence. The young girl, France, shares a set of mysterious rituals and rules with Protee but, as well as mentor, he is always and finally the servant. While Aimee's secretive intimacy with Protee exposes the exploitative reality of the colonial situation, he is a servant subject to the white man's rules: the rejection by Protee of Aimee's desperate gesture of desire, finally propelling him to the humiliating margins of the servant's quarters where he takes a small but cruel revenge on the child France.

We never really get to know these characters, who remain largely silent and inscrutable. There is no psychological exposition nor is there a conventional hero for us to follow. This challenges the spectator to examine the details of the film closely in order to work out what is going on; each gesture and action, the looks and glances between characters, demand our full attention. Causality in this world comes largely from the roles characters play in the colonial drama; unspoken rules determine how they can behave, what they can do and not do, to and with each other as masters and servants or men and women. Their freedom to act is limited by the part they have been forced to play by history. The film is full of long silences, ellipses and hidden emotion, and we never get close to any of the characters, as we might in a more conventional film.

This is part of their attraction: they are inscrutable, unpredictable, fluctuating characters, perhaps closer to our everyday experience and the mystery we sense in others and ourselves. In our fictions, too, we should be careful about seeming to know too much about our characters believing that two pages of backstory or a tick-box list of traits is what is required. They, like us, need to be free and, therefore, unpredictable: but whether in mainstream or art-house films, characters are almost always in trouble; their attempt to resolve their problems, creating the disorder and unrest of the plot.

CONCLUSION

In mainstream cinema, characters arrive in medias res (in the middle of things): we assume they have led a life before the story began, a life that has shaped their hopes and fears, and their dreams and desires. Whatever the age, they have a backstory, a social world that defines them and a psychology that drives them. They have secrets, vulnerabilities and surprising contradictions that will be used and revealed in the plot. They may lack some important quality or need to let go of an old way of being, but we enter their life at a point of change, a moment of disruption in the orderly flow of their everyday lives: a moment of crisis.

Dramatic characters, like characters in fairy tales, are usually in trouble and trying to find a way out. They are men and women who are often the cause of the trouble or subject to troubling misfortune when chance or unexpected circumstances come into their lives; they are the driving force of the narrative.

Characterization in narrative is what a character does or intends to do, but in film there are different ways to clarify these actions and intentions. The screenwriter has at her disposal the whole expressive vocabulary of cinema. The visual range is broad, from the round earth and the blue sky to the close detail of the human face, small gestures or significant objects. Landscape and light, the human environment and precise imagery can all represent the interior life of thoughts and dreams, and suggest hidden motives or desires. The language of cinema includes montage, juxtaposition, sound design and the ability to move back and forth through time and space to tell the story in the cut.

This means that character is created through fragments and countless details: physical appearance, body language; the way they move and interact in their everyday world. The screenwriter's task involves the selection and careful placing of these elliptical elements that become basic components of the plot: the specific features and traits of character behaviour, the network of relationships, the particular world of the protagonists that makes their lives alive and vivid for the spectator, as they set out on the journey together.

The journey metaphor assumes that the protagonist is in constant movement, both internally and externally. They have to move ahead, they have a need, a desire, a goal that drives them; there is something at stake that the audience can understand and experience for themselves. This need for character progression means that the screenwriter has to design challenging settings and situations that slow down or divert the protagonist from their goal or put pressure on them to change behaviour or strategy. Rhythm is an expressive element, a quickening or delaying of the storytelling that is also an important dramatic device.

The turns and twists of the plot mean the road is not straight: the journey of the hero or the heroine must involve defeats and delays, as well as momentary success and relief; moments of up and down, stages and steps, turning points. Each scene should be charged with importance and carry the mark of what is at stake for the protagonist. Each moment matters, as they press on relentlessly against all the odds to the end.

The next chapter will look in more detail at how to plot and structure the journey of your characters.

EXERCISES

1. Choose three people in your life who were important to you as you were growing up. They could be a parent, sibling, relative, neighbour, friend, rival or teacher. Describe them briefly and discuss why they were important and the effect they had on you. What qualities or traits were fundamental to their personality and what surprised or fascinated you? Try to remember an event involving them. Describe what happened and reflect on the emotional impact.

2. Write about an incident or situation that marked your shift from childhood to adolescence or adolescence to young adulthood: something that *changed* you. It might be, for example, an initiation into a new way of thinking, your first love or first encounter with death, disillusionment with an older figure or betrayal by a friend. Describe what happened and how you came to terms with the situation and what you think you learned from it.

3. Write about some key moments in your life – your moment of greatest: (a) fear, (b) courage, (c) sadness, (d) joy, (e) shame, (f) loss, (g) achievement. Be open and honest – it is more important than literary style.

4. Select three films that you have enjoyed recently. Identify the core desire and need for the protagonists. What is at stake for each of them? Do they change through the action of the plot and in what way?

5. Select a protagonist from a project that you are currently working on and write a two-page biography for them. This should include a brief physical description, as well as background information on the social and psychological elements that shape their personality. Include their name and place of birth, parents' names and occupations, and other relevant facts about family background; places where the character has lived; education and other training; occupations; significant and formative experiences; key figures who have influenced their life; important interests, traits or habits. You should also note any vulnerabilities, secrets or contradictions that could be used in character development and plot, and list their needs and desires. What do they want or need most at this point in their life?

6. Select three characters that you are currently working with. In what way are they vulnerable – physically, emotionally or morally? What threat or danger are they exposed to in the story? What action will they take to avoid or escape the danger?

7. Take three characters that you are currently working with. What secrets do they have? How does this affect their behaviour with other characters? Are any of the other characters trying to find out their secret? Why? Why not? What would happen if one character were to reveal a secret to another?

8. Take a story idea that you are working on and sketch out a map of the character relationships – how each of the characters are related to each other through family, friendship, work, need or desire.

9. Read the screenplay for *The Third Man* and draw a map of the character network and relationships. Select three principal characters and explore the triangular relationship between them. What are the lines of developing action? What does each character know or not know about the other? How is that knowledge used in creating conflict and tension in the plot? Describe the beginning, middle and end of each of the relationships. Now return to question 8 and review your current character-relationship map. What is missing in terms of fears, loves, hatreds, desires? What else do you have to learn about them to make the story work?

10. Select three characters that you are currently working with. Imagine each one in a stressful situation, e.g. an accident, violent fight, a problem at work or school. How do they deal with it? Take your time to develop the scene.

11. Select three films that you have enjoyed recently and choose three characters. Choose a key action that each of them make and explore their motivation. Was it a single cause or complex of motives that decided their action? Repeat the same exercise with characters that you are currently working with.

12. Take three films that you currently admire and identify the main characters. Who, if any, is the protagonist? What is their objective and what is at stake for them? Analyse the same three films. Who is the antagonist or the forces of antagonism that oppose the protagonist's objective? Do the same for a story that you are currently working on.

13. Examine the same three examples from question 11 and give examples of how the protagonist(s) reveal their determination to succeed. Does the protagonist change? How is that change set up and developed? Do they gain any insight into themselves or the nature of their problem? How does that insight relate to the climax of the film?

14. Choose three films with a clear antagonist or opponent. Analyse their characters. Do they have any positive qualities that make them more rounded characters?

15. Work on your own or in pairs. Decide on the following criteria for a protagonist: a job, a life problem and a personality type. Then use these three choices as a springboard for developing a short film.

16. Find a location that inspires you – it could be a park, a shopping centre an abandoned factory. Spend time there and observe what happens. Take notes and photographs. Think about how the location suggests characters. What kind of person would you find there? Describe them and develop a short story.

17. Choose a character you are currently working on and write a monologue on their obsessions, relationships and desires.

18. Describe an incident that reveals something normally hidden about the character.

19. Describe an incident that would challenge the character and perhaps transform them.

20. Describe a character with an internal tension of some kind. Find a scene that presents the tension dramatically.

SCRIPT ANALYSIS

Read the screenplay of *The Third Man*, then make notes from the following questions:

1. Who is the protagonist – i.e. physical, social and psychological? Describe his character briefly. What is his backstory? Why has he come to Vienna? How do we find out about his character, backstory and project?
2. What does he want and why is it important to him? What does he need? How is this different from what he wants? How does this difference help create internal conflict in the character?
3. Why can't he get what he wants and needs?
4. What's at stake for him?
5. How do the protagonist's characteristics or qualities help and hinder him in his plot quest?
6. Briefly describe the story world, including visual references. What part does the visualization of the story world play in the development and illumination of character, plot and theme?
7. Give a brief description of the secondary characters, including the antagonist (the one who opposes the action of the protagonist). What is their relationship to the main character and his objective?
8. How and why do the feelings, needs and objectives of the protagonist change during the development of the plot? Give examples from the beginning, middle and end of the plot.
9. Give examples of three key decisions/actions taken by the protagonist. How do they impact on the plot development?
10. How has the protagonist changed through the course of the plot? What is the character arc? List the main beats of his journey.
11. What part does the antagonist play in the protagonist's journey and the theme?
12. What do you think is the theme(s)?
13. What kind of clarity or illumination is achieved in the climax of the plot for both protagonist and audience?

Use the questions to guide a similar analysis of three films or screenplays that you admire.

5

STRUCTURE

It is in our nature to tell stories, to dramatize our relationships, our work, our love lives, our everyday encounters – to give them shape and meaning, to clarify and communicate to others. In dramatizing we give life a plot; we select and organize events in order to entertain and to understand what happened. For this we use dramatic tools: set-up, suspense and surprise, juxtaposition, ellipsis, irony, the compression and extension of time.

Dramatic stories engage an audience, appealing to our emotions, imagination and intellect. A well-designed, well-structured script will resonate more deeply, touch and amuse us in more complex ways than a script with poor structure.

Understanding structure is a way of thinking about the audience experience, about how to tell the story so as to involve the viewer. This requires getting a handle on concepts such as point of view, preparation and foreshadowing, cause and effect, exposition and revelation, as well as the role of dramatic conflict in creating momentum and surprise. Good structure is about keeping the audience involved and shares with the well-told joke a sense of rhythm and timing, including where and when to place the dramatic moments of a story for maximum effect.

In classical cinema, narrative structure provides a framework that brings together character, event and theme into an expressive whole, where character and meaning are revealed through a plot design that builds through conflict inexorably to an ending.

FORM AND CONTENT

Art Forms

Cinema has inherited theories of dramatic and narrative structure from theatre and literature but it also shares an interest in dynamic form with all the arts: the metrical and alliterative patterns of poetry, the importance of composition and perspective in painting, the structures of light and shadow found in photography.

Basic structures underlie most art forms, but in its harmonies, counterpoints and motifs, and in its rhythmical unfolding, drama has an especial affinity with the structures of music and architecture. As a symphony falls into three, four or five movements in the creation of tension and its resolution, so, similarly, a feature film develops its narrative in a number of movements or acts. Like the rhythms and proportions of a Gothic cathedral, with stones and stained glass placed in the right order and proportion, a well-structured screenplay interweaves form and content to create a space for the free play of imagination and emotion.

Drama shares with myth, religion and ritual this use of rhythmic movement, darkness and light, motif and music to give unity and comprehension to an essential mystery that an audience may not be aware of but which shapes their experience.

Ritual Space

The feature film screenplay has a formal equivalence to ritual in another sense: that of a special

A well-structured screenplay interweaves form and content to create a space for the free play of imagination and emotion.
IVAN VDOVIN/ALAMY STOCK

consecrated space with its own rules – a playground; a temporary world; a framed space like a card table, magic circle, soccer pitch or theatre; a place apart from the ordinary world with its own set of rules and expectations. Like twelve-bar blues, a sonnet or a haiku, or the relationship between phrase, motif and movement in music, these rules or principles of structure appeal to our love of pattern and order.

Pattern

We have strong emotional reactions to the perception of pattern, to the contrasting characters and clashes of antagonism in a story, just as we do to the relationships of melody and harmony in music. Pattern and design give us pleasure: we sense beauty in order over randomness, and in predictability over chaos.

The regularities of pattern suggest a meaningful, purposeful and, therefore, predictable world, rather than one ruled by mere chance: a world over which we have some control. As evolutionary creatures we have become pattern extractors, searching for repetitions and causal relations, recurring features that will allow us to predict what might happen next – because our lives might depend upon this knowledge. Pattern recognition in facial expressions, for example, allows us to predict mood and intention in others, and to anticipate likely actions and reactions, to predict threat or encouragement.

Similarly, structural elements in drama set up patterns of rising expectations that may be satisfied, modified or overturned, but which always attract our attention and offer useful information

We take pleasure in the repetitions and variations of pattern. BRIAN DUNNIGAN

about how to navigate our own lives. In this sense, the feature screenplay is an art form structured and elaborated to attract and hold attention and from which audiences can make rewarding and meaningful inferences.

Structural patterns also provide the basis for a kind of cognitive play where the repertoires and scenarios of narrative allow us to reflect on different strategies for problem-solving and survival. Breaking the rules and the patterns of expectation are, of course, part of the repertoire of the screenwriter as she seeks to surprise and intrigue the reader, but every new screenwriter has to develop their own dynamic relationship with convention, audience expectation and structure.

WRITING STRUCTURE

Structural Models

The current conventions in screenwriting theory include a variety of structural models that have been codified in recent screenwriting handbooks, most notably the *3 Act Structure* and *The Hero's Journey*. These books encourage the writer to build up and structure their story following specific story beats, turning points and progressions. They offer useful guidelines, as long as you know when *not* to follow them.

Rules

Every story has its own rhythm and structure, and this is something to be discovered rather than imposed. If you stay too close to the conventional form, you run the risk of constantly making the same film. Rules are never forever; they are always changing. The main rule is being entertaining, to capture and maintain the interest of the audience, which is, of course, one definition of good structure.

DISCOVERY

While writing is discovery, it is also planning and designing – or discovering – the shape of your

THREE ACT STRUCTURE

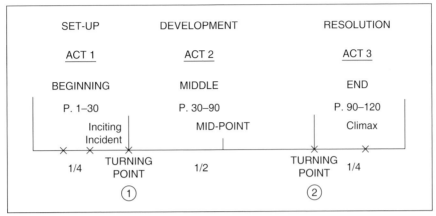

A structural paradigm for the feature film screenplay, as popularized by the American screenwriting teacher Syd Field.

story. Writing is surprising yourself and your audience with turns and twists, and character revelations that become elements of the plot structure. When the writing is going well, the story seems to grow organically. For writing is also discovering how one part relates to another and how suddenly they both relate to the whole.

Planning vs Improvisation

Finding the ideal structure for your story involves conscious and unconscious work, planning as well as improvising. Each writer has to find their own method of developing and structuring their screenplay without over-reliance on beat sheets or formulas. Most writing is rewriting, trial and error, a back and forth between the events of a story and the inner life of the characters. Finally, you have to make decisions about the plot.

Craft Skills

With this in mind, understanding conventional structural tools, concepts and techniques will give you a range of options with which to help you shape your story for an audience, as well as helping to solve story problems. These are the craft

skills and conventions of screenwriting based on a long dramatic tradition that can be studied, learned and, of course, ignored or reinvented.

PLOT

Character and Plot

Character is not a static element but is revealed in action and interaction with others.

The journey metaphor assumes constant movement internally and externally. It involves details of actions and reactions, the impact of events and surprising encounters, the relationship between back story and future goals – all of which have to be plotted and revealed or implied by a line of dialogue, a look or a glance, a gesture or action. Information about characters' thoughts and feelings, what they know or intend, what they are ignorant of and only now realize, all require the screenwriter to make strategic decisions about how to show this – and when.

Dramatic structure is not an arbitrary invention but a codification of how we make sense of the world and dramatic plots help us connect to, and make sense of, character needs and desires. An audience has to feel the cause and need that drives the protagonist forward, what is at stake and why a particular goal matters. On this journey every moment counts. This is why character is inseparable from the action of the plot; and why the plot needs a premise or controlling idea to give direction and meaning to that action: the underlying concept that is motivating you to write this particular story.

Character deepens and enriches the plot and audience experience. Character action affects every incident and event, creating momentum and sudden changes of direction. Think of Don Draper in *Mad Men* (2007–2015) or Daenerys Targaryen in *Game of Thrones* (2011–2019). Character motivation provides the through-line, the spine of the story, the progression of cause and effect. This is what Aristotle refers to as 'unity of action', which is essentially plot structure and was, for Aristotle, the most important element of dramatic writing.

Tragic Plots

Tragic plots show protagonists struggling against their fate, exercising their will and demonstrating their humanity in the face of great difficulty or suffering. The action of the dramatic plot, unlike the epic, is swift and focused, bringing the hero quickly to crisis and discovery, to the realization of some terrible truth or disaster. At the same time, a sense of foreboding and inevitability comes from the implication that the hero in some way contributes to his fate through some previous mistake or error of judgement – what Aristotle referred to as *hamartia*. Thus incidents in the plot that earlier seemed to have occurred by chance now in retrospect seem inevitable. Suffering (pathos) leads to discovery and realization – *anagnorisis* – 'a change from ignorance to knowledge' usually accompanied by a change of fortune for the protagonist.

For the audience there is a powerful emotional charge to this dramatic form that reminds us of the hidden unconscious forces at play in our own lives. There is a paradox that what we seem to choose freely has somehow already been determined, linked to a constant realization of our own mistaken perceptions and judgements and the impenetrable mystery of the human situation. The coherence and clarity of tragic plots, the surprising inevitability that links beginnings and ends is pleasurable for the audience. The final moment of realization and enlightenment is affirmative and cathartic for both spectator and protagonist.

This tightly bound progression of cause and effect and the driving through-line of action to a sudden realization and reversal, where every element contributes to the overall meaning, are not only constants of tragic dramatic form but also the underlying concepts of classical plot in mainstream cinema.

Plot Outline

While for some it may be the least important part of a narrative, without the structural underpinnings of a plot the other elements, including character, may fail to cohere or attract attention. Although it may come later in the creative process, plotting the story outline is crucial to a deeper understanding of the complex relationships at the heart of a drama. A plot summary may miss out subplots or ambiguities, but a careful reduction and linkage of the main story beats can reveal what is being imitated – what the story is really about, whether a moral action or a psychological state. The reader or viewer is herself constantly summarizing the links between motive and objective as she tracks and tries to make sense of the story, moving between the past and present, concerned not only with what will happen next but also trying to understand what is happening now.

Once the screenplay is complete, a plot summary can also be a useful tool for script editors or collaborators in illuminating the gaps of credibility or momentum. Plot gives form to desire, the desire of both protagonist and reader to know more, to anticipate future outcomes and to have their expectations confounded in surprising but meaningful ways.

A plot summary also reminds us of the two interacting levels of the audience experience: the character's journey and the author's organization of events that gives us selective access to the characters' world.

Story and Plot

We experience our lives in the same way as both story and plot: the memories, dreams and desires, the motivations and intentions, the truth, lies and moments of recognition, the actions and decisions of our lived experience that we shape into the stories and plots of our lives, where we are both participant and observer of our own drama. This is close to what the Russian formalists distinguished as *fabula* (story), the relationships in the characters' world, and *siuzhet* (plot), the relationships organized by the author or screenwriter and designed to have the spectator become involved and participate in the lives of the characters.

This distinction creates a tension between two levels of plot that can be exploited for emotional effect. For example, a plot always begins *in media res*, in the middle of a story, so there are events that the characters have already experienced but that we, the audience, have yet to learn about. This creates mystery; it triggers curiosity in the audience and a desire to know more. This is the basic structure of a detective story where certain characters know more than the detective or audience. The emotional impact of dramatic irony, on the other hand, requires that some of the characters are more ignorant of events than the reader or spectator.

In practical terms, this distinction between two dimensions of plotting might encourage the screenwriter to develop their story imaginatively from the point of view of both the protagonist and the audience. The writer puts himself in the character's mind and world, imagining how they will respond to plot events, what they would like to do next and what they *must* do; then switching focus and reading the screenplay for entertainment and asking himself what would be a fantastic twist or shift that would excite him if he were in the audience.

In fact, many of the interrupting and delaying techniques – foreshadowing, suspense, curiosity, digression – are aspects of the *siuzhet* rather than the *fabula*; but being aware of these different dimensions enriches the screenwriter's options for engaging with an audience.

Plot Relationships

For Aristotle, the most important part of plot was the relationship amongst the incidents; plots are ways of meaningfully relating incidents to one another. The types of relationship are limited – one event after another (chronologically), or close to each other (spatially); because of what came before (causally); resembling one another (associatively) or narrated within the plot (narratively), such as a character telling a story or reading a letter.

The most powerful relationships are causally connected, usually working in parallel with a before/after chronological system. This approach interacts most effectively with the basic patterns of our minds: when something happens, we seek to find out what caused it; or, before taking an action or making a decision, we may reflect on the consequences of this decision for others and ourselves.

Incidents

An incident or event, from the point of view of the screenwriter, is where something happens that moves the story forward, where the protagonist has to think and feel, act or react. It is one of the building blocks in constructing the plot and includes the inciting incident or catalyst that generates the main conflict and a series of transformations in the plot. Each incident and event of a plot is part of a larger whole, but the structure of each follows a familiar tripartite pattern – following Aristotle's definition of a good plot as something with a beginning, middle and end.

The French theorist Julian Griemas, analysing folk tales, described the basic structure of an incident:

1. The hero is in a special state.
2. He needs something.
3. He achieves it.

In *Code Unknown* (2000), a young middle-class professional is ironing while watching television. A noise from her neighbour's flat disturbs her and she picks up the remote and turns down the sound. We hear shouting and a child's frightened cries and watch as the woman decides what to do about an incident of possible child abuse. She points the remote at the television and turns the sound back up and continues with her ironing.

The Russian formalist Shklovsky finds a similar internal structure in early Trickster tales, where the protagonist is in a tight spot and forced to answer a difficult riddle:

1. We are given an explanation of the tight spot.
2. His answer.
3. A particular resolution.

Modern theorists generally agree with Aristotle that the plot and each of its component incidents has this tripartite internal structure, which the narrative theorist Robert Belknap summarizes as:

1. A basic situation.
2. A need.
3. An action.

For Belknap, this three-part structure works well for short forms like the narrative action in a fairy tale where the *fabula* is close to the *siuzhet*. But the model fails to account for 'the lyrical and reflective digressions'[24] found in the novel and, we could add, the short film or the feature screenplay, where the plot relationships may be thematic, an associative connection rather than causal. Thus, the structure of incidents in the plot is bipartite:

1. An expectation.
2. Its fulfilment or frustration.

In *Code Unknown* (2000) we are waiting to see what the woman will do, we expect that she might get involved but at this point she does nothing. The internal structure of the scene follows a three-part structure but the plot focus, the audience experience, is primarily on the two-part dynamic of expectation and resolution. The screenwriter, aware of this distinction, can organize and manipulate this interaction and tension between story and plot, playing on the internal tripartite rhythm of character need and action, while building the expectation/resolution dynamic of a scene or situation that will engage an audience.

UNITY OF ACTION

Mythos

For Aristotle, plot or *mythos,* which is the overarching through-line of action, was the central element in a play that shaped audience experience and created meaning, and was more important than diction, spectacle, music or even character. Defined as the 'representation of an action… an arrangement of incidents', whereas the 'action' or *fabula* is the arrangement of incidents in the characters' world and 'representation' belongs to the *siuzhet* or plot and all its constituent elements, including character, diction, music, spectacle and thought.

Emotion

The intensity and directness of dramatic plots evolved out of the limitations of time and situation in the Greek world. With audiences standing or sitting for a short period, a strong and focused plot was the most powerful way of engaging their emotions. Plotted action was the chief source of pity, terror and other 'dangerous' emotions, which would be generated then purged by the drama. This goal, and the limitations imposed by the time and place of performance, generated the classical rhetoric for modern drama – central to which is the through-line or 'unity of action.'

Action

This is what Aristotle means by the drama needing to imitate a single action, a series of causally related incidents linked by the action of the protagonist and triggered by *hamartia*, or error, which leads through suffering to recognition. This offers a clear and simple design that reveals a pattern of behaviour that seems probable but not inevitable. Take, for example, the anger of Achilles, which causes and provides focus and unity to Homer's account in the *Illiad*. The plot moves inexorably from Achilles's angry withdrawal from battle, to the gifting of his armour, which leads to the death of his best friend and the channelling of his subsequent grief into murderous revenge and the degradation of Hector before the walls of Troy.

Through-Line

The dramatic unity and causal through-line of Achilles's actions maximize the feelings of terror and pity for an audience and the recognition of the insecurity and incompleteness of a human life. Even though Achilles is restored to his humanity in the meeting with Hector's father Priam, it is tempered by the realization of the inevitability of human suffering and the unpredictability of the gods.

Clarification

Aristotle points out that it is Homer's art, the way he selects and structures his material, that enables us to see and understand the ignorance, vulnerability and contingency at the heart of human existence. Homer has imposed form and order on the chaos of life and made the particular story of Achilles's anger into a plot of universal significance. In this sense, structure or the imposition of order is not just an aesthetic matter, but also the very way that an artist or screenwriter clarifies and communicates his moral truth about the human world.

Causality

The causal connection between the incidents and events of the plot are crucial to its effect. For Aristotle, the causal connection was essential to our need for a well-ordered, interpretable world. The audience takes pleasure from the perception of causality just as they do with the imitation of human action on stage. This kind of intelligence, an ability to link past and future, cause and effect, has contributed to our evolutionary success: animals that can understand these temporal and causal relationships are more likely to survive. As humans mature we move from being able to describe events to perceiving the connection between them. We pay more attention to cause and interpret events in terms of goals and objectives. We seek coherence and explanation at a deeper level. This is fundamental to the pleasures of dramatic narrative. Buster Keaton is a master of this kind of causally rooted pleasure, with plots constructed around two causal epiphanies: 'I could see it coming' and 'I didn't see it coming' – just as useful in comedy as in tragedy, and allowing for endless variations in suspense, surprise and the creation of dramatic tension.

As the creators of the animated TV series *South Park* (1997–2019), Trey Parker and Matt Stone told an NYU audience:

> Stories are defined by cause and effect, this causes that and that causes this and so on. It is about set-ups and pay-offs. It's about action and reaction. Cause and effect lend meaning to events. They link scenes together. They give wholeness to seemingly separate ideas. Cause and effect are the linking in your chain. They make a story a story.[25]

Here they are talking about the importance of inventing strong causal relationships in the plot, as well as introducing surprising reversals that have been prepared for earlier. The Aristotelian plot is causally integrated, with every element and action playing its part in the shaping of emotion and the creation of meaning, such that if one part were dropped, it would diminish the emotional impact of the whole. This not only offers energy and clarity to the rising tension, but also creates the sense of inevitability that gathers around the protagonist's struggle.

This remains the dominant plot structure in mainstream American cinema – the causal relationship of incident to incident: a purposeful arrangement of experience that is clear and simple to follow, bringing redemption and a new harmony to the life of the protagonist, satisfying our need for order. But this very ease of connection and comprehension is what some film-makers reject as failing to reflect the world as they see it.

In the next chapter we will examine alternative structures that eschew this traditional cause–effect model. In general terms, the relationships in these alternative structures are associative and thematic, working with similarity and difference across parallel plot lines, rather than causally integrated ones.

Parallel Plots

In most of his plays, Shakespeare sacrifices 'the causal tightness of plotting' required by Aristotle for 'a thematic tightness around parallel plots'.[26] We have already encountered this style of film structure in Chapter 5, where we discussed the colonial and domestic relationships in Clair Denis' *Chocolat*. Here the plot of mistress and servant is paralleled by the contrast between the world of colonial women and children trapped at home with the autonomy of the masculine world of the colonial overlords.

Shakespeare's use of parallel plotting often also involves different social levels; masters and servants, kings and courtiers, townsfolk and peasants. They are not, however, so parallel that there is no interaction or overlap between the plots; though never enough to satisfy Aristotle's definition of a good plot. In *King Lear*, for example, the plot around Lear and his daughters runs alongside the Gloucester plot generated by his bastard son. While Edmund is ultimately responsible, directly or indirectly, for the death of all of Lear's daughters, the two plotlines don't need each other. Here, Shakespeare is sacrificing the tight relationship between incidents, the emotional impact of causality and rising action in order to explore the similarities and differences between parallel worlds – sinning fathers, cruel and faithful children – thereby asking us to think of the common thematic elements, such as arrogance and selfishness.

Similarly in *Henry IV Part 1*, the parallel worlds of Falstaff's tavern, Hotspur's rebellion and the King's court, contrast and illuminate each other. Each world, and their characters, have their strengths and weaknesses: zest for life, bravery and kingship. Each disparages the other as sinful, impulsive or pedantic.

The incidents in these plays are linked not by causality, but by similarity; they allow for comparison and contrast and create rich patterns of implication for the audience who are consciously and unconsciously following the overlapping and divergent plotlines. The movement between parallel plotlines is also an important aspect of many TV series like *Game of Thrones*, although these plotlines are contained within the over-arching objective shared by everyone – the Iron Throne.

This focus on thematic rather than causal unity and a series of parallel plotlines rather than a single plot is the basis for a range of alternative structures that the screenwriter should study. Multi-protagonist, ensemble, tandem and flashback structures can be found in films as diverse as *Citizen Kane* (1942), *Chocolat* (1988), *Little Miss Sunshine* (2006), *Code Unknown* (2000), *Pulp Fiction* (1994), *A Separation* (2011), *Timbuctu* (2014) and *Avengers Assemble* (2013). These structures offer different and complementary pleasures to the single-protagonist plot but all involve some degree of conflict as a technique for audience involvement.

CONFLICT

Protagonist and Antagonist

Aristotle says little about conflict in the *Poetics*, as it was assumed in the Greek world that *agon*, or the struggle between protagonist and antagonist, was central to any drama – just as we assume that drama, as an imitation of life, must always at some point be concerned with conflict.

Strength of Will

We are born vulnerable and dependent, and grow up experiencing a succession of conflicts at home and school, in work, play and love. Born into hierarchies, as well as the demands and expectations of others, we are at the same time encouraged to see ourselves as individuals, free to choose our lives. We are encouraged to seek fulfilment or satisfaction, driven by unconscious needs and wants, which are constantly frustrated or limited by our place in society.

The world will not necessarily give us what we want; there are always obstacles and complications involved in relation to our ambitions. This requires us to persevere, to develop strong wills and press forward in the face of the inevitable difficulties of life. How characters deal with life's challenges, and what they are prepared to do in order to get what they want, reveal what is at stake, what they value and who they are. Ree Dolly in *Winter's Bone* (2010) is a typical representative of this single-protagonist structure. The stress and pressure of opposition to her desire requires her to respond or change: to change direction, attitude or strategy.

Character Arc

The concept of a character arc is predicated on this idea of incremental change under pressure, a gradual revelation and interlocking of character and theme: Macbeth's destructive ambition and Thelma's quest for freedom provide the underlying meaning of the narrative. Character is forged and clarified through conflict with others and with oneself; characters become aware of unconscious needs that propel them into contradictory actions they never imagined possible.

Conflict is a technique in fiction that binds character and plot through surprising revelations and actions. Characters are forced to dig deep for the insight and passion that will carry them forward and, in the process, clarify their motivations and desire as they decide what to do. For example, in *The Godfather* (1972), Michael has to decide which family he will devote himself to. In *Thelma and Louise* (1991), the decision is when their journey to freedom, which began as recreation, becomes an absolute commitment. For an audience, the more complex or conflicted the motivation of the protagonist, the more intriguing the characterization.

Internal Conflict

Hence the importance of strong and nuanced opposition in a well-structured screenplay for the creation of not only external conflict between characters, but also an internal conflict that triggers an emotional response. External conflict alone leads to melodrama, angry exchanges, physical confrontation. Conflict within a character riven by self-doubt, guilt or fear, torn between conflicting values or motivations, is more involving for an audience and leads to a suspense based around tension and ambiguity, where the audience has to take sides as the conflict builds towards the climax.

SUSPENSE

In a famous interview for Truffaut's book on the film-maker, Hitchcock declared that there are two primary principles in drama: suspense and surprise. Suspense is when we know there is a bomb in the case and worry about where and when it will go off, while surprise is when the room blows up and we realize there was a bomb in the case. He added that while we need a few surprises, the basic principle in a good screenplay is suspense – making the audience want to know what is going to happen next. The creation of suspense is a key technique for engaging the emotions of an audience.

Suspense is clearly related to audience involvement and knowledge: how much they know and care about a character or situation. Hence, good structure is also about information flow or exposition: when and how to reveal knowledge of plot or character, how much and to whom.

The emotions are awakened, just as in music, by the creation of tension and its resolution. This is the strongest kind of suspense, more effective than simple mystery or overt conflict: a building of tension, from the Latin *tendere* 'to stretch'. Tension in narrative fiction has that effect: of something being stretched until it must snap; and it requires preparation. For example, in *Drive* (2011) where the unnamed getaway driver has a five-minute rule: the bad guys must exit from the crime scene within five minutes or he leaves. He always sets his watch on the dashboard and we know he will do it. The audience can feel his rigidity and repressed violence. It is not a question of will he or won't he, but when and how it will happen. We sense the outcome will be shocking. The incidents of the plot accumulate; we wait, knowing that the thread of tension will be taken to breaking point. This is central to the creation of suspense: letting us know there is a bomb in the case, a ticking clock on the dashboard, keeping something unresolved as long as possible, prolonging and delaying the outcome. It is through tension that foreshadowing and suspense achieve their most successful interaction. This is achieved simply by delaying an event that the audience knows about and, therefore, expects to happen.

Readers and viewers naturally want the tense and suspenseful feelings resolved; they seek release from tension, they want answers.

EXPOSITION

Flow of Information

The screenplay story is fragmentary, composed of subtle hints, conflicting opinions, partial revelations, mysteries and denials, secrets and lies that are organized to reveal character motivation, move the story forward and intrigue the spectator. Structure requires organizing this flow of information, the facts the audience needs to know in order to follow and experience the story. The specific story world includes character biographies and their traits, feelings, desires, flaws and aspirations that drive the narrative and will be paid off later.

Questions of Knowledge

Exposition is an aspect of plotting that involves questions of knowledge, such as: where are we; who are these characters and what do they want from each other; what does the audience know that the characters do not and vice-versa; what does the audience need to know; what do some characters know that others do not? These raise an over-arching question: where to place recurring lines of dialogue or imagery that add thematic texture and prepare for, or foreshadow, what is to come? The challenge for a screenwriter is how to convey this essential exposition without slowing the story or losing dramatic interest.

The characters in their world already know much of what the audience needs to understand in order to follow the story, but any crude attempt to have characters tell each other what they obviously already know will kill the drama. Characters should be shown simply and clearly pursuing their objectives and relationships in the present, going about their daily activities with no need to explain what is happening to the audience.

Pursuit of Objective

The richness of possible story information means the screenwriter must select only what is essential for understanding and dramatic effect. Let the audience work out what is going on through exposition that is elliptical, indirect and invisible. 'Show don't tell' is the workshop maxim that advises the writer to craft scenes using a subtle cinematic language of sound and image, actions and reactions, looks and glances, and suggestive lines of dialogue that allow the audience to explore, discover, make connections and experience the story for themselves.

Withholding Information

Withholding information can arouse our emotions and make us curious; misinformation or misunderstanding can prepare us for powerful surprises at the end. Many of Shakespeare's plots are constructed around lies and lying that create a tension toward the end. Exposition is the plotting and placing of action and image, dialogue and subtext that clarify and shape audience participation in what is happening now – and what might happen in the future.

Too much, but also too little, information can limit audience engagement. The audience need to know enough about character intentions and objectives to understand what is at stake and to experience the significance of the action for the protagonists. The basic principle is to reveal only what the audience need to know about characters and the situation for narrative comprehension and development. Arouse their curiosity, force them to ask the question 'why?' and this will create a tension that can later be resolved. Similarly with dialogue: anything that has to be said, hold back as long as possible until there is a compelling need for explanation; use oblique or banal lines of dialogue that deal with the present issue or point to the future rather than narrate what is already known.

Active Exposition

Apart from creating a compelling need for the audience to know, the most effective means of conveying necessary information to the audience is through dramatic conflict. What the film-maker Alexander Mackendrick refers to as 'active exposition' takes place in the context of a scene where the clash of wills or the questioning of foil figures forces the revelation of key story information.

Along with conflict, the use of humour is another useful technique to conceal exposition; they are often used together to disguise the release of key information. For example, *Up In the Air* (2009), where Ryan and Alex display their extensive collection of loyalty cards, competing to see who is the more skilled player of the system. We are amused by their ironical engagement in corporate status games, while learning more about their characters and the erotic charge between them, which prepares us for the following seduction scene. In this way, exposition is a by-product of a dramatic encounter and emerges organically from within the story, rather than being imposed from outside by a narrator.

Voice-Over Narration

Voice-over narration is, of course, a technique that allows a character to directly address and inform the audience, but should be used sparingly, unless it is central to the autobiographical or ironical nature of the story. It can be used at the beginning, as it is in both *The Third Man* (1949) and *Up in the Air* (2009), to set up the story and theme, and to draw us closer to the protagonist, but only if a more dramatically interesting way cannot be found.

Flashback

The use of flashback as a form of exposition is also to be considered carefully, unless it is part of the overall structure of parallel storylines interacting and playing off each other, as in *Reservoir Dogs* (1992) or *Martha, Marcy, May, Marlene* (2011). A flashback as information or an explanation of character trait or motive takes us out of the present drama and slows the narrative impetus. However, it can also add value, complexity and lyrical texture, develop character and set up clashing ironies, as used in the TV series *The Handmaid's Tale* (2017). As with everything else, it depends on the story you are telling. A TV series often has the time and space for more reflective, lyrical moments that cut away from the main storyline.

Tell the Story

The main point is to just get on with telling the story: thrust the audience into the middle of the action and let them work out the past. Show us the protagonists pursuing their objectives and characters getting on with their lives. Let the audience uncover the connections and mysteries behind these lives. Release exposition carefully and selectively, and spread it out slowly through the whole drama. The beginning usually requires a little more exposition to bring the audience into the story but less than you think, while certain critical facts should be left for the climax and revelation at the end.

Foreshadowing

A successful story integrates character and action, and there are a variety of techniques, including conflict and suspense, that support this interaction. Foreshadowing and preparing for what is to follow are complementary ways of weaving together character, plot and theme, and providing focus through the use of image, sound, a line of dialogue, a mood, a temporal inversion (the end at the beginning), a prophecy or simply the sense of inevitability in the progression of the plot. Like a tone in classical music, action can be prepared, suspended and resolved, themes introduced and developed or a troubling character trait observed that will take on dramatic significance later. This technique goes back to the earliest roots in oral storytelling: the setting-up or planting of an idea that will be paid off later.

The young drifter who, in the introduction to *A Short Film About Killing* (1988), casually flicks a stone from a motorway bridge and smiles at the sounds of breaking glass and screeching tyres prepares us for his later brutal murder of a taxi driver. The blank screen and the child cowboy rocking on his squeaking toy horse, which symbolizes the emptiness of the American dream, at the opening of *Midnight Cowboy* (1969) and the master at the beginning of *The Servant* (1963) declaring that he wants help with 'everything', which anticipates the complete take-over and collapse of his life, are examples of foreshadowing that are equally as intriguing and prophetic as the witches at the beginning of Macbeth. They pose a question in our minds, engage our emotions, prepare us for the plot action to come and, by provoking our curiosity and concern, enhance the effect of conflict, suspense and dramatic tension. For example, the description of Hannibal Lecter as a 'monster' before we meet him in *Silence of the Lambs* (1991), contributes to the suspense and wondering about what kind of monster he is – also preparing us for the surprise of meeting an apparently refined middle-class intellectual. The temporal inversion at the beginning of *Citizen Kane* (1942), where the dying man's last word 'Rosebud' prepares us for the biographical quest, foreshadows the end and prepares us for the lyrical meaning that transcends the final image of death.

Foreshadowing and various forms of preparation run through the entire screenplay, exciting our expectation, engaging our emotions and creating the sense of organic unity that makes the drama feel real. Techniques like this should by studied and practised by the screenwriter and filmmaker.

SURPRISE

The Unexpected

Another technique central to the pleasure of good narrative structure is surprise or reversal: the unexpected in life and art that cuts through the habitual and familiar, and excites in the audience an upsurge of feeling – a reminder that life can be surprising – in good and bad ways.

Pity and Fear

According to the classicist Martha Nussbaum, the tragic plots of fifth-century Athens were deliberately constructed to show us the significance of what happens to people through no fault of their own: the pity and fear of the characters confronted by chance events that could destroy them, and the concerns of an audience aware that the same thing could happen to them. How can you lead a good life, if so much is contingent and out of your control?

The Irrational

Amongst the unexpected ways in which our lives can be surprisingly turned are the powerful primitive emotions that can erupt at any time: for example, the desire for revenge and the passions aroused by erotic love, jealousy, need, fear. Ancient Greek tragic drama offered no easy answers but by showing the mystery and indeterminacy of human motivation and action, and the role of the unexpected in life, asked its audience to think about these things and to evaluate their ethical importance.

Design

For modern writers too, the invention of surprising events and revelations remains an important element in the design of the screenplay, requiring careful planning and preparation to be effective, although, paradoxically, the best ideas may surprise the writer herself in the process of writing. Technically, however, the preparation for, and the delivery of, surprising moments are elements of plotting related to exposition or the structured release and flow of information.

BEGINNINGS AND ENDINGS

Inciting Incident

The beginning of the screenplay is where we find the inciting incident or catalyst: the disturbing factor that disrupts the everyday world of the protagonist and provokes further actions, raises questions and triggers our curiosity. There is a secret lurking under the story and this is precisely the outbreak. We are invited to go on a journey to unravel this secret, which will not be revealed until the end.

In Media Res

Thrown into the world without our consent, we are born *in media res*, like characters in a story, and like them we have a deep human need to locate ourselves in time, to harmonize beginnings and ends, to connect the past, present and future in significant and coherent patterns. We tell a story to ourselves and to others of where we have come from and where we are going. Classic narrative structures and Aristotelian plots play on this need for explanatory fictions, which reveal a profound relationship between origins and ends – a relationship that moves us. Beginnings and ends are inextricably linked through a tension stretching toward some as yet unresolved expectation.

Prophecy

All plots in the beginning have this element of prophecy that anticipates the end – the witches in *Macbeth*, the arrogance and folly of Lear, the ghost in *Hamlet*, the birthday gifts and the arrival of Buzz Lightyear in *Toy Story* – all foreshadow future outcomes, hint at possible future discoveries and trigger a conflict that will intensify to the final crisis and climax. As Aristotle observed, the strongest plot is often where the end has arisen from aspects of the original situation that the audience thought insignificant. For the screenwriter, the message is clear: bury the beginning in the end.

Self-Knowledge

In tragic art, the end is cognitive – self-knowledge: let humans know for good or ill, to see things plainly, to confront what deep down we already know. There is a kind of redemption in recognizing our situation where we must act as if we are free but, in retrospect, it was always going to end this way. But we are not to be frightened: this is how things are; this is what we have to face. In the end, the emotions of pity and fear, and being aroused are purged, leaving us calm and able to reflect on what has happened and what we should now do.

Catharsis

For Aristotle, the purpose of participating in the drama was this catharsis or clarification brought about by paying attention to our emotional responses to the incidents and resolution of the plot. The discovery of what we value in human life, the attachments and commitments that matter to us, our passionate responses to events – are how we came to know ourselves.

Obligatory Scene

We are made to feel and think – moved, touched and shocked by small moments throughout the play, moments of generosity, comedy, courage,

vindictiveness, hubris or stubborn resistance. The key moments that move us to laughter or tears are the climactic moments where the tension, set up by the dramatic conflict in the beginning, is finally resolved in the end: the obligatory scene of recognition, repentance or reconciliation, the triumph of justice or the righting of a wrong.

This is the kind of end we expect in a classic melodrama – exploiting our need for truth, safety and justice, such as the family reconciliations in *Secrets and Lies* (1996) and *Little Miss Sunshine* (2006) or in Woody's new friendship with Buzz in *Toy Story* (1995). Depending on the story, the end of course may be ambiguous or open-ended, tragic or ironic.

The moral collapse of the aristocratic Tony in *The Servant* (1963) as his house and life are taken over by his servant, or the revengeful Emad whose anger leads to the death of the old man who has violated his wife in *The Salesman* (2017), remind us that the action of the plot is also concerned with the moral conflict of the protagonist and the clarification of theme through the resolution of that conflict.

Open Endings

In *Do the Right Thing* (1989), the ending is more ambiguous. The initial argument over Sal's all-Italian Wall of Fame builds to an explosion of violence initiated by Mookie, his African-American delivery boy and ends with the burning of Sal's Pizzeria – likened by Mookie to a colonizer's outpost. In the aftermath, Sal and Mookie reconcile but the underlying bitterness of racism and violence remains. The dichotomy of theme and moral conflict is represented by two quotes. The first, from Martin Luther King, who argues that violence is never justified under any circumstances. The second, from Malcolm X, who argues that violence is not violence, but 'intelligence' when it is used in self-defence.

Do the Right Thing has an innovative structure but still relies on a through-line of rising tension

Do the Right Thing has an innovative structure but still relies on a through-line of rising tension that connects a small, seemingly trivial incident at the beginning with the explosive violence of the end. PICTURELUX/THE HOLLYWOOD ARCHIVE/ALAMY STOCK

that connects a small, seemingly trivial incident at the beginning with the explosive violence of the end. In a classical screenplay there is no structure without this dynamic movement toward the end that also shapes the middle and, finally, determines the meaning of the drama.

A Good Ending

A good ending, of course, does not have to resolve everything – there are always narrative lines left open that are capable of further development: a possibility that underlies the seductive power of a TV series and the endless branching pathways of computer games.

The ending of things matters to us. Our concern for how things turn out is a fundamental aspect of our human existence; we need to know how the story works out as a whole. Like in a football match where a late goal can erase earlier pleasures, endings matter. This is why sometimes the best place for the writer to begin is at the end.

FAIRY TALE STRUCTURE

Fairy Tales and Hollywood

In the simplicity and universality of its structure, the Hollywood film shares with the fairy tale the kind of emphasis on plot and endings that underlies Aristotle's *Poetics*. Screenwriting as storytelling is close to the kind of oral wonder-tale that was the basis of the literary fairy tale developed and refined by the Brothers Grimm. In the clarity of their storytelling, through vivid images and actions, fairy tales offer a useful model for film-makers.

The fairy tale knows when to begin and where to end; it cuts out any elements that are extraneous to the plot by following a logical progression from beginning to end. By keeping focused on the story, fairy tales decide what is crucial and cut out what is elaborate or irrelevant. The screenwriter constructs her screenplay in the same way with clear and simple actions and images, showing us the protagonist's struggle, the obstacles to their desire, the persistence of their endeavour to succeed in a difficult world. At the end, as in a fairy tale, the truth will be revealed, justice will prevail, the moral order will be restored. Fairy tales, like certain types of Hollywood films, are forms of wish fulfilment and usually end happily, though this may depend not only on where you stop, but who your intended audience is.

Audience

At the end of the Charles Perrault version of *Little Red Riding Hood*, the wolf swallows the little girl and she is left in the darkness forever, with no further development. Writing for aristocratic ladies in the French court at the end of the seventeenth century, Charles Perrault's iteration is a cautionary tale pointing out the dangers of straying from the path of duty and offering a punishing image of death and darkness from which there is no recovery.

The Brothers Grimm, on the other hand, with a nineteenth-century bourgeois family and children in mind, introduced the woodcutter father who saves his daughter by cutting open the wolf's stomach with his axe. They turn a tale of violent rape, in which the child is somehow complicit, into one in which the father becomes a symbol of redemption.

Saved from the darkness of the wolf's belly, *Little Red Cap* is a tale of death and rebirth, and shows traces of earlier stories such as *Jonah and the Whale*, *Cronos Swallowing his Children* or

even earlier solar myths about the return of life-giving light and heat. It is also an image used in later structural models to point up a low point in the hero's journey, when the protagonist is trapped in the belly of the beast or in the dark night of their soul. This is the moment, paradoxically, when out of despair the hero or heroine changes their understanding completely and, now reborn, finds the resolution to finish the journey.

Feminist Re-Working

However, like the structural paradigms of screenwriting, fairy stories are not fixed and eternal but malleable and open to multiple re-interpretations. Later feminist versions, for example, from Angela Carter to the more proactive heroines of twenty-first century Disney films, recover the basic plot dynamic of the original wonder-tale, where the young protagonist devises tricks and strategies to overcome obstacles and defeat brute force with wit and imagination. These heroines take charge and responsibility for their actions and keep life and narrative moving forward, just like Clarice in *Silence of the Lambs* (1991) or Ree Dolly in *Winter's Bone* (2010), although the Hollywood heroines in these movies still rely on men for their final success.

The central figures in the original wonder-tales were opportunistic. Needing to change in order to survive, they were ready to take advantage of any opportunity, just like a good Hollywood protagonist. So, Clarice will placate the psychopathic beast that is Hannibal Lecter in order to catch the serial killer and win her place in a man's world. She is too smart to allow herself to be eaten by the monster and knows how to play the game if she is going to succeed.

Themes

Fairy tales share many themes with Hollywood films – the struggle to survive, getting in and out of trouble, finding your place in the world, encountering terrifying monsters but discovering the power of friendship and love, moving from isolation to a satisfying bond with another human being. These tales were originally for grown-ups and their underlying concerns show how childhood fantasies and anxieties still disturb the adult psyche with terrors and utopian hopes. This is why fairy tales still have a grip on our cultural imagination: we continue to find in them ways of knowing more about ourselves and the primitive fears and desires that drive, inspire and betray us. They remain a great source for contemporary stories.

There is no one ideal type of fairy tale but *Little Red Cap* (Brothers Grimm) has some of the basic symbolic patterns that we find also echoed in contemporary cinematic storytelling: the departure from home in search of independence; the forest where the protagonist is lost or abandoned; the encounter with a villain pretending to be good; the fork in the road and the decision that begins the conflict; the apparent success of the adventure in the discovery of a beautiful new world; the arrival at a place of apparent safety; and the sudden reversal and shocking discovery of the wolf's true identity. At this point too, the central theme is clarified: in *Little Red Cap* it is the fear of being devoured. The Freudian conflict between the pleasure and reality principles builds to the climax of violence and denouement of redemption.

Initiation

There is a rich and varied interpretive literature on both the structural organization and psychological meaning of fairy and folk tales but a general agreement about their origins in ritual drama. The symbolic settings, the enchanted forest, mysterious underground caves, the magic objects and gifts that enable you to fly, disappear or defeat evil, all have their origins in the drama of initiation.

As discussed in earlier chapters, the rites of passage involved in moving from one stage of life to another, the movement from ignorance to knowledge, from darkness to light, is fundamental to the hero or heroine's journey and the structure of classical narrative that underlies contemporary screenwriting.

SHORT FILM CASE STUDY: *ALICE* (2010)

This short film, written by established British screenwriter Abi Morgan, is a rites of passage story that incorporates many of the classic fairy tale themes: the problems of growing-up, Oedipal dilemmas, the anxiety and excitement of sexuality, the need to be loved. The exposition is elliptical, requiring the audience to make the causal connections, but the underlying structure of action and the release of information offer a clear through-line of gradual revelation and rising conflict to the reversal and discovery at the climax.

The screenplay is organized around a young girl's trip to the theatre that turns into a disturbing encounter with adult duplicity and sexuality. The basic plot pattern of the fairy tale – leaving home, encounters with friends and helpers, a mysterious other world, the threat from a powerful person, the demonstration of resourcefulness and renewal in the form of a perfect union – are all present in the film.

The causal through-line of conflict and resolution, the action of the Aristotelian plot, is strategically organized by the writer to deliver the emotion and meaning at the end, while provoking our curiosity at the beginning. Why is the mother so angry? Why is the child so passive? Where are they going? In the *fabula* the characters, of course, know exactly where they are going but the writer of the *siuzhet* is holding back on this information to create curiosity and suspense. She also has a surprise that she is holding onto for the end, where everything becomes clear.

This is film too that is more about feeling than plot and more interested in the internal world of the characters than in external conflicts. It is structured around inference and hints at the truth rather than assertion, and the rhythms and musical effects of a cinematic language rather than an externally conflict-driven plot. To engage the audience and gradually build the tension, the screenwriter has designed a journey with a clear objective and a reversal for the protagonist that also gives a through-line of expectation for the audience. The encounter with her father and the discovery of his affair reveals the source of the mother's unhappiness and leads to a new bond of empathy between mother and daughter.

Abi Morgan has thought about the set-up of the story in relation to the end and carefully arranged and planted key information, foreshadowing what is to come and creating an underlying pattern, a causal thread and unity of action, which prepares us for the surprise at the end. As she notes: 'Screenwriting is very mathematical. It is about structure, order and rhythm… finding the shape, creating order out of chaos.'[27]

The structure of the screenplay is designed to makes us curious ('Curiouser and curiouser' cried Alice) and draw us into the story that is also a journey of initiation for Alice: an encounter with the dark father and renewal in the form of a deeper relationship with her mother. As Morgan herself has discovered, making the meaning of Alice's journey clear to an audience requires a good understanding of structure.

CONCLUSION

How to work with the director in structuring the story is one of the key tasks of the screenwriter and in the next chapter we will deepen our understanding of the structural issues as applied to the feature film – as well as exploring alternative ways of organizing story material for an audience.

EXERCISES

1. Fairy tales and myths are organized around clear and simple story structures. They usually focus on one main character, who goes on a quest or journey with a clear objective. The narrative proceeds in a linear way without explanation or characterization. Secondary characters either help or hinder them in their quest. Write a linear story about a character on an important quest with specific obstacles and reversals to a point of final crisis and climax. Decide on a powerful antagonist or forces of antagonism that oppose the protagonist's objective.

You could use the summary of Vladimir Propp's key functions as a guide:
   - Disruption or transgression/a task given/departure to the wide world.
   - Encounter with a villain or mysterious individual/protagonist who is in trouble is given magical gift or help.
   - Threat from powerful person/test/battle.
   - A sudden fall in the protagonist's fortunes but only a temporary set-back. A wonder or miracle is needed to reverse wheel of fortune.
   - The protagonist makes use of a magical gift or insight to achieve her or his goal/the hostile forces are defeated.
   - The success leads to renewal in the form of wealth or perfect union.

2. Read the following short story by Leonard Michaels:

I smacked my little boy. My anger was powerful. Like justice. Then I discovered no feeling in the hand. I said, 'Listen, I want to explain the complexities to you'. I spoke with seriousness and care, particularly of fathers. He asked, when I finished, if I wanted him to forgive me. I said yes. He said no. Like trumps.

Now analyse the story in terms of its narrative structure. What, according to Aristotle's definition, are the beginning, middle and end? What is the incident that begins the conflict? How is that initial conflict developed? How is the exposition used to create tension, suspense and surprise? Discuss the double reversal at the end. What does that achieve? How is the dramatic unity of the story achieved?

3. Character and plot interact with a story moving forward into plot through a character's decision and action. In a few sentences outline a specific character in a specific situation, e.g. an encounter in a cafe, a mugging, a car crash, shoplifting, finding a bag. Introduce opposition and alternative outcomes to the circumstances of the situation. What would your character want and do? What other elements could you introduce to complicate the situation? What actions and reactions would provoke further story developments to a point of crisis and resolution? Sketch five mini-plots.

4. The beginning of a story is often most clearly discovered when you know the end. On each of five 3×5 index cards, write down an occupation and on a second set of cards write down an odd behaviour, a gesture, an action that will become the last scene. Shuffle each of the packs separately, then turn over a card from pack A and one from pack B and ask the question: why did A act or behave in the way described in B? Provide a setting, a motive and a conflict that might be resolved by this behaviour. Think of a scene near the beginning that sets the story up and one near the end that demonstrates the severity of the conflict.

5. Write five mini-stories based on a single event or set of circumstances, e.g. a theft, a violent encounter, being locked in a building, a friend from the past. Each story should be different in terms of character, plot and theme.

6. Write a story about two married people who are considering divorce until something unforeseen happens.

7. Outline the beginning, middle and end of a story in three paragraphs. Each paragraph should be not more than three sentences. Just describe what happens without dialogue. What begins the story? What is the turning point at the end of the beginning that moves the story into the middle and from the middle to the end? What changes at the end? How does the end relate to the beginning? Now tell the story to a friend or partner and listen to their questions and feedback. Where are the gaps and confusions? Rewrite.

8. Find an event from your childhood that changed you or led to a new discovery or realization. Describe the situation, the circumstances and what happened. Now use this as a basis for outlining a short film where a child finds out something new, shocking or surprising that changes them. Use sound and images, actions and gestures to build the film story to the climax. You want to convey the child's inner life and feelings through action and image. Look again at *Gasman* and *Alice*. What can you learn from studying these films? Write an outline of the key moments of your story and then write a first-draft screenplay. Remember to focus on how you establish, develop and resolve the story through action and ellipsis.

9. Write about rites of passage, e.g. your first day at school, university or work, or your first kiss, falling in love or your first experience of death. Use the story as the basis for a short film script.

10. Read *Little Red Cap* by the Brothers Grimm or find a fairy tale or myth that excites you. Use it as a basis for writing a contemporary short story. How do you adapt the story into a short film script? What is the difference between prose and screenwriting implied by the maxim 'show don't tell'?

11. Find three short films that you like and analyse how they are structured. Who is the protagonist? What do they want? What is at stake? What are the obstacles and the turning points? What do the characters know that the audience does not? How is that used in the dramatizing of the plot? How does the end relate to the beginning? How is the conflict initiated and developed to crisis and climax? How does the exposition gradually reveal character and theme?

12. Select three feature screenplays that you like. Analyse and break them down: protagonist, objective, obstacles, complications, the through-line of conflict and action to crisis and climax.

13. Write a plot summary for three feature films. Compare with a partner who has done the same exercise. What have you learned? How has the unity of action been achieved? How have things changed for the protagonist by the end?

14. Look at the beginning and set-up of three feature films. How have the characters and plot been set in motion? How is the end prepared for earlier in the screenplay? Give examples.

15. Study a favourite feature film. How have the key elements of exposition been released or revealed to the audience? Give specific examples. List the visual and aural motifs and lines of dialogue that are repeated or modified to create structural patterns. How do they contribute to character, theme and the overall structure?

16. Analyse three feature films. Describe the relationship of character and plot following Henry James's definition of character as 'the determination of incident' and incident as 'the illumination of character'.

17. Select one of the films from above and describe the different and varied ways in which lines of tension are established, developed and resolved. What is the difference between conflict and tension? What is the relationship between external and internal conflict?

18. Go through a story outline or screenplay that you have written with the following questions in mind: What does the audience already know? What does each character already know? To whom is each piece of information revealed? How and when is it revealed? Ask yourself how you could improve clarity, curiosity, suspense or surprise by adding or taking out information or releasing information at a different time.

19. Write a plot treatment for a feature film of ten to twelve pages describing in prose what is happening from beginning to end. Use paragraphs to break up the blocks of action. Review again the basic structural relationships of character and plot, exposition, beginnings and ends, as well as the narrative elements of protagonist, objective, obstacle, turning points, crisis and climax.

6
THE FEATURE FILM

The classical feature film is both a narrative and dramatic art form with the screenplay enhanced by storytelling skills and knowledge of film-making, but primarily rooted in a feel for the human drama. Dramatic stories, as Aristotle reminds us, focus on humans in action and the emotional engagement of the audience with the struggle of the protagonist who is just like us: incomplete, vulnerable, desiring.

The drama explores what it feels like to be human: our emotional experience, our vulnerabilities and mistakes, our arrogance and ambition, our ignorance, envy and compassion. In this very human sense, small details of action and re-action are often more important than large-scale conflicts: not the big external actions so much as the consequences of the action on the soul of the protagonist.

In the classic Hollywood feature film, the protagonist pursues clear objectives, overcomes problems, learns new things and is forced to make difficult choices. The plot is a series of dramatic moments or crises on the way to a final confrontation. Drama is seen as the struggle of the hero or heroine to get what they want, so it is important to clarify the protagonist's objectives early on. This struggle to find order and kindness, to resolve inner conflicts, is the redemptive myth at the heart of mainstream films, where the complexity of being human is played out around themes of sex and violence, cruelty and greed, belonging and loss.

Drawing on Aristotelian ideas of drama, including the importance of point of view, causality, plotting and rising action, classic American cinema has created its own repertoire of principles and standards of plot construction and characterization that are a conventional part of professional screenwriting language and a point of departure for considering the writing of a feature screenplay.

CLASSIC NARRATIVE PRINCIPLES

Premise

The premise is a writer's underlying concept or idea uniting the story elements. This is usually expressed in terms of the initial situation that generates the main conflict/dilemma for the protagonist as they move toward their objective. So the premise is also connected to the protagonist's backstory and the inciting incident. High concept refers to a plot-oriented premise; low concept to a character-centred story. The premise can be summarized in a tag line or a one-line pitch of the story idea that reveals the potential for conflict and the dramatic spine of the story.

Story World

The story world is a location or setting that provides the context for the character and story events, whether naturalistic or fantastic. It has its own rules, which need to be clarified for the reader, so that the reader can believe in the story world. The environment of the scene or story creates mood, tone and atmosphere, as well as contributing to the meaning and dramatic unity of the film. The setting may be basic to the original conception or the result of a conscious and deliberate choice, but the writer should be concerned with how it enhances or contributes to the narrative. In a classical film, everything works together and the story world is an important element in the more subtle and visual dimensions of the story. Research is the key.

Characterization

Characterization refers to the totality of physical and personality qualities, backstory motivations, relationship networks, intentions and objectives of any given character: the qualities of a unique individual selected as a specific element of contrast or conflict in the narrative. Each major character has their own objective and way of going about attaining it, either in conflict or harmony with the protagonist and others. It also refers to the attitude a character takes to the facts of their personality and backstory – how they feel about who they are. The essence of characterization is how they reveal different and hidden aspect of themselves in interaction with other characters and the events of the plot.

Tone

Tone refers to a feeling or inflection: the mood and atmosphere of the story, usually set by the writer's attitude to the characters and theme, for example serious, humorous, ironical.

Protagonist

Protagonist comes from the Greek, meaning 'the one who struggles'. The main character whose story we are following is defined by their backstory, motives, needs, fears but, especially, their desire,

The protagonist is the main character defined by their backstory, motives, needs, fears but especially their desire: embodied in the pursuit of an objective that is difficult to achieve. But in some stories, the protagonist discovers that what they want is not what they need. RGA

which is embodied in the pursuit of an objective that is difficult to achieve. An audience will be involved in the film to the extent that they identify with the protagonist's dilemma, objective and central conflict. It is the protagonist's movement toward the objective that determines where to begin and where to end and, therefore, the backbone of story structure. The protagonist's desire is what provides focus and intensity to the story.

External Objective

The external object of the protagonist's desire is what the protagonist is struggling to achieve. The story begins when the protagonist clarifies their objective, usually after the inciting incident that motivates them to move toward a goal. In Hitchcock's terms, this is the 'McGuffin' – something the protagonist must have because it is important to them. The protagonist's objective provides focus for the audience and emotional tension as it comes into conflict with the goal of the antagonist or the forces that want to block it. The objective should be difficult so that the protagonist changes as he moves toward it but not so overwhelming that the protagonist has no chance of overcoming it. In pursuit of the objective there must also be something at stake, something the protagonist cannot afford to lose – whether it's their life, family or self-esteem. The unity of the story depends on there being one main objective, but the nature of the objective can change during the development and create unexpected turning points in the plot. Each scene and sequence, as well as the overall plot, is usually structured around a specific objective of the protagonist.

Internal Objective

The protagonist's internal need, which is less apparent than the external objective, emerges gradually in interaction with other characters. In some plots the final revelation becomes the major discovery and reversal of the climax, where the protagonist realizes that what they want is not what they need, such as in *Midnight Cowboy* when Jo achieves his external goal of hustling for money, he realizes that what he really wants is to be loved for who he really is and not for his idealized self and money. The internal need is an element of characterization and plot development, defined by the protagonist's flaw or lack and their consequent internal journey toward realization. An example is in *Toy Story* – Woody needs to realize that he cannot force Andy's love and has to let go of his desire to regain his original place. Woody's character arc from anger and rejection of Buzz to friendship and acceptance also defines the theme. The character arc often defines the theme.

Stakes

The stakes are what the protagonist stands to lose or risk, if they fail to achieve their external or internal objective. Raising the stakes means increasing the risk for the protagonist and enhancing the emotional engagement for the audience, as they progress through the screenplay. Let the reader discover through the action what the protagonist cares most about and, therefore, what is at risk

for them. There can be more than one thing at stake. While the screenplay will have major stakes, it should also have minor stakes underlying individual scenes and sequences. You can raise the stakes by keeping the objective out of reach.

Obstacle

Obstacles include all opposition and antagonism to the protagonist's objective in a scene, sequence or in the overall plot, including the external world of people, circumstances and events, as well as the internal world of the protagonist's fears, flaws and unconscious needs that block them from getting what they want. In some stories the obstacle to a protagonist's external desire is a need for something they were unaware of that becomes the discovery and reversal at the end. The plot depends on a series of incidents and events that impede, as well as aid, the hero or heroine in quest of their objective. Obstacles to the protagonist's desire play on the audiences' emotions through turning points, reversals and set-backs in the plot. Without obstacles to the protagonist's desire, there is no conflict and no story.

Motivation

Motivation involves the complex of conscious wants and unconscious needs, the causes of the protagonist's desire that move them into action and are usually connected to what is at stake for them, what they stand to lose if they don't act. In mainstream films, motivation is clarified and focused by being placed at an early crisis point for the protagonist during the set-up of the story and revealing what is motivating them to action through conflict rather than explanation. Clarifying why a character is doing something is also a technique for involving the audience in the action, while competing motivations create internal conflict and are gradually revealed through character change. Withholding information on what motivates a character can weaken credibility and, therefore, audience involvement or it could be the deliberate choice of the writer to create a story where uncertainty of motive is an aspect of characterization and theme. The deeper and more complex the characterization, the less clear we become about character motivation.

Sub-Text

Sub-text concerns the thoughts and feelings a character wants to hide, as well as the inner conflicts, fears, insecurities and secrets of individual characters. From the writer's point of view, what the audience doesn't see but feels is often more emotionally effective than actively showing something. The sub-text is suggested, through hints, gestures, looks and glances, small actions rather than through dialogue. However, confrontation and intimate exchanges can reveal a character's inner thoughts and feelings – especially at the climax.

The Inciting Incident/Catalyst

The catalyst is an incident or event chosen by the writer to start the story and is the first cause of action that sets the plot in motion. It could be a disturbance in the everyday world that produces a conflict or a central dramatic problem for the protagonist that will not be resolved until the end. The inciting incident usually occurs near the beginning at a point of crisis and vulnerability for the protagonist and awakens their desire and the need to find a solution to the problem. A story conventionally begins in media res and, therefore, requires back-story exposition during the plot development.

The Dramatic Question

The dramatic question is provoked by the inciting incident and creates tension, uncertainty and suspense, and excites audience participation. The question takes us all the way through the story and

keeps the audience interested in the outcome. Plot incidents and events develop and reformulate the question, providing thematic focus and dramatic unity. It is a technique for unifying the action, raising the emotional stakes and clarifying the meaning of the action.

Dramatic Unity

The spine or through-line of action that links the dramatic question and protagonist's objective with the central conflict and climax is known as dramatic unity. It is based on Aristotle's belief that a dramatic story must have a unity if it is going to move an audience. For the action to be unified, there must be probable connection between the incidents, each incident following the other and at the same time moving the story forward – thus making the parts fit together to form a single image that depicts the transformation of the protagonist's fortunes.

Journey

The journey is the protagonist's search for an answer to the dramatic problem and a test of character. The journey metaphor refers to both the external incidents and events of the plot and the internal/emotional changes within the protagonist. In a classical screenplay, both narrative levels are linked in a constant movement of transformation as the protagonist faces increasingly difficult obstacles and choices. In the process, they gain knowledge and insight about themselves and the world. It is related to metaphors of pilgrimage and quest, where the journey is the human need to leave home for a sacred place, a new home in the world, where wounds are healed and life renewed.

Development Sequence

A block of dramatic action that carries the story forward as part of a steady development of character and plot is called a dramatic sequence. It is a series of linked scenes united around a common action or theme, which moves the protagonist closer, or further away from, their objective. In each sequence the protagonist has an immediate objective and obstacle to overcome and a dramatic problem structured around a beginning, a middle and an end. A mainstream feature film is usually structured around eight to twelve major sequences.

Exposition

Exposition refers to information that the writer needs to convey in a selective and subtle way to an audience, so that character action, motivation and relationships are clear and credible. It should be used strategically, as it is a narrative rather than a dramatic device, and best revealed through conflict or humour or as a by-product of a dramatically interesting scene. Explanations are not dramatically interesting, it is better to use visual hints and dialogue clues that involve the audience in working out the backstory, as well as the intentions and secrets of the characters. In a well-structured screenplay, the reader will understand subliminally what is going on but still be surprised by the ending. The audience may want to know more, but it is the not knowing that keeps them hanging on.

Ellipsis

An ellipsis is an important element of cinematic language meaning literally 'waiting in silence'. It refers to a hole in the plot that gives it shape; moments where the writer deliberately leaves out information in order to heighten the sense of mystery or suspense. It can also be used to speed up the narrative, requiring the audience to use their imagination in bridging the gaps. In a classical ellipsis, the omission can be filled in without reasonable doubt, but it is an important formal property of modernist plots that that we cannot supply the missing piece with any certainty.

Dramatic Irony

Irony is a dramatic device where the audience knows something that one or more characters don't know: this creates suspense and heightens the audience's involvement in the story. Placing the audience in a superior position is intrinsically dramatic and, therefore, at the core of the dramatic experience. The writer often has to choose between dramatic irony and surprise, in other words letting the reader in on the secret or startling them with it later.

Suspense

A delay in fulfilling an established expectation, dramatic suspense is one of the writer's most powerful techniques. Creating anticipation and uncertainty in the audience means making them concerned about what will happen next and whether the protagonist will succeed in solving their immediate problem or in achieving their overall objective. The audience must care about the fate of the protagonist, be aware of all the facts involved and have a sense of what is at stake for suspense to be effective. It is a way of drawing the audience into the action that runs through the whole screenplay, including scenes, sequences and acts.

Discovery

Discovery is the principle of surprise, which may be an unexpected character or a plot revelation. Surprise helps to keep the audience involved in the story by reminding them that their expectations will not always be fulfilled. It creates tension and excitement around the unpredictability of human actions but needs to appear as an organic part of the plot and be logically connected to something earlier that seemed insignificant at the time – rather than imposed as a *Deus ex machina*. It is a less effective tool overall than suspense, which depends on irony.

Preparation/Foreshadowing

Foreshadowing is a detail or action carried out in the immediate moment that prepares us for later action or revelation; for example, the planting of a piece of information, a line of dialogue, a characteristic or gesture that may arouse our curiosity but whose meaning or significance does not become clear until later in the drama. This includes appointments and deadlines that build up expectations and momentum, as well as the 'dialogue hook' that links into the next scene and the 'dangling cause' that leaves some important issue unresolved at the end of the scene. These devices heighten audience involvement by creating an expectation of future outcomes and possible conflicts. They make credible a later action that might otherwise appear contrived and they contribute to a sense of dramatic unity through repetition.

Motif

A motif is a dominant or recurring theme or subject in the screenplay that can be verbal or visual. It is a shape or design repeated in a pattern, as in music, that illustrates character change or a theme, for example in *Toy Story* the line 'To infinity and beyond'.

It can be introduced earlier and paid off later and paid off more than once and with variation to become a running gag. The use of motifs creates resonances akin to rhyme in poetry, such as the visual motifs in *Silence of the Lambs*: cocoon/death's head moth/diamond pattern on

Kieslowski uses images of glass to add thematic resonance: a window that you can see through but that separates you from other people; a telescope that brings you closer but keeps you at a distance. PHOTO 12/ALAMY STOCK

the dress – threaded through the screenplay to build meaning, suspense and dramatic unity.

Image System

An image system is a series of images that are repeated throughout the screenplay, which add texture and poetic resonance to the theme, for example in *A Short Film About Love* (1988) Kieslowski uses images of glass to add thematic resonance: as a telescope that brings you closer but keeps you distant; as a window that you can see through but that separates you from other people; as a mirror that reflects and shatters. The writer should select her images carefully and place them subliminally throughout the screenplay.

Reversal

A reversal is a plot twist, which involves a reversal of fortune; setbacks build tension and heighten concern. In a conventional narrative, the plot usually builds through a series of minor reversals to the major reversal of crisis and climax. It is often accompanied by the protagonist recognizing or realizing the true meaning of events for the first time.

Crisis

A crisis is a culminating moment of discovery, where the protagonist is under the greatest pressure and seems likely to fail in her objective. At this point, the final nature of the problem she must face is revealed. It is an incident near the end of the protagonist's journey: a point of no return that sparks the climax.

Climax

Everything in the screenplay has been leading to the climax, sometimes referred to as the 'obligatory scene', where the principle characters reveal their moral weaknesses or strengths, as well as their true feelings about themselves and others. It is the highest point of interest, tension and catharsis: the culminating moment of action, where the complications are reversed, the conflict resolved and the protagonist overcomes their flaw or weakness. The climax is the final showdown with the antagonist and the answer to the dramatic question provoked by the inciting incident at the beginning; it is usually followed by the resolution.

Denoument or Resolution

Denoument is a derivative of *denouer* 'to untie', where the knots of the plot are undone: a tying up of loose ends; a pay-off for every set-up. It is the falling action of the screenplay, where all the problems and narrative lines not resolved in the climax are unravelled and any needed explanations given or feelings expressed. It is through the resolution of the protagonist's moral conflict that the theme of the screenplay is stated.

Theme

The theme is the underlying dramatic meaning of the story revealed through the actions and interactions of the protagonist with other characters. It is an idea or image that repeats at various points in the screenplay but is clarified at the climax: what the story is about.

STRUCTURAL MODELS

These principles and techniques drawn from literature and theatre, combined with influences from painting and photography, as well as cinema's unique language of editing and close-up, have provided the dominant model for visual storytelling during the past 100 years. They are principles not laws or fixed rules, and, therefore, open to interpretation and improvisation. They embody a view of the world and human endeavour as comprehensible, dynamic and time-bound, with individualized characters pursuing important objectives for a reason, and their actions unified by a chain of cause and effect. Incidents and events are foreshadowed, conflict and tension build progressively to the climax in a way that feels inevitable and the protagonist is changed through interaction with the plot. The protagonist in a drama is ultimately in pursuit of himself or herself, incomplete, conflicted and needy, seeking their object of desire – be it knowledge, love or self-worth – with time running out.

Exposition in the classical form is gradual and elliptical, with the audience involved in trying to fill in the gaps of understanding and meaning. This is how we see and make sense of the world: emotionally engaged in working out the links between intention and action, cause and effect, the past and the future. The plot action is designed precisely on this basis, assuming the impulse to understand and the desire to become involved and stay involved in the story as a source of audience pleasure and enjoyment.

The structural template of mainstream feature films has evolved to reflect this kind of audience expectation, with the plot divided into three large-scale units, like acts in a play. The pattern reiterated in screenwriting manuals since the 1970s is the three-fold movement familiar to oral storytelling and described by Aristotle much earlier:

> Tragedy is an imitation of an action that is a whole and complete in itself and of a certain magnitude… a thing is a whole if it has a beginning, a middle, and an end.

Three-Act Structure

In the Hollywood structural pattern, this basic rhythm of beginning, middle and end is reformulated in a theatrical language of three acts – where an act is a series of scenes in a strategic sequence ending in a major reversal or turning point, and where the protagonist's response to the dramatic problem is the through-line of action that is shaped into three movements, building in intensity and complication to the climax in the third act.

Act 1: introduction of protagonist and problem.
Act 2: struggle of protagonist to solve problem, building to a severe test.
Act 3: protagonist solves problem.

If this sounds familiar, it may remind you of the apocryphal story of the screenwriter who woke up in the middle of the night with a brilliant idea – and when he looked in the morning found written on his notepad:

Boy meets girl.
Boy loses girl.
Boy finds girl.

This three-part movement is the familiar structure found in jokes and folk tales. A pattern of desire frustrated, of things going well for a while then suddenly not so well, then all is lost, before a surprising solution to the initial problem is found. The turns and twists of the plot engage the hopes and fears of the audience and then deliver a satisfying resolution.

Hollywood movies have a similar act structure as formally organized as French classical tragedy and as universal as a fairy tale, while its emphasis on plot underlines the continued influence of Aristotle. You could also say the feature film has a unique form in the same way as haiku, a sonnet, twelve-bar blues or the three movements of a classical concerto, with each act variously defined by a variety of theorists over the years.

There are other structural models, of course, including the Shakespearean rhythm of five acts or Chekov's four-act plays and the twelve stages of the hero's journey, as outlined by Christopher Vogler. There is no absolute rule about how you structure your feature screenplay or at what stage you organize your story material, but the underlying pattern of all structural models and mainstream

Three-Act Structure

Act 1	Act 2	Act 3
Exposition	Conflict	Catastrophe (AC Bradley)
Thesis	Antithesis	Synthesis (Lajos Egri)
Separation	Initiation	Return (Joseph Campbell)
Conflict	Crisis	Climax (Brady and Lee)
Establishing	Building	Resolving (Michael Hauge)
Set-up	Confrontation	Resolution (Syd Field)

cinema remains the template first fully articulated by Syd Field in his book *Screenplay* (1979). For him the three acts are the classic blueprint, a way of keeping the audience on track, ordering our thinking about the action and articulating the dialectic of change and growth undergone by the protagonist.

It is not a static model but a set of flexible guidelines to help the writer to think about the audience experience and how to order and focus their own branching pathways of story options. The paradigm only comes alive through vivid characterization and a great story. It is a foundation, not a formula.

ACT 1: SET-UP

The writer establishes the world of the protagonist, then creates the disturbance or problem in the world that defines his or her objective and the difficulty in achieving it. This act focuses on everything before the protagonist's objective becomes clear in the audience's mind; it introduces the inciting incident and establishes the basic lines of conflict. It can be seen as two parts – before and after the inciting incident.

ACT 2: DEVELOPMENT

Act 2 covers the extended struggle of the protagonist, often marked by a major change in tactics or a new situation or an element that requires a counter set-up and a refocusing or recasting of the protagonist's goals. This leads to further conflict, setbacks and complications that raise the stakes. Despite some minor successes, there is a period of frustration where the protagonist seems to be making little progress. By the end of the act, he feels he has failed in pursuit of his objective. This is the longest act and sub-plots, montage sequences and comedy are often used to sustain audience interest.

ACT 3: RESOLUTION

The pace of the screenplay accelerates to the climax as the protagonist surprises the audience, takes over and succeeds by his own efforts. The climax is a point of major reversal and discovery for the protagonist and the spectator, and where the question triggered by the inciting incident is answered. The protagonist must be seen to change as a result of the action over the three acts.

Dramatic Turning Points

This is a conflict-driven model with the protagonist as the focus, actively driving the plot by making decisions and choices that resolve a series of escalating crises. The plot is structured around obstacles and reversals with major turning points taking the story in a different direction, building momentum and heightening audience suspense. Some turning points help her progress; others produce further problems and setbacks.

In the three-act structure there are major turning points at the end of Act 1 and Act 2, as well as the climax. Along with the concepts of inciting incident and mid-point, they track the protagonist's motivational through-line and can be used to break down the act structure into key dramatic moments that can provide the basis for a plot outline and the first draft.

The Set-Up Introduction to the story world, main characters and relationships: the everyday world before the disturbance. A sequence of scenes that situate your characters in the settings and locations that ground your premise and introduce their desires, strengths and weaknesses, beliefs and cultural influences before the dramatic hook.

Inciting Incident/Catalyst The dramatic hook or triggering event that sets the plot in motion, incites our curiosity and raises questions: the disturbing action or event that upsets the normal balance of the protagonist's world and, therefore, guarantees further action. It usually happens within the first ten to fifteen minutes and helps to define the protagonist's purpose. It can be an apparently harmless event that leads to serious trouble, such as Thelma and Louise turning-off to the roadhouse or Tony interviewing Barrett in *The Servant* (1963), or a visual image that creates a moment of emotional resonance, for example in *Toy Story* (1995), Woody being replaced on Andy's pillow by Buzz. The emotional progression of every film springs from an incident that establishes the through-line of action on which the plot incidents hang. It is further reinforced or complicated by the next turning point.

Act 1 Climax A surprising challenge or event and a major turning point that shifts the story in a different direction, propels the protagonist into a new world or way of being and drives the action. A point of no return for the protagonist – the world will never be the same again. It is related to the dramatic question triggered by the inciting incident and illuminates the theme. This turning point can also be a key moment of defeat or challenge where the stakes are raised and the protagonist realizes their simple efforts to solve the problem created by the inciting incident have failed and they have to take the initiative and reformulate their objective. The path they have chosen may lead to partial success but they will come to realize it is the wrong one. The audience will be ahead of the protagonist at this point, foreseeing future problems, difficulties and even disaster.

The Mid-Point The point almost half-way through where something profoundly significant happens, the jeopardy increases and the protagonist realizes there can be no return to how things were before the initial disturbance. It is a moment of truth or realization when the protagonist draws on what she has learned so far and tries something new to solve her problem: a false victory or crushing setback around which the Act 2 pivots and where the protagonist is forced to take control of her destiny.

Act 2 Climax A major crisis and reversal to the protagonist's objective at the end of Act 1, where all seems lost, but that allows the protagonist to take stock of the situation and revaluate all the efforts so far. The lowest point and biggest crisis from which there seems no way out but is also a deliberately reflective moment where the protagonist finds the means to defeat the forces of antagonism without revealing to the audience how this is going to be achieved. A turning point need not be a moment of high drama – often a turning point is a small but decisive action that determines the direction the next block of action will take.

Act 3 Climax The pace of the screenplay accelerates as the revitalized protagonist takes over and surprises us with a new approach to solving the problem: a final confrontation with the forces of antagonism, where the protagonist is faced with her biggest challenge and most difficult decision. The climax is the highest point of the drama, where all the story elements come into conflict and where the success or failure of the protagonist's objective is decided and where the theme is revealed.

The Resolution This occurs after the final climax and provides an opportunity for the writer and the protagonist to show how the dramatic and emotional conflicts triggered by the initial dramatic problem have been resolved. The denouement is where all the narrative threads and loose ends are tied up, order is restored and there is a new harmony and balance in the protagonist's life.

Summary

This three-act pattern provides a shape in which a protagonist is tested, where their strength of will is pitted against increasingly overwhelming odds but where, finally, the truth of their situation is revealed and the audience is encouraged to reflect on the meaning of all that has led them to this point.

In the beginning, the writer defines a problem and elements of threat, then designs a strategy for dealing with them that needs constant revision and digression in the face of difficulties and defeat. This is arguably how we perceive and order the world, and how mainstream drama is structured around the quest of the protagonist in pursuit of a single goal. In the long second act, the audience is misled, misinformed and disappointed, in order to keep their attention. It is also at this point that something new emerges for the protagonist, something unexpected but concealed in the beginning that overwhelms them and threatens their entire project. They discover the true nature of the struggle and that realization forces them to change their understanding completely. They had wanted to give up but now they realize how wrong, foolish or arrogant they had been and are ready and determined to force a final confrontation.

Dramatic structure tracks this maturing process to the point where the protagonist has to face the truth and what has been ignored or denied now prevails. What was hidden is revealed, what was lost or missing is found. We remember the beginning when our world was disrupted and we made that fateful choice, and how we were wrong – until we were right. At the end we can see that the pattern of event and consequence was not accidental

Structural Outline: Thelma and Louise

Premise:	Two women seek fun and freedom on a road trip.
1. Set-up:	Introduction to the main characters and their repressive everyday lives: Thelma a child/woman trapped in an oppressive marriage, Louise a hyper-organized waitress in a dead-end job. They both need a change and are on the point of escaping to the freedom of a cross-country road trip where they hope to have a good time and bond with each other.
2. Inciting Incident:	Thelma persuades Louise to turn off the road and pull into the Silver Bullet roadhouse.
3. Act 1 Climax:	The attempted rape of Thelma then the killing of Harlan by Louise. They are now on the run from the law.
	Story beat (a key moment or action that moves the plot forward): they pick-up a hitchhiker – Thelma has liberating sex with him and picks up tips on how to rob a store.
4. Mid-Point:	The hitchhiker steals the money they need to escape. Louise despairs; Thelma takes charge and remembering the hitchhiker's advice proceeds to rob a store.
	Story beat: hitchhiker picked up by police and reveals where to find Thelma and Louise.
5. Act 2 Climax:	Driving across the desert they learn they are wanted for murder and with the police now closing in, they realize they will never make it to Mexico.
6. Act 3 Climax:	Thelma and Louise are surrounded by the police on the edge of the Grand Canyon and faced with a choice of surrender or…
7. Resolution:	They exchange looks of agreement, Thelma puts her foot down and the car drives over the edge of the canyon.

but shaped by the nature of the person we have chosen to become.

In *Thelma and Louise* (1991), the external and internal journeys of the protagonists can be tracked by noting the key turning points.

If you add the additional plot points before and after the mid-point, where the hitchhiker is picked up by Thelma and then later by the police, you will have ten story beats around which to develop the screenplay.

You should also see that by introducing a mid-point and breaking the second act into two large units of action, you would have a four-act not a three-act structure as a guideline for outlining the dramatic moments of your screenplay. We will look again at this breakdown when we discuss outlines and treatments in Chapter 9.

CONCLUSION

The story beats of *Thelma and Louise* shaped around rape and murder, sex and love, guns and cars are on one level a parody of the male-bonding buddy movie, but at its heart it is a road movie celebrating female empowerment; it is about freedom and finding yourself. The act structure without the writer's passion to subvert a male genre and celebrate female autonomy, friendship and sexuality would be empty and hollow. It is important to remember, when thinking about structure, that what is primary is having a subject, a passion, something to say – then working out the best way to express that idea, rather than trying to fit your story into a pre-determined mould.

In the next chapter we will consider a range of different methods and models as a basis of organizing your story material – exploring this relationship between structure and meaning, and the interplay of form and function that combine in the best films.

EXERCISES

Read the feature screenplays of *Winter's Bone* and *Silence of the Lambs.* Make brief notes in response to the questions below.

1. What is the premise/logline of the two scripts? How are the stories similar or different to each other?
2. Write a brief story outline on each screenplay beginning 'This is a story about...'. Use only three sentences and cover the beginning, middle and end.
3. Who is the central character/protagonist?
4. What do they want? (external objective). What is the difference between what they want and what they need?
5. What do they need? (internal objective). How is this need established and how does it relate to their character development?
6. Why can't they get what they want?
7. What happens if they don't get it?
8. What's at stake for them?
9. What is the disturbance/initial conflict that begins the story?
10. What is the central dramatic question?
11. What are the major obstacles to their want and need? List.
12. What are the key turning points of the story? How do they relate to the internal as well as the external objectives of the protagonists?
13. List five key moments in the plot that trigger internal change or conflict in the protagonists. Suggest three other incidents or events that could have been used in the plot to the same effect.
14. Describe the final crisis and climax. What do you think the ending is saying? Suggest other endings.
15. What do you think the theme of the story is?

7
CLASSICAL AND ALTERNATIVE STRATEGIES

The classical Aristotelian model and its conceptual framework offer a way of thinking about how to structure your film idea for an audience: the tools and techniques that involve the reader in your story. In the Hollywood version, the screenplay is designed around a vulnerable, contradictory but determined protagonist in crisis, with clear personality traits pursuing an objective that forces them into conflict with others.

In a classical feature script, pacing is varied because the drama needs variety, as well as unity: the flow and rhythm of highs and lows, and the contrasts of fast and slow, comic and serious, day and night require the skilful manipulation of character, sub-text, setting and mood; an understanding of where to place the major and minor plot points and story beats for maximum effect.

The dominant structural model in Western cinema is that of a three-, four-or five-act structure or eight to twelve sequences with the purpose of each act or sequence clear and simple and shaped to keep the audience informed and, therefore, tense and engaged in the protagonist's problem. As in other art forms, timing is crucial: not only what to show and what to exclude, but when to show it are critical to the emotional impact of the drama. The writer works within a narrative framework that helps them organize their ideas but one that has many variations: it is a form not a formula.

Reading and analysing a range of feature screenplays are useful exercises in understanding the rigour and variety of these formal conventions and should be part of a new screenwriter's regular practice. This chapter will offer some examples in a series of feature film analyses that relate the films under discussion to earlier outlines of classical storytelling principles and to the different ways in which the key elements of character, plot and theme interact to create meaning. Alternative models to the mainstream approach will also be discussed: screenplays and films where the protagonist is powerless or passive, where the structures are less linear, goal-oriented and logical, and more elliptical, impressionistic or episodic; films where the focus is on theme and mood, rather than character and conflict.

By implication, the classical model assumes a self and world that is legible, stable and coherent, but there are many other kinds of stories that entrance us not by concision and schematic concentration, but through their openness, ambiguity and non-linear organization, and where the self is not coherent but complex, fragile and unknowable. We will look at films of this kind shortly, but we will first explore further the classical model and its variations.

CLASSICAL STRATEGIES

Thelma and Louise (1991)

Screenplay: Callie Kourie.
Keywords: dual protagonists/backstory/structure/characterization/change.

Thelma and Louise (1991) is a film often referenced in screenwriting manuals because of the simplicity and clarity of its characterization and plot – an exemplar of classical style. The main characters, their relationships, their objectives and what is at stake are simple and clear, expressed through image and action. The opening shots reveal Louise's control and mastery in the world of the diner; her clean, uncluttered kitchen and small suitcase are contrasted with the chaotic world and erratic behaviour of Thelma.

The closed, patriarchal world they both need to escape from is deliberately juxtaposed with the open road of possibility, adventure and self-knowledge. The story beats of attempted rape and murder, escape and set-back, realization and acceptance are organized to engage our emotions. The gun foreshadowing the murder, the money arriving then stolen, the hitchhiker who is both sexual liberator and betrayer, are all good examples of structuring motifs and reversals: elements that foreshadow, characterize and drive the action forward; that create suspense and surprise.

Similarly, Louise's past trauma in Texas is not only used as a critical obstacle to their escape, but deepens her character, implying the roots of her repression and her impulse to shoot the rapist Harlan. The inciting incident is the result of three elements from the backstory of the main characters: Thelma's innocence, Harlan's brutal attitude to women and Louise's suppressed past. When these three elements collide, they provide the catalyst that begins the story.

The point of view is split between our dual protagonists, each with her own character flaw that establishes a need for change. Louise is shown during the set-up and the initial crisis to be the adult in the relationship: rational, focused and organized, with experience and knowledge of the wider world. She is also repressed and, as we learn, deeply wounded by something from her past. Thelma is the child-woman married to a pompous idiot husband and the one who changes most through the plot action: her irresponsible, playful

An image of the open road, of possibility, adventure and self-knowledge sets-up the metaphorical journey of the two protagonists. KEN KISTLER/ALAMY STOCK

pleasure-seeking self, contrasts and conflicts with Louise and lead to the two moments of disaster that become major turning points in the plot.

From a structuring point of view, it is Thelma's story at the centre of the drama: she is the one who needs to change most and who takes the most important decisions, including to finally drive off the cliff. Both characters need time, escalating pressure and a moment of crisis to come to the realization that they need to face up to, and let go of, the past. They help each other do this in scenes of fraternity and conflict.

The real issue in the screenplay is this relationship between the two women, and not between them and the law; that would just make for an entertaining but forgettable road movie. How they help and challenge each other to grow and flourish is the real subject and theme; the structure emerges from their emotional journey. Thelma's passivity has allowed her to be pulled into Louisa's trauma, another form of subjugation from which she has to break free and take action herself.

This is a story about liberation; liberation from a limited view of oneself and the demands of others that paradoxically depends on relationship. Louise also has to face up to her demons, rather than running away, and the trucker scene is there to show us this moment complementing Thelma's witty put-down and dismissal of her husband on the phone.

With two female protagonists, this appears to be a radical revision of the road movie highlighting sexual politics, but it is a movie that ultimately punishes its heroines. Their quest for freedom and equality involves stereotypical male characters and offers simplistic solutions to complex situations, especially the use of guns as emblematic of their new-found power, eschewing a deeper engagement about the abuse of women, the murder of Harlan (did Louise need to kill him?) or what happened to Louise in Texas.

Without confronting these issues, the bonding implied by the silent exchange of looks before they go over the cliff feels contrived; especially as the spirit of the film is full of fun and sex as pleasure and women finding themselves – the suicide makes the ending troubling and distressing. Later road movies, like *American Honey* (2016), show women having fun without the punishing consequences or driving off a cliff – but then road movies rarely end happily, the journey haunted by a fatalism that usually ends in death or destruction.

Ozark back-country, a place of rural poverty where many families depend on drug dealing and a code of silence for survival is integral to the characterization, plot and theme of the film. IMDB

Winter's Bone (2010)

Screenplay: Debra Granik and Anne Rosellini.
Keywords: single protagonist/story world/quest/character network/sub-text.

The protagonist of *Winter's Bone* (2010) is Ree Dolly, a seventeen-year-old girl living in the Ozark back-country, a place of rural poverty where many families depend on drug dealing and a code of silence for survival. This is the story world established visually and through the interaction of the main characters during the first act.

Ree is part of a network, including her immediate family and her kin, who live in the surrounding hills and woods. She is the main carer for two younger siblings, teaching them basic survival skills like cooking and hunting. Jessup, her father, is often absent but, with her mother depressed, she depends on the money Jessup sends from his shady deals to keep the family together. When she learns from the local sheriff that Jessup has skipped bail, leaving the house as collateral, she sets out to find him. He has to turn up for the court hearing within the week or she will lose the house. This is the set-up and the inciting incident.

Ree's objective is clear, as well as her motivation and what is at stake for her family. Without the house, the family would be broken up or live a hopeless life in makeshift shacks or in the woods. There is also the pressure of a deadline for Jessup's return. The screenplay is stripped down and spare, building the tension through a series of escalating dangers and difficulties facing the young protagonist. Jessup seems to have disappeared and no one knows where he is or at least they are not saying. There is a disturbing and threatening undertow to Ree's encounters with her friends and relatives.

A sense of danger escalates visually, reflected in her slow climb up the hill to confront the most powerful local dealer, Thump Milton and his family. We gradually learn that Jessup was cooking crystal meth, might have been caught by the police and turned snitch and, therefore, may now be dead. This is a close-knit community, where some people are prepared to kill anyone who speaks to the authorities – and that might include Ree, if she continues to ask questions. She is in over her head, scared, threatened and, finally, beaten up, but she will not relent until she finds her father or his body: evidence of his death will be enough for the court.

This is another variant of the classical pattern – a quest story. A threat has arisen and the heroine sets out across hostile terrain, putting her own life in danger in order to gain the knowledge, boon or treasure that will save the kingdom. The obstacles are many – discouragement at the beginning, temptations (she is offered drugs, a cousin is prepared to take her little sister), the deadly opposites (caught between the corrupt Sheriff and the violent Thump family) and the journey to the underworld – a harrowing ordeal where she is finally shown the murdered body of her father and has to cut off both his hands as proof of his death.

Although the focus is on the single protagonist and the forces of antagonism, Ree has a network of friends and companions who add nuance to her character and assist her on her quest, give her money, food, and truck. There is also her father's brother, Teardrop, whose complementary qualities of physical strength and violence help her survive. At first encounter he is sullen and antagonistic but Teardrop's surprising appearance at the second act climax, when all seems lost, not only saves her life, but his promise not to seek revenge for his brother's death, along with Ree's tenacity and the advocacy of her case, ultimately persuades the community to show Ree where her father's body lies.

Though Teardrop provides critical support, this is Ree's story: she is the one we are following, the one who is fearless and relentless in the face of danger, the one who suffers and who gradually matures to the point where she is finally ready for the decisive confrontation with darkness and the terrible truth that releases her from the quest.

Along the way, a key relationship is with someone we never meet – her father.

The moments of discovery and reflection around Jessup chart her internal journey. Objects belonging to him that she touches or picks up, make his absence present – his clothes, boots, banjo. The conflicted sub-text is triggered by encounters with the Sheriff, Teardrop and external demands. Feelings of perplexity, love, anger, fear, shame and horror complement the external quest and lead to resolution and catharsis: an acceptance of what he has been and what he has done that allows Ree to let her father go and sink down into the swamp of the past.

Ree's change of character is not dramatic but the change in her circumstances is – as we also learn in the denouement about the boon of cash from an unclaimed bond. Her family's future is now assured: the denouement of the quest narrative is life renewed.

At the centre of the labyrinth is a monster who must be slain.
PICTURELUX/THE HOLLYWOOD ARCHIVE/ALAMY STOCK

The Third Man (1949)

Screenplay: Graham Greene.
Keywords: internal journey/myth/morality/melodrama/theme.

Graham Greene's screenplay for *The Third Man* (1949) is also a quest narrative: Holly Martins' quest to penetrate the mystery surrounding his friend Harry Lime's death and to find out the truth about his friend and himself. He is as equally determined to succeed as Ree in *Winter's Bone*, but he is clumsy, arrogant and naive – flaws that endanger not only himself, but others and make the audience fear for the success of his venture.

The film is set in the powerfully visual and cinematic story world of post-war Vienna – a perfect labyrinth of obstacles, of bombed-out buildings, borders, black markets, spies and underground sewers that make Holly's search difficult and give the story the atmosphere of a dream or myth. At the centre of the labyrinth there is a monster that must be slain – a monster of egoism and self-interest that happens to be the protagonist's best friend, who he is destined to kill.

According to Joseph Campbell, the essential passage of the mythical hero is psychological and inwards, to his own centre of love and knowledge, and this, ultimately, is where the plot trajectory leads. The external elements of this journey, the twists, reversals and discoveries of the plot, are also moments of insight and realization; a rites of passage, that turn a naive, idealistic writer of sentimental fiction into someone capable of betrayal and murder. So the screen story is also a melodrama, a drama of morality, a series of heightened and expressive encounters, of confrontations and choices around primal ethical forces that resolve in a final confrontation with evil.

The protagonist, Holly Martins, is an innocent abroad, an American writer of pulp westerns who turns up in Vienna looking for his old friend Harry

Lime. He has been offered a job, but when he discovers that Harry has recently died in a mysterious car accident, and that the police seem pleased at this outcome and would prefer that he leave, he decides to stay in Vienna and clear his friend's name.

As he encounters those who saw the accident, or who were friends of Harry's, he is assaulted by ever more shocking revelations: that Harry isn't dead, that he is a racketeer dealing in fake penicillin; that this has led to the death of dozens of innocent children. The complications are many: Harry's devious friends, the lies and half-truths, the murder of the porter who said there was a third man – and then there is Harry's old girlfriend Ana, with whom he falls in love.

Holly himself is a problem: cut-off and isolated by his lack of language skills in a city of several languages, handicapped by the romantic clichés of pulp fiction and his limited knowledge of human nature, he is a clumsy anti-hero and misguided idealist whose actions lead to the death of three people – the porter, the British policeman and Harry himself.

Through the action of the plot, including his love for Ana, Holly's character changes. He discovers his conscience, a deeper sense of right and wrong that leads him to reluctantly accept that Harry's cool, amoral charm conceals something terrifying that needs to be opposed. Ana will never forgive Holly's betrayal of Harry; she is guilty of moral blindness, preferring her memory of the charming man to the revelations of his wicked deeds. She walks away in the famous last shot in the cemetery where Harry has been buried, leaving Holly sad and alone, watching her walk out of his life.

Themes of love and friendship, betrayal and guilt, loss of faith add depth and texture to a story structured as a thriller but experienced as the internal journey of a flawed innocent in a fallen world. Loss of innocence is the over-arching theme that gives unity, meaning and mythic resonance to the screenplay and film.

Silence of the Lambs *(1991)*

Screenwriter: Ted Tally, adapted from the novel by Thomas Harris.
Keywords: dual antagonist/four acts/detective story/adaptation.

Thelma and Louise and *The Third Man* were both original screenplays, but many mainstream feature films are adaptations of novels or plays. Comparing a novel with a feature film adaptation is a useful way of gaining insight into classical feature form.

Ted Talley, who was trained as a playwright, found adapting *Silence of the Lambs* to the screen to be his training in screenwriting, forcing him to think in a logical way about telling a story. Faced with a sprawling novel that shifted point of view between three characters, he quickly realized that, for the cinema, he had to cut and focus on a single protagonist and their journey.

Tally broke down the book scene by scene, following the story logic, then put the scenes on index cards. He decided it was Clarice's story and cut anything that did not follow her journey. The director Jonathan Demme continued this emphasis on Clarice, eliminating any strong scenes that deflected attention away from her story. Some scenes from the book were conflated into one, new scenes were written, visual and aural transitions were invented – all in order to keep the action moving. As Tally and Demme worked on the screenplay they began to reference their own storyline more than the novel: it had developed its own logic and meaning.

While this storyline had a single protagonist in smart, desperate Clarice, one of Tally's inventions was the creation of two parallel antagonists in Lecter and Gumb. This relationship added to the complications for Clarice and to audience interest. It also offered a surprising helper in her objective to capture Gumb, as well as an antagonist that deepened and developed her character. Clarice has three objectives: her immediate goal of catching the serial killer Gumb; her long-term goal of becoming an FBI agent; and her internal goal to silence the lambs. These objectives add complexity and interest to her character and provide forward momentum and motivation for the plot.

While it is Clarice's maturation from student to professional that helps to structure the large-scale parts of the film, it is her developing competence in dealing with Hannibal Lecter that marks her growing confidence and knowledge. This is the single most important structuring device in the film, as she moves from the awkwardness and nervousness of the earlier scenes, to learning how to play his little games and coming to an understanding of Hannibal's true nature.

Silence of the Lambs is a longer movie than *Thelma and Louise*, *Winter's Bone* or *The Third Man* – and requires more key turning points to maintain audience engagement. This means the screenplay breaks down into four, rather than three, acts, based on a shift or refinement of the protagonist's objective.

The set-up ends with Clarice achieving the help of Hannibal, confirmed by the finding of Raspail's head and the new urgency to find the serial killer. The complicating action resets her goal of capturing Gumb, reveals her internal trauma and implicit goal to silence the lambs, and ends on a brief scene with the abducted woman, Catherine, realizing she is going to be killed; her screams are used as an aural transition into a third development section.

This third act is built around delays and complications: Hannibal's prison move and escape, a meeting with Senator Martin, the abducted woman's mother, and ends with the realization that the killer knew his victims. This insight propels us into the climax section where Clarice saves the girl and kills Gumb. Clarice's reward is her achievement of Special Agent status and the healing of her traumatic memories.

This is the story of a young woman haunted by her failed attempt to save a single lamb from slaughter, contrasted with two serial killers who butcher their victims. In the end, just like in *The Third Man*, she kills the monster/butcher and silences the screaming voices inside. As it is a screenplay with two antagonists, it requires the phone call from Hannibal for closure. He has his room with a view, which was his original objective. He won't pursue her. She is safe – for now.

Toy Story *(1995)*

Screenwriters: Joss Whedon, Andrew Stanton, Joel Cohen, Alec Sokolov.
Keywords: premise/inciting incident/writing team/sequence structure/motifs.

The original idea for *Toy Story* (1995) was that it would be about a group of toys and the boy who loved them. The twist was that the story would be told from the toys' point of view, with a team of writers eventually agreeing that the story should focus on Andy's favourite toy – a cowboy called Woody.

The catalyst was to be the arrival of a shiny new rival – Buzz Lightyear – who would become Andy's new favourite and shake up Woody's world. At one stage, and under pressure from Disney Studios, the character of Woody became edgier and mean, throwing Buzz out of the window in a jealous rage; but this proved a false step.

The screenwriter and director Andrew Stanton was brought in because of his insight into story structure and he immediately realigned the story around the more emotionally appealing idea of a toy cowboy who wanted to be loved. For Andrew, having a character that an audience can relate to is an important part of his writing process. He is always looking for that moment that hooks an audience emotionally and in *Toy Story* that was the image of Woody being knocked off Andy's pillow and replaced by a space-age Buzz Lightyear. It is a moment a child can connect to, a very human anxiety that we are not loved or lovable, or that we can be easily replaced or abandoned by those we thought loved us.

The screenplay has, to begin with, an action or image that connects to something primal; to feelings of jealousy, fear or anger that communicate directly with an audience; an image that works on an emotional, not just a plot, level and has consequences for the protagonist. What is Woody going to do about this dramatic change to his world? How is he going to regain his place in Andy's affections?

Stanton was brought into the *Toy Story* project to help redesign the plot and chart Woody's journey from fear and anger to recognition and acceptance. His method was to strip down the plot to its key development sections and then rebuild from the ground-up through a series of eight sequences within the convention of a three-act structure. This is another way to plan and structure your screenplay – to think in terms of key development sequences, rather than acts.

A sequence is a series of linked scenes, a block of dramatic action, complete in itself and united by a single idea, like arrival/escape/pursuit, that helps you map out the protagonist's journey by focusing on the immediate problems, encounters and objectives of each stage of the journey. Most feature screenplays are organized around eight to twelve sequences, each with a beginning, a middle and an end, and a specific objective and obstacle that are steps toward the overall goal of the protagonist.

Each goal meets an obstacle and each setback or reversal requires the protagonist to pause, rethink and devise a new strategy that provides the energy and direction for the next sequence. There are also usually moments of character and relationship development that contribute to the overall character arc. Sequences are the spine of your structure and offer an organizational framework for your screenplay that focuses on how the audience experiences the story by manipulating dramatic tension to maximum effect.

In *Toy Story*, the sequences build around Buzz's arrival and Woody's initial attempts to get rid of him. After Buzz is accidentally knocked out of the window, the aim of getting him back home before Andy moves house is complicated by the evil kid Sid capturing and imprisoning both of them, ending with Buzz's despairing realization that he is just a toy. At this low point, Woody finds a way to re-inspire Buzz, then devises a plan of escape involving the other toys in defeating Sid.

The climax sequence has both Woody and Buzz pursuing the moving van carrying Andy and his family to their new house, making good use of the previously planted match and Buzz's line of dialogue 'to infinity and beyond'. The potentially life-saving match and the dialogue hook remind us of an earlier time in the story and how far we have come. They are also examples of visual and aural motifs, planted and paid off, that contribute to the sense of unity and reality of the story world.

Every sequence in *Toy Story* leads to the next and each is emotionally gripping with turns and twists and serious threat and danger for our heroes, with the end sequence especially moving and uplifting. The image of Andy's family driving

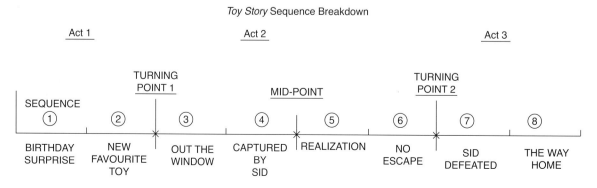

Toy Story Sequence Breakdown

You can structure your screenplay around a series of development sequences, each with their own set of objectives and outcomes.

away, and the desperation of Woody and Buzz to catch-up and finally make it home, stirs powerful emotions in the audience. Nobody likes to be left behind.

Like Odysseus, we invest in the emotion of return to an idealized place of safety and fulfilment; the desire and emotion of finding our true home, our place in the world, where we are acknowledged and accepted for who we are, rather than how powerful, important or successful we are.

In fairy tales it is always a transformed home, opening a way to a new life and destiny that you had not anticipated. If you add in Woody's willingness to sacrifice himself for his friend, you have the full resolution of a theme parallel to Woody's acceptance of his new place in Andy's life – that of friendship – a theme that adds to optimistic emotion of the film amplified by Randy Newman's feel-good theme song.

> Friendship is a kind of virtue or implies virtue and it is also most necessary for living. Nobody would choose to live without friends even if he had all the good things.
>
> Aristotle – *Ethics*

ALTERNATIVE STRATEGIES

Little Miss Sunshine (2006)

Screenwriter: Michael Arndt.
Keywords: parallel plots/ensemble structure/individual storylines/comedy.

Michael Arndt was the screenwriter on *Toy Story 3* (2010) and subsequently big budget movies such as *Hunger Games* (2013) and *Star Wars: the Force Awakens* (2015), but his breakout screenplay was the low-budget comedy *Little Miss Sunshine* (2006). The script offers another variation on the typical Hollywood model of three-act structure shaped around the action of Ree Dolly in *Winter's Bone*; in this case, an ensemble movie where the story of a group provides the over-arching narrative within which we follow the storylines of individual group members.

This is a form of parallel storytelling that includes a range of alternative structures, where conflict and tension build across different time periods or narrative lines often involving several protagonists, or the same protagonist at different (real or imagined) moments in their life but woven together around the same theme. These include a variety of structural approaches, for example flashback: *Citizen Kane* (1941), *The Killers* (1946), *Momento* (2000), *Martha, Marcy, May, Marlene* (2011); sequential: *Blind Chance* (1987), *Run Lola Run* (1999), *Moonlight* (2017); tandem: *Magnolia* (1999), *Code Unknown* (2000), *Crash* (2005); ensemble/multiple protagonist: *Saving Private Ryan* (1998), *Little Miss Sunshine* (2006).

Ensemble films focusing on a group of characters can be found across a range of genres but typically in films of siege or horror, where a group is trapped and surrounded, such as *Night of the Living Dead* (1968), *Assault on Precinct 13* (1976), or come together in a reunion, such as *The Big Chill* (1983), or set out on a joint quest, such as *Lord of the Rings* (2001). The group is usually under threat both from external forces and internal division that may include a group member who will betray them.

The macro- or over-arching plot involves the survival of the group, why and how the group is threatened and develops the theme. An ensemble film also has to show the different responses of individual protagonists to the events of the plot, as well as the conflicts and shifting loyalties of the interweaving narrative lines. Individual characters and storylines create problems and possibilities that are woven into the main plot. The common element that threatens the group puts pressure on all the individual characters to reveal themselves, with each character a protagonist on their own journey.

The macro plot is shaped conventionally from inciting incident through turning points and rising action to the climax. In *Little Miss Sunshine* the catalyst is ten-year-old Olive's winning a place in the final of a children's beauty contest and her desperate desire to attend. The first act involves her mother, Sheryl, persuading her dysfunctional family to come and support her in their beat-up Volkswagen bus.

The family members are a bunch of comically flawed, self-absorbed, narcissistic men that includes: Frank, a suicidal Proust scholar; Dwayne, a teenage Nietzsche fan who has taken a vow of silence; Granpa Edwin, a heroin-snorting porn addict; and her husband, Richard, a pompous self-improvement guru. Richard's speech to his daughter, where he asks her if she thinks she can win because there is no point in going otherwise, sets up the central theme key to the writer's impulse in developing the story: the worship of success and the demonization of losers. If you add in Arndt's anger at the sexualization of children, you have the ideas and emotional energy that make the film more than an exercise in structure.

Setting out on the road to the competition final is the first-act turning-point, with a series of accidents, encounters and discoveries providing the obstacles and rising action of the plot, as well as moments of despair for each of the protagonists on their individual journeys. The car breaks down and ever after can only be started by everyone pushing it downhill before jumping in – thus giving the film a simple but powerful visual metaphor: because this is about a group, in this case a family, putting aside their individual obsessions and coming together to support each other, but especially the youngest and most vulnerable member of the family.

Each of the protagonists has a simple storyline, driven by a clear desire to be a success in the world: Frank wants to be the number one Proust scholar and win back his lover; Dwayne wants to be a jet pilot; Grandpa wants to lead a life of total excess; Richard wants to publish his self-help book; Olive wants to win the beauty competition. Each has to face up to different types of failure and a reckoning with their idealized selves but, in the process, discovers new meaning and the value of loving something beyond themselves.

The low mid-point, where the family are at rock-bottom and grandpa dies, becomes a revitalizing moment of action that takes them to the climax of support for Olive, allowing her to decide for herself that she will go on stage – despite the doubts of her father still obsessed with the importance of being a winner.

Her mother, Sheryl, has the smallest character arc but, structurally, she is the moral centre of the drama, the one who holds the family together and around whom the boy-men revolve. It is she who interrupts Richard's concern about success and failure with 'Let Olive be Olive'. Richard is the one who changes most, his final beats telescoped into the climax scene. Here he goes from thinking Olive might win, through denial, bewilderment, to the realization that his daughter cannot win but it doesn't matter. Released from his obsession with winning, he is able to leap onto the stage and join Sheryl and Olive and the rest of his family. Olive, caught between the two voices of winning or enjoying herself, makes her own decision.

Relationships of all kinds, family or otherwise, can be a prison but they can also be the means by which we flourish. This is a comedy not a tragedy and so involves the defeat of the dark, rigid, life-denying forces of selfishness, division and fear of failure by the energies of life and liberation. Just as in Shakespearean comedy, recognition of what is really important leads to a change of heart, reconciliation and the discovery of one's true identity. The group and individuals involved in *Little Miss Sunshine* have survived the challenges of the journey and can now celebrate.

Code Unknown (2000)

Screenwriter: Michael Haneke.
Keywords: network narrative/anti-psychological/modernist/music.

Another form of parallel storytelling that involves multiple protagonists is the network narrative – this is where storylines run in tandem to each other and characters are linked through chance encounters, rather than causality. Dramatic unity is provided not through the point of view of a single protagonist, but by a setting or theme.

This is a form of storytelling popular in the novel from Charles Dickens to David Mitchell, but also in contemporary soap operas, television and web series. The shifting points of view and the interconnectedness of the storylines draw us to network narratives because they seem to make sense of the multiple realities, hidden patterns and the constantly moving complexity of our lives in a digital world.

Crash (2005), written by Paul Haggis, would be an example of this kind of multi-protagonist approach, where a range of characters literally crash into each other's lives, with sometimes fatal consequences, but where characters also learn often harsh life lessons. This is a Hollywood movie and each of the individual storylines is coherent and comprehensible, shaped around principles of causality and character desire and need – where all the factors, external and internal, are neatly clarified and resolved by the end.

This is exactly the kind of cinema that Michael Haneke, the writer and director of *Code Unknown* finds over-determined and sentimental. He wants to break the Aristotelian enchantment and, like Brecht, to deliberately make the audience uncomfortable: to encourage them to reflect on the manipulation and illusion of fiction; to provoke questions rather than provide false answers. Life is too fragmentary and reality too complex to capture. Mainstream cinema pretends to know it all, but Haneke wants to have a dialogue with the audience, to make them think, not to give them explanations.

Code Unknown opens with a child trying to communicate what she is feeling to a group of deaf children by look and gesture. The children are intensely engaged and committed but cannot seem to understand, their attempts at interpreting dismissed with a shake of the child's head.

Then we cut to a Parisian street with a man trying to get into, what we realize later, is his lover's

apartment, but he can't get inside because he doesn't know the new code. A central theme is set-up at the beginning – the difficulty of communication, of understanding the code that would help us to understand and get close to one another. The film plays out the consequences of this miscommunication and our ignorance of each other's true lives.

A title on screen tells us we are about to see 'Incomplete tales of several journeys' and the film proceeds to introduce us to a range of characters: a struggling farmer and his angry teenage son; a street beggar who is a respectable mother and breadwinner back home in Romania; a young black musician and his African father; an actress and her war-photographer boyfriend. Their lives intersect in moments of anger, misunderstanding and underlying racism and violence. Images that, as an audience, we believe to be real, turn out to be part of a fiction film; while the reality of brutalized bodies from a contemporary European war puncture our fictional reality. Scenes and sequences stoke our indignation at some apparent cruelty, then thwart our desire to reach an easy judgement by showing us another side.

The focus is on how people relate to each other: the everyday cruelties and kindness; the guilt and recklessness; the petty acts of bullying; people not listening or thinking; the delusions of authority, class and privilege. Rather than goal-driven heroes and heroines and big character arcs, we have fragments that we have to piece together and reflect upon.

There is no diegetic music until the very end when the background rumble of unease and dislocation running through the film is picked up and amplified into a relentless drumbeat that is pointing to a threatening future for us all, or a hopeful message of communication. Perhaps it is both.

Haneke's objective camera keeps us at a distance from the characters and resists any easy psychological interpretation or explanation of their actions. Rather than a single unified plot, we have a multi-perspective collage of modern Europe, with scenes separated by a Brechtian device of black space, jolting us out of the fictional enchantment. The plot is disjointed, focusing on several unrelated people and random acts of violence, but to a purpose.

It is also a film concerned with moral questions about inequality, immigration, guilt and responsibility. It asks what responsibility we have to each other. Unlike the Hollywood formula, it does not seek to reassure us that things will work out, that there is an explanation for everything and a remedy. Characters don't really change; it is not clear if anyone learns anything and, if they do, what that might be. The film is more disturbing than cathartic.

Each fragment feels authentic and true to life, rather than didactic or fantastic, showing us situations that we encounter on a daily basis. Without a compelling plot, the skill is in the crafting and staging of scenes that are contradictory and conflicted enough to engage an audience in the moment.

The structure of the film is bound by the idea that reality is always fragmentary and episodic. The individual narratives may be open-ended and ambiguous but, like theme and counter-theme in music, the internal conflicts and rhythms within and between each scene create a kind of unity and tension that offer an alternative to the classical way of storytelling. Film is about rhythm – it is closer to music than literature. One aspect is conventional, however: in the end, something happens to each of the characters, the events have consequence for them and their lives, however incomplete or mysterious, they all go on a journey.

Vagabond (1985)

Screenplay: Agnes Varda.
Keywords: research/dramatic question/observational/episodic structure.

Agnes Varda is, like Michael Haneke, a writer who also directs and her film *Vagabond* (1985) was originally conceived as a network narrative of eight characters whose lives criss-cross, but resolved itself into the portrait of a young female drifter who wanders in the south of France during a bitterly cold winter. Like Haneke's character journeys, the portrait remains incomplete; the protagonist, Mona, remains opaque and mysterious.

Based on several months of research, Varda originally developed a conventional backstory for her character that she then dispensed with to focus on her real interest – how Mona lives and survives the cold and solitude, where she goes and who she meets along the way. All she has is a tent and a rucksack, but the emphasis is on walking and movement, rather than the interactions. This is a woman on the move, a moving figure in the landscape; but where she comes from, or where she is going to, remains hidden from us.

The film has two openings: the first is the discovery of a young woman found frozen to death in a ditch and the second a flashback to the same woman emerging naked from the sea. There is, therefore, no conventional suspense as to what happens to Mona. We know that she will die in the end but, like the opening of *Citizen Kane* or any murder mystery, a conventional dramatic question is posed – how and why did she die? Although we follow her through the last two months of her life, the question is never really answered. The film is more interested in how she survives, and in the gestures and actions of her daily life. It is observational, rather than psychological; as if the camera is recording a strange creature in their habitat.

On her journey, Mona meets several people who help her, or give her food or shelter. She says very little about herself, while the episodic structure is further punctured by testimonials to camera of those who met her briefly and tried to help or understand her: a hippy shepherd, a tree surgeon, a garage mechanic, a fellow drifter; some envy her freedom, others despise her rootless and dirty existence, but the film refuses to judge or interpret.

Vagabond is a film that breaks with classical film narrative in several ways. The protagonist has no clear motivation, desire or ideology; we have no access to her inner life and, therefore, no sense of an internal journey; the forces of antagonism

The choice between love and hate – *Do the Right Thing*'s ultimate question about what guides our actions. IMDB

that drive her to her death are unclear. Although Mona is clearly vulnerable and exposed to many dangers, she does not seek our pity and the film is not constructed in a way that might elicit it.

The fragmentary episodes reflect the random quality of her existence but break with any coherent account of what is happening to her. There are some causal links between scenes and there is a background of rising tension around her gradual deterioration, but this is a film that deliberately eschews the conventional redemptive or cathartic ending. Like Haneke, Varda prefers ambiguity rather than explanation and opacity of character over psychological interpretation. Who was Mona? We will never know… or maybe that is the wrong question.

Do the Right Thing (1989)

Screenwriter: Spike Lee.
Keywords: ensemble/morality/political/ambiguity.

Spike Lee is one of a group of independent filmmakers who take a contrary view of American life to that of mainstream Hollywood and is resistant to the fantasy and formula of commercial cinema. His subject is the dark underbelly of the African-American experience – a history of slavery, violence and murder, police brutality and discrimination – but also an engagement with power relations, gender and class in a multi-cultural world.

His films are disturbing and ambivalent, humorous but often tragic; his characters flawed, excessive and unpredictable. He wants to disturb you; he is driven by a passionate desire for social justice and equality. He, too, wants to ask questions rather than offer easy answers and consolations. Questions such as how we live together in a multicultural world torn by class and ethnic hatreds, and how we live with our own secret hatreds of the other – our violence and paranoia.

He is not afraid to break with screenwriting conventions in order to wake us to the social disaster that awaits us if we do not confront our fears and hatreds. His narratives are often ambiguous with no particular voice privileged. Characters address us directly from the screen: punching up a clear choice between love or hate; tell stories within stories; burst into energetic, pugnacious dance; an uneasy mix of seduction and threat that sets up the theme. The hip-hop music that Tina dances to 'Fight the Power' is obsessively played by Radio Raheem and becomes the trigger for an explosion of violence in the climax.

Tina's powerful dance is the opening of *Do the Right Thing* (1989), Lee's third feature as a director. The setting is a single city block in working-class Brooklyn during the hottest day of the year. Here tensions build between a multi-cultural ensemble of neighbourhood characters, who are complex, contradictory and less than heroic. The film is structured around their competing voices and different points of view: angry, belligerent, tribal but also rational, religious, nostalgic. The older generation carry memories of an earlier political radicalism now being replaced by a new, aggressive, consumerist individualism. Music in the film reflects these shifts in mood and tone – old school jazz and orchestral to rap and hip-hop.

We meet them all one by one: Mr Senor Love Daddy, a local community DJ who delivers the wake-up call at the beginning of the film; Mookie, a feckless, defiant urban youth; his feisty feminist sister, Jade; Da Major, alcoholic and wise old man; Sal and his two sons opening up the pizzeria; Mother-Sister, the block's unofficial matriarch observing life passing from her window ledge. The passing black youth include: Buggin Out, an angry would-be political radical; Smiley, disabled and stuttering with his postcards of Michael X and Martin Luther King; and Radio Raheem, big and silent with a boom box constantly playing the film's hip-hop theme song, 'Fight the Power'. His knuckles are the ones we see later, inspired by *Night of the Hunter* (1955) emblazoned with the choice between love and hate – the film's ultimate question about what guides our actions.

At different points of the day and night, they all converge on the Italian pizzeria run by tough but affable Sal and his two sons: Vino, decent and fair minded and, Pino, a racist bigot. Mookie works here and argues with Sal about his mixed-race interest in his sister Jade, at the same time as confronting Pino on his racist attitudes. But it is Radio Raheen's demand for black heroes on the Italian Hall of Fame and the relentless noise of Raheen's radio that finally breaks Sal's good humour when, in a screed of invective, he smashes Raheen's radio. In the mayhem that follows, Raheen is choked by the police and killed.

Mookie, a voice of reason up to this point, throws a garbage bin at the glass front of the pizzeria and begins a riot that ends with the burning down of the building. In the cold light of day, Mookie returns to meet Sal for the money he is owed. There is no apology or reconciliation between the two. Every character plays their part in the build up to the climax but Mookie and Sal are the main players, the structural elements that represent two apparently irreconcilable points of view.

In a coda, Smiley holds up his two postcards – one of Martin Luther King, the other Malcolm X – which is it to be, integration or separation? A list of the fallen, those African-Americans killed in police custody, runs over the end credits. There is no real catharsis. The ambiguous tone, the ambivalent characters, the multiple perspectives, the tangled web of racial and power relations ensure there is no easy answer to the original question of what is the right thing to do.

Despite the complexity and radical disruptions of the screenplay and film, there is a mix of conventional elements in *Do the Right Thing* that keep the audience on track, even through the digressions and Brechtian intrusions.

The underlying shape of set-up, development and climax, along with the unity of time and place, the careful plotting of the rising tension, the visual and aural repetitions, and the role of Mookie and Sal as protagonist/anagonist, are the Aristotelian elements that ensure the audience remains engaged with the action and the uncertainty of outcome. Although Lee plays with conventional form, the integration of character, structure and theme aligns with the classical model in ways that create dramatic unity and audience engagement.

CONCLUSION

Classical American cinema has absorbed the experiments of art and independent cinema over many years. The wide range of political film-makers and artists who have moved into film-making, illustrates the range and flexibility of the classical model.

It has always been like this. Hollywood has always encouraged the exploration of new ways of storytelling and from the beginning, but especially in the 1940s and 1950s, experimented with flashback structures, dream sequences, multi-protagonist and network narratives. As with most recent experiments, including time-loops, hypothetical futures and complex plotting, unconventional storytelling has largely taken place within the patterns of a classical tradition that the audience can understand. Hence, for a new screenwriter, the importance of studying that tradition *and* its variations by readings screenplays and viewing a wide range of films drawn from world cinema. This should include the kinds of cinema that challenges, or cannot be contained within, this model.

Alternatives to the Classical Model

A list of innovative films and screenplays will be found at the end of the book but, from the films analysed in this chapter, you should already begin to see that there are a number of different ideas and techniques that you can use to add an original twist to your screenplay.

You could, for example, have:

- a looser structure – more elliptical and ambiguous, fewer explanations, less linear and logical;
- an episodic, tandem, ensemble, multi-protagonist structure;
- a flashback structure that plays with time and rearranges events;
- events ordered by psychological rather than chronological links;

- a minimal narrative – with attention given to small details of everyday life;
- an emphasis on the internal drama of a character, rather than plot twists;
- mood and atmosphere over plot;
- poetic and lyrical elements;
- no single point of view;
- characters directly addressing camera;
- a lack of psychology;
- stories within stories;
- passive or powerless protagonists;
- four or five acts rather than three;
- incidents and events linked by chance and coincidence rather than cause and effect;
- the presence of dreams, fantasies, memories;
- elements of different genres;
- documentary style;
- the use of voice over.

Models that emphasize active, goal-oriented protagonists and three-act structure can fail to catch the ambiguity, the randomness, the arbitrariness of the everyday world. They can seem predictable and formulaic, but from the earlier analyses in this chapter, you can see that there are ways of working within the tradition that can allow you to play with audience expectations and give an original twist to your screenplay.

In the next chapter, we will turn to the basic building block of the screenplay – the scene.

EXERCISES

Winter's Bone (2010)

Screenplay: Debra Granik and Anne Rosellini.

1. What is the central dramatic question of the screenplay? What is the central dramatic question of your screenplay? How does this question relate to audience engagement?
2. Describe how the question is raised, developed and answered in the screenplay.

3. Describe briefly the emotional journey of the reader/audience. How is that journey organized by the plot structure? What does it mean?
4. Describe briefly the action taken by the protagonist at four key moments: (i) the inciting incident, (ii) the Act I climax/turning point, (iii) the mid-point, (iv) Act II climax/turning point.
5. Find examples of how the following dramatic devices are used to create tension: anticipation, suspense, sub-text and raising the stakes.
6. Give an example of surprise in the screenplay. How is this achieved? Why is it an important element in a story?
7. Give examples of what the audience is hoping for and simultaneously afraid of. How is this achieved?

Toy Story (1995)

Screenplay: Joss Whedon, Andrew Stanton, Joel Cohen, Alec Sokolov.

Read the screenplay of *Toy Story* by Andrew Stanton and make notes on the following:

1. Write a half-page synopsis and a logline for the film story.
2. How does the story begin (*in media res*) and how are we made curious?
3. From whose point of view is the story told and what is at stake for him?
4. Discuss briefly how audience identification is achieved? Why should we care for the protagonist? Why should we care for your protagonist?
5. What do you think is the main dramatic question? Can you do the same for your feature project?
6. How is dramatic tension created and sustained through the length of the story?
7. What is the difference between the protagonist's want and his need, and how does the conflict between the two relate to the concept of the character arc?

8. Who is the antagonist and what is his function? What does that mean in terms of the structure of the plot? Describe briefly the main beats in the relationship between the protagonist and the antagonist. Do the same for your own project.
9. Select one dramatic scene and analyse the structure. Describe the set-up, development and climax. How does the scene pick up on what has come before and prepare us for what will happen later?
10. Break-down the screenplay into sequences. How many did you find? What fictional techniques are used to sustain the flow of events and the sense of organic unity between the sequences? Select one sequence and analyse the structure.
11. Give examples of visual and aural motifs. How are they used?
12. Give three examples of ironic tension in the screenplay.
13. Do you still play with toys or dolls or both? Do you believe they come alive at night when you are sleeping? You can keep this answer secret.

Little Miss Sunshine (2006)

Screenwriter: Michael Arndt.

After reading the screenplay (www.dailyscript. com), write brief notes on the following:

- **Genre:** romantic comedy, road movie or mixed genre? What kind of audience is the film aimed at?
- **Logline:** provide a one-sentence encapsulation of what the film is about.
- **Concept:** what is the controlling idea/theme of the film?
- **Synopsis:** write a short summary of the film (half page – one page).
- **Plot Structure:** list the inciting incident, key turning-points, major sequences, crisis and

climax. Does it have a conventional narrative structure? If not, how would you describe the structure?

- **Character:** list and describe the main character types. What are their defining qualities? What are their problems and objectives? Select three characters and describe briefly the main plot points of their journeys. What is at stake for each of them? Do they change? If so, how and why? How do their stories connect to the theme?
- **Dramatic Scene:** choose a scene that (i) dramatizes a turning point for a character, (ii) involves a moment of crisis for a character. Describe briefly in the context of their narrative development.
- **Personal:** what did you find in the film/script that was interesting or useful in the development of your own screenwriting or project? Brief notes.

Crash (2005)

Read the screenplay for *Crash* written by Paul Haggis and Bobby Moresco and view the film of *Code Unknown* written and directed by Michael Haneke. Then answer the following questions:

1. What are the key characteristics of classical narrative in cinema?

2. Define briefly (i) a three-act paradigm, (ii) a character arc, (iii) the hero's journey. Discuss with reference to your own project how useful these theories were as practical guides to writing to your screenplay.

3. What other models or elements of theory have you found most useful in developing your screenplay or deepening your understanding of screenwriting?

4. What alternatives to the classical model can you name? List different approaches. What is their attraction?

5. How many key storylines in *Crash*? List them and summarize the main story beats.

6. What is each character frightened of? Take a character from your own screenplay. What are they frightened of losing? What do they most fear? What would they do if they were forced to face their fear?

7. How does the screenplay of *Crash* maintain interest and focus with so many characters?

8. What is the theme?

9. *Code Unknown* is also constructed around interweaving storylines. In what way is it different from *Crash*? For example, characterization, style, tone, theme. What do you think the writer/director wants to say?

10. Select a scene that you admire and analyse its structure.

8
SCENE WRITING
AND DIALOGUE

A classical feature screenplay follows the journey of the protagonist and their struggle to achieve an objective; but this takes time and is developed in stages. Every step of the journey is also a trial, a test of character, a series of encounters and obstacles, revelations and setbacks, partial success and opportunities that are dramatized scene by scene. Audience interest is sustained over 90–120min, with major reversals at two or three key turning points or act breaks, but in every scene there are also minor or individual moments of change that are important stages in plot progression and character transformation.

A dramatic scene is one in which something happens: an incident or event takes place, the situation between the characters is different at the end of the scene from what it was at the beginning. The balance of power has shifted and this new situation prepares us for the next scene. A scene is the basic building block and a part of the overall pattern of the screenplay, where part and whole depend on each other. Every scene drives the story forward toward the end and each scene ends in a crisis that makes us wonder what will happen next.

Of equal importance is the question 'What is happening *now*?' Without the significance of the present moment, there is no desire to look forward. While the audience may be intrigued by the onrushing sequence of plot events, the same amount of attention needs to be given to the conflict or tension in the present situation: it could be a visual clue, a mood or atmosphere that suggests danger or something hidden; this may

be information, knowledge or intention that the audience discovers as the scene unfolds, but it should engage them in the moment, as well as raising expectations about the future.

The writer must also think about how to reveal or hint at what characters might be thinking or feeling: the sub-text of emotion that adds complexity and texture to the scene; how body language, movement and gesture betray feelings but also add depth to a character. This involves paying attention to not only big actions but also to small details of behaviour, such as how a character drinks their coffee or walks to the door. These behaviours will be watched closely and interpreted by other characters in the scene as well as the audience. In this sense the individual scene is a place of both visible conflict and an underlying subtext of thoughts and feelings that create tension and expectation in the mind of the audience.

THE SCENE

Definition

A scene can be defined by the word *drama*, meaning 'something done'. In a scene, something specific happens – a moment of tension that may or may not be resolved. It could be quite trivial, such as asking, 'How was the party?' but there must be a reason for asking the question. The scene may be short or long, visual or dialogue-driven, an action or a transitional scene; but always a scene takes place in one location, is part of a sequence and a key element of a larger structure that moves the story forward.

The Dramatic Scene

In a classical screenplay, a dramatic scene is usually two to three pages long and has four elements:

- Setting – visual/dramatic potential – atmosphere and props.
- Action – what the characters are doing.
- Dialogue – what the characters are saying.
- Sub-text – what is really happening below the surface/the emotional core of the scene and often the most important aspect.

Each dramatic scene is internally structured as a microcosm of the overall screenplay structure into a beginning, a middle and an end, with the protagonist of the scene pursuing an immediate objective and encountering opposition; the ensuing conflict building to crisis and climax through key turning points. There has to be something at stake for the protagonist, something to gain or lose, possible danger or jeopardy that motivates them to action. Take, for example, the scene in *Thelma and Louise* after the money has been stolen and Louise collapses in defeat.

The discovery that the money has been stolen is the set-up, and the development is Thelma's efforts to deal with Louise's defeatism and the turning point or crisis – Thelma's plan to rob a store as a solution to their problem. It is also the moment where Thelma changes and takes charge for the first time. The emotional complexity of their relationship and their interior lives is the deeper sub-text of the scene, revealed in action and dialogue, and through debate and the rising conflict between them.

Layers

A well-written scene is layered and textured; it is not just about moving the story forward. It explores character and theme, establishes a mood and atmosphere, provides important information and prepares for later events. In a dramatic scene, we see characters weigh options, reflect on new possibilities, make choices, take on responsibilities, come to a realization of what has happened and what might happen in the future. They are forced to face the consequences of their actions. Once thoughts and feelings are externalized, they can be acted upon; but there is no going back.

Action

Action takes us out of our solitude into the world of other people: what we do, as opposed to what we say we will do, reveals who we are and forms a link between our interior thoughts and external experience. By the end of the scene there is a shift in the overall balance of the story: a movement from positive to negative or vice versa. Thelma turns apparent defeat into an opportunity and takes responsibility for the first time. For the audience, this is a mood swing from fear to the hope that Thelma and Louise can both still escape to freedom.

Beats

Every movement in the scene, each gesture and line of dialogue, breaks down into the story beats of the scene. These are the actions and reactions of what one character says or does, and the response of the other character. The scene develops in this way, in action and reaction, a series of minor internal crises that are externalized and build in intensity until a point of major crisis that forces a decision or a revelation that changes the whole balance of the scene. This could be a turning point where one character wins out over another or where the protagonist is faced with a difficult choice that is resolved by a decision that becomes a first step in character transformation.

Structure

In classical cinema, a scene is structured around three key elements:

- The set-up:
  - Introduces the basic situation.
  - The problem is established.
  - A dramatic question is posed.
  - Prepares us for what is to follow.
- Crisis:
  - A major turning point.
  - A crucial or decisive moment.
  - An action or decision required that forces change.
- Climax:
  - The pay-off that resolves the major crisis.
  - A new state of affairs.
  - Creates the set-up for next scene.

Drama is built around the conflict and confrontation between one or more characters, but some films, such as *Cold War* (2018), and especially TV series, intensify the narrative pace by dispensing with the set-up and resolution, and focusing entirely on the crisis and confrontation. We are thrown immediately into the scene with little or no preparation other than our knowledge of what has happened previously and we cut out quickly at a new moment of crisis. Questions remain unanswered but the lack of any explanation or resolution excites our curiosity for what is to follow.

The maxim 'arrive late, get out early' is a technique for increasing narrative intensity and audience engagement, with crisis points in a scene subverting our expectations and propelling us into the next one. Contemporary films have many more such short, sharp scenes and five times as many cuts than earlier classical movies. Longer developed scenes are still important to many screenplays and certainly should be studied by the novice screenwriter.

From the viewpoint of the protagonist in a dramatic scene, another three structuring elements are crucial:

- Objective: what the protagonist wants in the scene.
- Obstacle: what prevents them from getting what they want.
- Action: the strategy chosen by the protagonist to overcome the obstacle and to continue the pursuit of their objective.

Inner Tension and Outer Action

A protagonist may have more than one attempt to overcome the obstacle, with each of these failed attempts creating the beats and the minor turning points of the scene until the original question posed by the set-up is fulfilled or answered. More often, the protagonist fails in their objective or only partially achieves what they set out to do in the scene, but this only forces them to reflect, change strategy or goals, and come out stronger and more determined. This happens at every stage of Ree's journey in *Winter's Bone* and with Holly, the protagonist of *The Third Man*. In a classical screenplay, setbacks and moments of failure are steps on the journey of character change.

For this reason, the end of many scenes requires the protagonist to think of what they are going to do now and the crisis becomes a moment of insight or change of heart. At key moments, and especially major turning points in the screenplay, this is what the protagonist has to do and what the writer has to show. The character processes the emotional impact of what has happened and what their options now are: how they plan to move forward.

At the end of the second act, we usually don't see the protagonist's plan for solving their problem and are, therefore, surprised and excited to see the outcome of this period of reflection. The important point being that a character's inner struggle, their thoughts and feelings, rational and moral, need to be linked through choice, decision and action to plot events. The tension between inner and outer action is another form of drama that also provides an opportunity to reveal a contradiction between what a character does and what they truly feel.

SCENE ANALYSIS

Toy Story: *Context*

Woody is a toy cowboy who has lost his place as Andy's favourite, to toy spaceman Buzz Lightyear, who also happens to be delusional, thinking he is a real spaceman and not a toy. Woody in his anger has accidentally knocked Buzz out of the window, but the other toys think he has done it deliberately. He must get Buzz back to save face and before Andy and his family move house.

But both Woody and Buzz are captured by the evil child Sid, who tortures and destroys toys, and Woody is trapped under a crate in Sid's room, unable to move. His long-term goal of reclaiming his place on Andy's pillow has been replaced by the immediate objective of escape and getting back to Andy's house.

Woody's goal in this scene is to get out from under the crate, so that Buzz and he can both escape from the clutches of Sid, who has threatened to destroy them when he wakes up. Buzz is free and could help but the problem is that he is depressed, having just discovered that he is not a real spaceman but just another toy.

Sample Scene

The scene begins at night. Sid is sleeping and there is a rumble of thunder as Woody tries and fails to shift the crate. He needs the help of Buzz. He goes for the easy option of asking for his help and realizes that Buzz is too depressed. He tries other forms of persuasion, finally opting for flattery – trying to convince Buzz that he is special, a cool toy, a toy that is loved by Andy. Woody thus stumbles into a sincere truth that reminds him that he is no longer the special one and his head drops so he doesn't see what we see – Buzz is looking at his foot on which Andy has written his name. From his reaction we see Buzz come to the realization that Woody is right – he is loved and that is what matters.

But when Woody looks up, Buzz has disappeared. Then 'suddenly the entire milk crate begins to shake' – Buzz to the rescue! Buzz, inspired by Woody's insight, has recovered his self-belief and come to help his friend. Together they begin to push the crate off, redoubling their efforts when they see out of the window the removal van arriving at Andy's house. A space is created for Woody to jump to the floor but, in a final twist, the crate crashes down on his head. However, with the help of Buzz he fights free of the rubble, just as Sid's alarm goes off...

Summary

The structure of the scene is clear and simple from the opening image through the turns and twists of rising action to a point of crisis. The set-up establishes an atmosphere of darkness and danger, and an image of Woody's dilemma – he is trapped under a milk crate, the slats like prison bars and he needs to get free before Sid wakes up. His attempts to persuade Buzz to help him escape build to a turning point where the reanimated Buzz helps free him, only to realize they are still trapped in Sid's room and Sid is waking up. So the climax of this scene becomes the set-up for the next scene.

From Woody's point of view, his objective – to get free of the crate with the help of Buzz – meets the very real obstacle of his friend's depression. But Woody finds a strategy to get Buzz involved in helping him escape and is now ready to re-engage with the overall goal of getting Buzz and himself back home before Andy and his family move house.

The scene is built up through a series of action/reaction beats but is also a stage in the developing friendship between Woody and Buzz, and the gradual changes in their character. These changes come from inside the characters as they process what is happening. We can infer from their body language, their gestures and facial expressions what they are thinking and feeling, and see their inner life and struggle externalized in what they say and do.

WRITING THE SCENE

Looking for Clues

As social creatures, we are primed to pay attention to facial and vocal expression, and are able to infer the desires, intentions and even the beliefs of others. This includes building into our behaviour an awareness of what others may infer about our motives and how they might respond to our actions. We are able to detect a contradiction between what they say and how they say it; we may suspect that we are being deceived. Like a detective or the protagonist in a scene, we are looking for clues about the intentions and sincerity of others and working out what we need to say or do to get what we want or to conceal our intentions.

When we encounter others in a social context, we have learned to pay attention; what we see or hear may be crucial to predicting what might happen next or what is expected of us. As animals we have become aware of others as volatile and unpredictable, but how we interact with each other is tempered by a developed moral capacity, the social emotions of generosity and kindness, and our need to maintain the delicate fabric of sociability that all too easily can be ruptured by fear and loathing.

All the World's a Stage

The sociologist Erving Goffman[28] uses a theatrical metaphor in his analysis of the fragile and deceptive quality of everyday interaction. The idea that all the world's a stage is, of course, as old as theatre itself, but he was interested in the mutual influence that takes place in day to day encounters:

the ways in which the part one plays is shaped by the parts played by others who constitute the audience. While the individual who presents himself before others will try to control the impression they have of him or her, the audience in their turn will form their own impression not only from what they already might know, but also from the conduct and appearance, the psychological traits and involuntary gestures of the individual who appears before them.

From this perspective, every dramatic scene involves a series of strategic games, an exercise in impression management and the repression or concealment of true feelings, desires and needs in order to achieve individual or social goals. The possibilities of breakdown, embarrassment or violence make it important to have some control in the definition of the situation, to know what to expect and how to behave in order to get what you want or to avoid revealing what you want to conceal. But this is not always possible. We don't have all the information about those present, so we could easily misread the situation or be derailed by an unexpected revelation or our own unconscious responses.

We are also sometimes powerless or have limited power to influence the situation. This is often the case, for example, in neo-realist films where characters are constrained or determined by their environment; unlike in the classic Hollywood film, where the determined individual can shape their world and the outcome of their desire.

Social interaction can be a tricky business, so we have to remain alert not only to surface appearances, but also to what might be going on below the surface: the hidden aspect of the person or the scene. Understanding what is really going on could be important to our success or survival.

In reading a screenplay or watching a film, the audience are also paying attention to the gap between what is being said and what is meant, and to the subtle ways in which the writer and performers offer a glimpse of this hidden world through small gestures and involuntary reactions.

The audience may realize from what they already know that what is being said is a lie but not know why the truth is being concealed. This conflict between what appears to be going on and what is really going on, the unspoken sub-text of the scene, increases audience involvement by building the tension and conflict between the external and internal worlds of the characters.

Sub-Text

Finding ways to suggest this emotional sub-text is critical to both characterization and good scene writing. The inner life and internal conflict of individual characters, their insecurities, fears and unconscious needs, are the deeper levels of both scene and story. What is in a character's heart and soul, what truly motivates or torments them, what they are ashamed to acknowledge or deal with: this is what you write around and imply through setting, staging and facial expressions. Without this understanding of sub-text, scenes will lack

energy and purpose. Showing the contradiction between thought and action, between what is said and felt, adds complexity and ambiguity to a scene.

It is through action, rather than dialogue, that characters reveal their struggle to resolve inner conflicts. The development of their moral thinking is a crucial tool in that struggle, as they work out the right thing to do. You construct your character and plot in such a way that forces them to feel, reflect and act, to disclose in action and reaction certain features of their psychology, their complicated, contradictory, vulnerable natures; their fears and desires.

Because in the end it is not the action that is most important but the consequences of what has happened for their moral and emotional life. This is the real meaning of sub-text. By adding a layer of dramatic tension between the spoken and the unspoken it makes the audience an active part of the drama, they have to work out for themselves what is really going on and be moved by consequences of the action; the discovery of the truth.

Sub-text – the conflict between what appears to be going on and what is really going on below the surface increases audience involvement. AKG-IMAGES/ALBUM

Preparing to Write

Dramatic scenes advance the plot, reveal character and develop the theme. Each scene escalates the rising conflict in the overall story and sets up what is to follow. Scenes are structured around the protagonist's objective, but every other character in the scene should be considered in selecting the moments of conflict. Every line of action and dialogue is there for a reason and the writer needs to be clear about what he chooses to show and what not to show.

Ask yourself the following questions and use any notes as preparation for writing the scene.

1. What is the purpose of this scene in the overall story?
2. What is it about?
3. What happens in the scene? What is the main conflict?
4. Where and when does it take place? Could it be set elsewhere to heighten impact?
5. How does it move the story forward?
6. Why is it there?
7. Who is the protagonist of the scene?
8. What do they want or need?
9. Why can't they get it?
10. What happens if they don't get it?
11. Is there an antagonist in the scene? Who are they?
12. What do they want? Why do they oppose the protagonist?
13. What do each of the other characters want or expect?
14. What does the audience know? What do they need to know to understand the scene? How do you release that information?
15. What do the other characters know? Do they know more than the audience or vice versa?
16. How do you reveal the inner lives of characters – their fears and vulnerabilities?
17. What are the main story beats in the scene?
18. Where is the scene going and when is it finished?
19. What is the major crisis and climax of the scene?
20. What has changed at the end of the scene from when we first entered it?

Remember also that you are writing for actors and that if the scene is not dramatically written, it will not be dramatically acted. You are responsible for making sure every scene is dramatic.

Writing the Scene

OVERWRITE

One way of achieving the compression of experience that gives the scene its dramatic focus and intensity is initially to overwrite. Write long scenes, several pages in length, taking in everyone's point of view, covering every story beat, and allowing characters to talk to each other in expansive and exploratory ways. This is a method for making sure that you will not miss anything in the scene and to clarify what are the crucial elements that need to be dramatized, such as backstory information or the glimpse of a character's real motives.

Another technique that can help you explore the scene is to improvise the scene from the point of view of each of the characters, including secondary characters. Everyone is at the centre of their own drama and views the world or the scene from the vantage of the part they are playing. You should anyway be thinking through the scene from each character's point of view, but this is a way of making that idea visible and concrete, forcing you to imagine yourself inside the heads of all your characters. You will come up with ideas on how to solve problems in the scene and moments of action and reaction that will add interesting detail and texture to your final draft.

EDIT

After this exploratory phase you can now begin to edit and distil: cutting back on dialogue and repetitions; replacing lines of exposition with looks and glances; building rhythm and contrasts through silences, small actions or elliptical cuts; finding visual and aural ways of conveying character and story information; planting information that will pay off later. Think of moments that add depth and texture to character and theme; juxtapose image and sound to move the action forward, foreshadow and create atmosphere. Good scenes have layers of meaning and possibility.

Write five or ten or pages then distil and focus the scene down to two or three pages constructed around the point of view of the scene's protagonist.

FOCUS

A key focus will, of course, be the protagonist of the scene, so you need to be clear who is driving the scene and what their objective is. Whatever they want or need will be part of the larger conflict, and the outcome of the scene will take them closer or further away from their over-arching goal. The scene will be part of the movement between hope and fear that takes place as the story develops and the action intensifies. Drama will come from the struggle of the protagonist to overcome the obstacle to their desire, so you need to be clear

Within any scene there will be a protagonist who is our focus; their motives and desires are what drive the action and the interest of the audience. IMDB

about what they want in the scene. You are writing for actors who, ever since Stanislavski, will want to know what their objective is.

CHOICE

In a well-constructed dramatic scene, the protagonist is brought to a place where they make difficult choices that will change their lives. What drives them, what they want, how badly they want it and what they are prepared to do to get it, reveal what is in their heart. It is one thing for a character to say 'I love you', but how do we judge that this is what they really feel? Drama arises when the protagonist fights for what they want and, however overwhelming the obstacles, keeps going and does not give up. This is how we know what they really feel.

CHANGE

A dramatic scene is a short film and needs time to build to the dramatic moment. You should be looking for conflict between the characters in the scene and the moment where something changes in the scene, something inside them. The protagonist understands something new before our eyes: she realizes that she needs to change in order to get what she desires. What matters is what is happening now, before our very eyes. What does she want? What happens if she doesn't get it? Why now? It is also going to make writing the scene a lot easier if you know where you are going and when you have finished.

WORDS ON THE PAGE

There are only four kinds of word on the page:

1. Title: interior or exterior, location and time of day or night – all capitalized, e.g. INT. KITCHEN. DAY.
2. Description: of setting and character.
3. Action: a large action or a small gesture. Details of behaviour.
4. Dialogue: what characters are saying and how they are saying it.

Location

Location or setting and time of day are important elements in the scene providing a context for the action, as well as props that you can use to dramatize the events taking place. Choose a setting that enhances the dramatic potential of a scene, for example a constricted location like a bathroom or basement from which the protagonist cannot escape or move your scene from private to public or from interior to exterior or from day to night. Where you set your scene should have a profound effect on the action, maximizing the conflict or underscoring the emotion.

Description

The element common to all good descriptive writing is detail: two or three words or lines that create a vivid image of character, setting and atmosphere. Such detail will contribute to the reader's emotional involvement in the scene.

Action

Your primary goal in writing action is clarity. Describe clearly and simply what the camera shows us, including any detail that enhances the impact of what we are seeing.

Dialogue

Dialogue is also an action and contributes to the momentum of the scene, as well as revealing character psychology and providing exposition, but in the classic feature film, dialogue is secondary to the visual. Ideally, screenplay dialogue is oblique, underwritten and economic, leaving space for sub-text. To find the essential dialogue and its place in the overall rhythm and meaning of the scene – give yourself permission to overwrite and then edit down, replacing lines of dialogue with silence, gesture and action.

Flow and Rhythm

Think of the screenwriting text as a form of poetry as much as prose, conveying the elliptical flow of image, sound and dialogue in short paragraphs of description and action, broken by bands of clear white space. Go to the screenwriting websites and read a range of screenplays to become familiar with the variety of writing styles and textual approaches that evoke a movie in the mind of the reader.

There is a flow and rhythm also to the progression of scenes that contribute to the overall impact of the film. The classic pattern of a feature screenplay is one that moves from crisis to crisis with increasing intensity but with quieter, more reflective moments in between scenes of high tension.

To vary the rhythm contrast:

- Dialogue with visual scenes.
- Fast tempo with slow.
- Light with serious.
- Long with short.
- Night with day.
- Interior/exterior.
- Static/dynamic.
- Noisy/quiet.

You can also vary scenes according to the focus on character, mood or plot. Variety and contrast are important elements in your toolkit.

THE WRITER AS ACTOR

Questions

When actors are given a screenplay, they will ask the same questions of their character as the writer should. They will want to know why the character is in the scene and what they have been doing since we last saw them. What they were doing immediately before the scene begins and what they will be doing after. What are the points of conflict and where does the scene change? Most importantly: what is their purpose in the scene, what is their immediate objective and their overall objective in the film?

Performance Skills

In this sense, the screenplay becomes a point of departure for the actor discovering their role, working backwards to the impulses and ideas the writer originally had when writing the scene. The writer too is a performer, inhabiting all of his characters, imagining their biography, understanding where they have come from and where they are trying to get to; knowing the intention and what they fear or want to conceal. He will inhabit the feelings and thoughts of the character and act out the physical behaviour, the small gestures and actions that break-up the dialogue. He will know what to say and how to say it and what not to say. Writing, acting and editing are all performance skills.

Build a Character

For these reasons, many talented writers are ex-actors who have learned how to build a character and develop an emotional sub-text for the roles they play. Every actor has their own method of inhabiting a role, but the techniques developed by Stanislavski in the early part of the twentieth century, including his emphasis on the objective, emotional memory and the through-line of action, had a profound and lasting impact on modern acting and screenwriting across Europe and America in both theatre and film. His books, including *An Actor Prepares* and *Building a Character*, remain provocative and useful for screenwriters and film-makers.

Exploring Character

Joining an acting workshop and exploring character from text or improvisation is also an enlightening experience for any screenwriter. You will gain insights that will enrich your screenwriting life and develop skills of empathy. It is one thing to know characters from the outside – their behaviour, appearance and actions – but to create convincing characters and to write convincing dialogue for your characters, you have to enter imaginatively into their thoughts and feelings. Understanding the inner life of a character is crucial to understanding what a character will do and say. Writing from inside a character is critical to scene writing but also to the writing of dialogue.

DIALOGUE

The Language of Cinema

Characters speak for a reason: they want something or they want to conceal something. Dialogue is a product of desire; the words characters speak to themselves and each other and to the audience. It is also what is not said. Silence is a form of dialogue and one of the most effective ways of communicating emotion. Through improvisation an actor learns to communicate something directly without mentioning it. This is important to all forms of dramatic writing but especially to screenwriting because it is a visual medium.

A picture can communicate more directly than words and the camera can catch the emotion behind the screen of language. What counts is the emotional and dramatic content of the scene, the fleeting moments of emotion picked up by the camera or an observant audience. It is what is going on in the minds of the characters that intrigue us. What is not said is often more dynamic to an audience, so it is usually better to imply than to have characters say what is on their minds.

This means that the writer should first of all try to make her story understandable without dialogue; to build the screenplay on actions and reactions, image and sound, body language and gesture. The writer should learn to use the expressive language of cinema and only use dialogue when all other means of expression are exhausted.

The spoken word can, of course, be an important element of storytelling, but because cinema is uniquely placed to explore small movements and gestures, it is less dependent on words than the theatre. The theatre depends more on words to carry information; but in a film you see more and you see it quicker. Therefore, what you hear has to be different or complementary to what you see. Good dialogue works harmoniously or in counterpoint with action and image.

The screenwriter writes for the camera. A good film story is always told in visual terms: the visual atmosphere of the film shapes the dialogue and the image often communicates thoughts or feelings more profound and resonant than any spoken line. Thus, the first rule of screen dialogue: less is more. Dialogue should be used sparingly; it can be direct or elliptical but it is always subject to possible intervention by the camera. It should emerge organically out of the interaction between characters. It may sound natural but it is crafted and directed, an integral part of the story action and the scene structure that it helps to create.

That is not to say that conversational or elaborate dialogue is not important in many films. Audiences take pleasure in the quick-witted exchanges of screwball comedies, the intellectual debates in Rhomer films and the literate gangsters and killers of Tarantino's world. However entertaining, even in the most dialogue-dependent films, the dialogue is intrinsic to the action from which it derives its energy and power.

Functions

Dialogue is a dramatic device that serves many purposes, including (as above) moving the story forward. If properly employed, it enriches the screenplay in several ways – through action, characterization, exposition and sub-text. Good dialogue can energize the screenplay and it is worth remembering that actors play close attention to what they say.

But you have to think why the dialogue is there. What it is about? Why is a character speaking – and why now? Dialogue may sound like everyday speech, but it is selected and shaped and directed to the main dramatic goal of a scene.

You can use dialogue to hide the meaning behind the words or to create ambiguity between what a character says and what they do. You can exaggerate, use elaborate metaphor or understate.

Dialogue is best when it has an immediate purpose in the scene and more than one function, including when dialogue:

- Reveals something about the character of the speaker.
- Reveals something about the character of the respondent.
- Reveals something about their relationship.
- Implies a hidden sub-text of desires, antagonisms, frustrations.
- Develops character and conflict.
- Gives the audience information relevant to story development.
- Provides exposition of backstory or off-screen events.
- Foreshadows or plants information that will be paid off later.
- Moves the story on.
- Offers information about time and place.
- Develops theme.
- Connects past and future scenes.
- Entertains.

Writing Dialogue

Dialogue should grow out of the developing action and conflict of the scene and not be used to conceal weak points in the structure. You should write from a sense of the inner desires and frustrations of the character but especially informed by what they want out of the scene. It is not their actual words that are important, so much as the underlying meaning or intention of what they say. Dialogue is a facade, an aspect of performance, of how a character would like to be seen by others. The true intent may be glimpsed between the lines. As we know from earlier discussions, sub-text adds a layer of tension making the audience an active partner of the drama.

Dialogue should be integral to the action of the scene. Characters act and move before, during and after they speak: they pick-up their coat, turn at the door, hesitate – you should pay attention to the physical actions that accompany the words; actions that might suggest hidden emotions, un-spoken thoughts. Actions and gesture also help to break up the dialogue or the speech, introducing rhythm and contrast to the page, and combine with dialogue in revealing character.

Don't make what you have to say more important than what the character has to say. A screenwriter must also know when to say nothing at all. Silence is a form of dialogue, like a pause in music it is an extremely effective way of communicating emotion. Silence can amplify or contradict what is being said, as well as opening up a moment of suspense, expectation and thereby dramatic tension for an audience.

Sparse, minimal dialogue, free of exposition is an ideal; the real feeling and meaning emerging between the spoken words. Use expository dialogue as a reaction to what has happened and invent actions that provoke comment after. This is always more interesting than unprovoked explanation, which flattens the dramatic energy. Remember that dialogue is best when used to get a reaction from others.

In a scene, characters engage and conflict with each other, their desires clash, drawing out the internal complexities, the emotions and values that define them. The protagonist may try several actions to overcome the antagonist or the obstacle in the way of their objective: dialogue is one of those actions.

The back and forth of dialogue in action–reaction is a good way to build the conflict and revelations in the scene. Dialogue can be dialectic in this way; with challenge followed by a counter-challenge, resolved in a new synthesis: a way of conceptualizing change in a scene and throughout the entire screenplay.

Good dialogue feels natural but is compressed and works with, or against, the grain of the visual storytelling. Every word is there for a reason, adding layers of information, emotion and characterization. As an important element in the overall scene, dialogue too can be overwritten in earlier drafts – but then cut, compressed and distilled in the rewrites to leave room for visuals and sub-text. Save longer speeches for a later pay-off, revelation or turning point.

Listen to how people speak – most people are not very articulate and good dialogue reflects this. It should be fragmentary and disconnected to give the illusion of reality; but it should also be concise, clear and strategic – contributing to plot, character and action. Once written – read aloud. Dialogue, whether conversational or dialectical is written with performance in mind and it is useful, therefore, to have actors or friends read the dialogue. From this you will hear where you might have overwritten or lost track, and you will gain insight into what you will do in the rewrite.

CAUSALITY

Dramatic Unity

A scene is a part of a larger conflict that brings the protagonist closer or further from their goal and swings the audience from hope to fear as the story progresses. A scene dovetails with earlier and subsequent scenes and is part of a causal chain; the dramatic unity gives organic life and vitality to the plot.

Connections

As a writer, therefore, you are always looking for what connects one scene with another. This includes not only linking what has happened with what happens next, but also deciding on moments or events in the scene that will pay off later.

Causality is an essential element in the screenplay that helps you in constructing your plot and in creating narrative momentum, leading to reversals and surprise. In constructing your plot, make the causal link: this happened *therefore* this happened *but* this happened.

One scene following another in time, with no necessary connection between the two scenes, often lacks excitement and tension. Good plotting requires strong causal links between scenes that build suspense and allow for the unexpected.

Episodic

You can, of course, break the strong causal link between scenes if you want to make a film that is more episodic or fragmentary. Michael Haneke does this in many of his films because he believes this is closer to how we experience reality – in isolated moments, rather than in a continuous flow. The challenge then for the writer is how to keep the audience engaged with the discontinuous action.

Transitions

In mainstream cinema, there are also gaps and ellipses between scenes, where the audience is expected to make the connections. The writer, therefore, has to pay attention to this unwritten space.

The art of cinematic writing comes from the choices you make between what you show and what you leave out that still allows the audience to piece together the story on their own.

Sequences

Many contemporary screenwriters plot their screenplays through sequences, which are a series of scenes; linked by a common theme, for example the sequences of capture and escape in *Toy Story*.

In a mainstream film, each sequence is around 10–15min with a beginning, a middle and an end that propels us into the next sequence. There are usually eight to twelve sequences in a feature film.

REWRITING THE SCENE

The maxim 'start late, get out early' not only highlights the emphasis on momentum in many contemporary screenplays, but also the focus on what is the essential conflict in any given scene. The aim is to get to the point quickly, to focus on what happens in the scene and to where the dynamic between characters changes. This is not always immediately apparent and requires overwriting and rewriting to find what the key focus of the scene is, and where to place the story beats.

One approach is to edit the original draft of a scene down to the essential moves between the characters and the key lines or actions that trigger a shift in the dynamic and web of relationships. Turning points in the scene can be discovered by rewriting or improvising from the point of view of all the characters – a technique that might also uncover previously unnoticed problems.

Characters can be permitted lengthy exposition to explore the reactions of other characters and important lines may be reassigned. You should make sure that every character arrives in the scene with aims and intentions, as well as information or knowledge that other characters don't have, so that they are prepared for what might happen.

A GAME OF CHESS

Intelligent characters will arrive at the scene ready to make certain moves and anticipate the moves of others. They will have thought out not only what to say, but the likely way in which it will be received. An argument is like a chess game with opening moves and gambits, defensive tactics and counter-attacks. Confrontation between two characters can be developed around dialogue exchanges that probe for strengths and weaknesses, building the tension through the ensuing clash of wills.

After the initial moves, with one of the characters having the upper hand, there will be a moment of important and surprising exposition, information that makes one of the characters vulnerable, leaving them exposed: a move that could reverse what has come before and shift the power balance from one character to another.

This game, however well plotted, will be effective only so long as the character work has been done earlier to provide the emotional depth and the variety of contradictory feelings that make for the possibility of change. The audience needs to care about the protagonist and what is at stake for them in the scene for the moves to be dramatically engaging.

CONCLUSION

The tension of the interlocking conflicts and multiple narrative lines, the writing and rewriting to find the essential focus, the moves and counter-moves of the shifting power plays, reveal screenwriting to be less a linear art form and more like weaving or jazz – with the various narrative threads or lines playing off against each other in harmony and counterpoint, each note and sequence contributing to the overall melodic and thematic unity of the scene.

EXERCISES

Read the screenplays for *Thelma and Louise*, *Winter's Bone* and *The Third Man*. Now select a key dramatic scene and answer the following questions below.

Then do the same with three feature screenplays that you admire.

1. Where and when does the scene take place? Could another time or location serve to heighten the impact?
2. Whose scene is it, and what does he or she want?
3. What are the obstacles to that objective?
4. What's at stake? i.e. what happens if they don't get what they want?
5. What are the objectives of each of the characters?
6. What is the central conflict of the scene? How are the internal conflicts externalized?
7. What is the scene about? e.g. indecision, elation, deception, fear, sexual tension etc.
8. What does the audience know?
9. What do the characters in the scene know?
10. Where were the characters before the scene started, and where are they going after it ends?
11. How is the scene related thematically to the rest of the story?
12. Does the scene prepare us for further action?
13. What are the main beats in the scene?
14. What are the key turning points?
15. How does the scene advance the story?
16. Why is this scene necessary?
17. Give an example of dialogue that: reveals character/provides exposition/foreshadows or plants information/conceals sub-text/is supported or contradicted by physical action or non-verbal communication.
18. Select a scene from a short or feature script that you are currently working on and apply the same questions.
19. Write down moments of failure or shame, guilt and loss that you have experienced. Explore and reflect on how you felt, the fear or despair or how the experience changed you. How did you move on from there or how has the experience remained with you? Identify the people who inspired you or helped you to face up to what you were doing. Write from there.

Select one of those moments and write a scene or a short sequence of scenes based on that experience. Rewrite using the notes in this chapter. What have you learned?

20. Give yourself sufficient time and go to a quiet place. Write down three pairs of contrasting characters, e.g. young/old; extrovert/introvert; black/white. Now decide on the relationships, e.g. lovers, parent–child, friends, work colleagues. They have an unresolved problem between them. Decide what it is and what one of them knows that the other does not. Give each of them a secret. Choose a location and a point of view. Write a scene. Write at least five to six pages, then edit down to two or three pages.

Rewrite using a different location.

Rewrite using a different point of view.

What did you learn?

21. Draw up a list of five scenes from films that have moved you deeply. Identify what it is in each scene that you find so compelling. Why do you think you find the scene compelling and how does it connect to your own writing and personal themes?

9
DEVELOPMENT

A feature film is the outcome of a process of collaboration that begins with the writer and the development of a unique screenplay: the screenplay itself beginning with an idea for a film – an image, an aspect of human life, a situation or a character, and its gradual development into an outline, then a first draft. The development process is not linear but involves a continuous internal dialogue and a dialogue with others, a moving back and forth, writing and rewriting, trial and error: a process of discovering the basic humanity in the project.

A screenwriter needs to develop not only an understanding of film-making and dramatic principles, but also the ability to outline and pitch her ideas, as well as deal creatively with notes, feedback and comment from a range of film-making collaborators. The screenplay is continually changing and evolving with the creative input of many others and is never completed until the finished film. In this sense, screenwriting is film-making.

This chapter is concerned with both the development of the screenplay and the screenwriter, and is followed in the concluding chapter by a range of advice for the next step in screenwriting development.

WRITING THE SCREENPLAY

Make it Personal

A screenplay develops from the imaginative interplay of dream and memory, experience and observation, research and planning. There are no rules but there are craft skills that can be studied and practised, and dramatic principles and audience expectations to guide the shaping of a story, which we have discussed in earlier chapters.

Certain questions can help direct your thinking, as can observations about recurring narrative problems and differing approaches to artistic practice. The essential idea for the screenplay will come from you: your thoughts, feelings and obsessions. What interests or troubles you? What makes you angry or curious? What do you want to write about and why? If you are not interested in the story, nobody else will be.

What kind of film do you want to write: a genre film with heroic characters and fantastic worlds, a high-stakes political thriller on themes of idealism and corruption or a low-key drama focusing more on everyday life and recurring human problems and feelings?

Whether you are writing a genre movie, an art-house film or a low-budget digital feature, you have to be personal. How you see the world, what your values are, what you think is important, exciting, funny, tragic or absurd are the original qualities that you bring to the work. This is what will surprise and excite an audience – to be taken into worlds, ways of seeing and points of view that they have not quite experienced before. The audience can learn something, but in the writing you may also discover something new by thinking about your life in more depth and detail.

As a writer you need to use your sensitivity, your perception of life and an understanding of yourself in shaping your story. This self-knowledge creates

What is the world of your story? What is your point of view on that world? IMDB

an imaginative link to your characters. What you have observed about yourself and others, how we interact, what we believe and hope, opens the door of insight and empathy, and makes the work more particular and specific – more personal. And the more personal, the more it reminds us of our common humanity and resonates with our own experience of life.

Structure

As a film writer you also need to study the language of film, the power of telling stories through images and the place of order and structure – the backbone of the screenplay. Personal voice and original ideas are worked through a common architecture of underlying structures that can be studied. All artists select, arrange and concentrate the events and actions of their screenplay to give them focus and meaning. The rhythms and patterns of plot structure are ways of drawing attention to what is concentrated and to what we might otherwise miss.

Improvisation and Order

The process is a synthesis of improvisation and order: you write and rewrite, you interact with

In this film the protagonist goes on a journey to develop her own relationship to creativity – this is the journey of every writer. IMDB

what you are writing and begin to understand what you are trying to say and then start to put some order into what is emerging. This does not require a specific set of rules but responsiveness and flexibility to new combinations and situations, and a developing understanding of craft skills and techniques, which have been highlighted in earlier chapters.

What we do and feel, slowly takes shape within us. Writing is discovery not just of what happens next or surprising character revelations, but discovering how all the parts work together, how they relate to each other and the whole.

Development is writing and rewriting, a movement back and forth between the events of the story and the inner lives of characters. It involves asking the right questions, listening to yourself and thinking deeply. It is also a dialogue with yourself and significant others, including the audience.

Audience

You must be interested in your story and themes because it is your passion that will connect with an audience. They will want to know what excited you to write this story, what the secret of the film is – the hidden meaning that will not become clear until the end.

The audience will have certain expectations; they will want to be surprised but also to empathize and identify with the characters, to experience their hope and fear at the events of the plot. They will expect coherence and clarity in the storytelling and the plausibility of character actions and outcomes.

You should also be able to tell the story in terms of how the audience will experience it, the turning points that will keep them watching and the gaps in their knowledge that will create the suspense and surprise.

To keep the audience engaged requires not only the energy and passion of the writer's vision, but also storytelling skills of selection and timing, and the application of craft skills and techniques of plotting that will lead the audience step by step to the truth of events: a truth that will resonate with their life and experience.

STAGES OF DEVELOPMENT

In your dreaming and imagining, your exercise work and notebooks, through observation and research, you now have subjects, characters and conflicts that you want to explore. What you are searching for is an idea for a dramatic story that you then have to develop and structure for an audience.

Every professional writer has their own method of development: some begin by writing scenes and working backwards and forwards to discover the story; others spend a long time working everything out before they start by making notes, drawing diagrams, creating character networks and biographies, planning scene outlines. Most writers like to have an idea of the end so they know where they are going but not necessarily knowing how they will get there.

For the novice writer, and many screenwriting professionals, a plot outline is usually a necessary stage in the process; the structure of your screenplay having as profound an effect on the audience as vivid characterization and dramatic themes.

The following stages are indicative and interactive, rather than fixed and linear: a starting point for working out your own method of story and screenplay development:

1. The idea.
2. Research.
3. Premise and logline.
4. Character biography and networks.
5. Outline.
6. Treatment.
7. Step outline.
8. First-draft screenplay.

Ideas

The word idea comes from the Greek *eidos* meaning a new perspective, a new way of seeing. Ideas for stories arise all the time, from something seen or heard, a place, an encounter, an image, a news item, a childhood memory, a feeling. But ideas may just as quickly fade or be forgotten. We need to have time to ponder, to hold the idea without judging it, to see how persistent it might be or what it wants from us. Often it requires a further period of reflection and gestation, research and note taking, waiting and

The Dardenne brothers sum up their complex film: 'We wanted to tell the story of a man who, to accept paternity, has to sell his child.' RGA

not knowing, before a second or third idea provides the catalyst for a character and basic situation to emerge that can sustain the 90–100min of dramatic development required for a feature screenplay.

For the Dardenne brothers, their film *The Child* (2006) began with an image.

> While shooting *The Son* (2003), we would see this young woman pushing a baby carriage, very violently, as if she were trying to get rid of the child.[29]

In looking for their next film this vision reappeared and through discussion they decided the missing character, the baby's father, would be the main character – combining with an earlier idea about a father selling his baby. So now the essence of their new idea could be distilled in one sentence:

> We wanted to tell the story of a man who, to accept paternity, has to sell his child first.[30]

The French film-maker Agnes Varda more often looks to a particular place for inspiration, then uses research and interviews to develop character and action. This was the approach used in the writing of *Vagabond* (1985). In imagining the film she was initially moved by news reports of people still dying of exposure in the modern world, and she connected this with her previous work on exploring and documenting the lives of those who lived in poverty. She chose to use the harsh landscape of the rural south, with its isolated villages and abandoned farms, as her starting point, waiting for ideas, emotions and images to emerge. Out of this research arrived the idea of showing how a young female vagabond survives on the road – with the focus being on the day-to-day encounters and the material conditions of her life and not on her psychology. A tough young woman who did not want to talk or communicate, who, despite the various accounts offered to camera by the people she encounters, we never get to really know or understand. The opaque nature of her character and a resistance to a psychology of cause and effect, motivation and objective, was a clear part of Varda's intention and idea for the film.

Lee Chang-Dong, the South Korean novelist and film-maker, was initially inspired in the writing and development of *Poetry* (2011) by true events.

The idea for *Vagabond* grew out of Vada's earlier work on documenting the lives of those who lived in poverty. The protagonist is defined by the material conditions of her life, rather than psychology. IMDB

The idea came from a news report of a group of teenage boys in a small town who had raped a young middle-school girl, an incident that he kept remembering but that in itself did not provide a basis for the kind of film he wanted to make. It was only some years later, while watching a television channel for travellers with a peaceful river and meditative music in the background, that he had the idea of dealing with the atrocity through poetry and beauty.

> The main characters would be a woman in her mid-sixties who learns how to write poetry for the first time in her life, and her grandson who has committed a violent crime. These characters, a basic plot, and the title *Poetry* simultaneously came into my mind.[31]

YOUR IDEA

Everything springs from your original idea about the kind of film you want to make. It may be a theme or subject that intrigues you, an interesting character or a dramatic situation, but you need to clarify to yourself what it is you are going to write about.

Explore your idea in response to the questions below. Your answers could be included in a research file or work-book that you are encouraged to begin as a method of further exploration.

- What was the initial inspiration for your film idea?
- Why do you want to develop this specific idea?
- What is it about? i.e. the premise or dramatic question.
- What makes it cinematic?
- What makes it a feature film and not a TV series or short film idea?
- Who is the target audience – who do you think would go and see this film?
- What is the world of the story? Give examples.
- Who is your main character(s)? What do they want or need?
- What are the obstacles or forces of antagonism in the way of their desire?

- What do you want to communicate to others with this story?
- What kind of film do you want to make? Give examples of other films that have inspired this film idea.
- What are your hopes and intentions for the script?
- What are the main obstacles to you writing this script?
- What are the main assets that will help you write it?

Research

At this point, you might want to look again at Chapter 2, where creative work is explored in more detail. In Chapter 2 there are several other questions and exercises designed to trigger ideas and thoughts for further development, including a focus on the importance of research as a way of enriching the visual and thematic context before you begin to develop the story.

The research file or work-book will be a source of insight and inspiration and open up branching pathways of connection and association to enrich your original idea.

It might include some, or all, of the following:

- Initial idea/visual references.
- Why I want to explore this subject/characters/situation.
- Research notes.
- Observations.
- Details of story world.
- Interviews with people who are in the situation you are exploring.
- Clips from published interviews.
- Images that might appear in the film or inspire powerful emotions.
- Photographs.
- Sound or music clips related to the atmosphere/theme or associated with specific characters.
- Quotations.
- Lines of poetry.

- Something overheard or remembered.
- Anecdotes from your own experience.
- Diagrams and drawings.
- Character biographies and networks of relationship.
- Film references.

You can document your research as you please – in spiral notebooks or old-style scrapbooks, using a box file or computer or a combination of them all. The important point is that you have a period of exploring your initial idea, finding new angles and options for the development of the story.

The Premise

After exploration and research, you should try to condense your new idea into two or three sentences, focusing on the essential elements and the direction you want to go with the story. This should be a brief encapsulation of what the film or movie is about, including reference to the protagonist and the dramatic problem or intention. The search for a premise is a meditation on what the story means and, in the early stages, it means finding your main character and the defining action. It should arouse our curiosity and give a strong sense of why an audience might be interested in the story. Try the idea on friends and family, listen to their feedback and comments, then rewrite.

The premise is not fixed – writing is discovery – you are still in the process of discovering the core concept that will guide you through the stages of development. It will evolve as your story and characters will. You are trying to define the basic structure of your story. For example:

An amoral and carefree young thief sells his new baby to a black market adoption ring with the intention of making some quick cash. But when he tells his wife what he has done and shows her the money she collapses in shock and despair.

Realizing his terrible mistake and that his wife is pressing charges against him he buys the baby back at a premium that sets him on a downward spiral of debt and petty criminality that threatens his efforts to win back the trust of his wife but awakens in him a new and profound sense of responsibility.

Dardenne brothers – *The Child*

With your premise, you don't need to be able to answer all the questions but you certainly want to stir the emotions of your audience, indicate where the story is going and excite them to find out more. There is no formula but your premise should suggest the potential in your idea for conflict, visualization and audience appeal, and be a guide to the future development.

The Logline

The logline is another tool for both analysing and checking the story potential of your idea and the basis of communicating the essence of your idea in a short, pithy form. It is the short, sharp answer to the question that you may be asked at any point: 'What is your story about?' It is also a way of finding out for yourself if you know the answer and a reminder of work that still might need to be done if you don't.

An example of a good logline:

- It has a title.
- It is the essence of what your film is about.
- It hooks the reader with a surprising conflict.
- It is clear and concise.
- It has an element of irony or contradiction.
- It suggests a time-frame.
- It gives us a sense of the overall film.
- it helps you to find the dramatic spine of your film.

The logline for *The Child* (2006) on IMDb (the Internet Movie Database) ticks most of these boxes, except what the film is really about:

Bruno and his partner Sonia live off benefits and thefts committed by his gang but they now have a new source of income: their newborn son.

Whereas the Dardenne brothers see the core of their idea as being:

The story of a man who, to accept paternity, has to sell his child first.

The one-line distillation written by the Dardennes focuses on the protagonist and the paradoxical journey he will take to become a responsible father to his child. That is the dramatic essence of the idea. Compare this with the three-sentence premise as outlined above and you will see how the exercise of distilling the dramatic idea to a few lines was a useful basis for coming up with a one-sentence pitch of the idea.

What their one line lacks, however, is the marketing bite and dramatic hook of the IMDb version. Both are works in progress when it comes to finding the killer one-liner that is also the essence of the film idea.

Being able to describe the central concept is an important skill in analysing others' work, as well as providing a guide for the development of your own idea. As with all the other stages of writing, you will return several times to this one-line summary, and rewrite and revise as your screenplay evolves.

You can practise this skill by trying to write and refine loglines for your favourite movies or try rewriting your own loglines for some of the films below:

- A young FBI trainee must confide in an incarcerated and manipulative killer to receive his help in catching another serial killer and fulfil her ambition of becoming an FBI agent. (*Silence of the Lambs*)
- With the help of a German bounty hunter, a freed slave sets out to rescue his wife from a brutal Mississippi plantation owner. (*Django Unchained*)

- An African herdsman protects his wife and daughter from the Taliban group that has taken over their local town – until an impulsive action endangers all their lives. (*Timbuctu*)
- A weak-willed and dissolute aristocrat hires a new servant to take care of all of his needs, which the servant fulfils but in the process makes himself the new master. (*The Servant*)

Some ideas can be captured in even fewer words:

- The servant becomes the master. (*The Servant*)
- A monster shark terrorizes a small town. (*Jaws*)

Here is the famous pitch for *Alien*:

- Jaws in space.

The last two, especially, are examples of high-concept ideas.

High Concept/Low Concept

Most Hollywood or commercial movies are high-concept, with a startling or unusual idea easily summarized in a few words that grab your attention. For example:

- A psychopath wires a bus so it will explode if it falls below 50mph. (*Speed*)
- A struggling puppeteer discovers a portal into John Malkovich's head. (*Being John Malkovich*)
- A lawyer suddenly loses his ability to lie. (*Liar Liar*)

'Hollywood' movies are usually high-concept genre movies aimed at mass audiences with fantastic and fairy-tale elements, big budgets, glamour and spectacle.

Low-concept refers to arthouse/independent films, often low-budget and character-focused, but also darker, more realistic and subtle than big-budget movies. Rather than the escape into fantasy, these films dramatize ordinary feelings, family life, love and friendship – the strangeness and wonder of everyday life and our basic humanity. The narratives can be minimal or slow-burning but still centre around a dramatic encounter or problem embedded in the logline. For example:

- An ageing movie star lost in Tokyo befriends a twenty-something young woman who feels lost in her marriage to a hotshot photographer. (*Lost in Translation*)
- The day-to-day life of a young female drifter and the people she encounters on the road before the loss of her sleeping bag threatens disaster. (*Vagabond*)
- After her mother dies, a successful black optologist goes in search of her birth mother and discovers that she is a lonely and unhappy white woman who intends keeping her new relationship secret from her working-class family. (*Secrets and Lies*)

There is an obvious overlap and interaction between the two ideal types – big-budget movies that are also intimate character studies and gritty low-budget films with flashy dramatic hooks. But describing the concept involves thinking about the tone, as well as the audience and budget of your film.

Another element that you need to consider when developing your idea is the genre – what type of story is it?

Genre

Is your idea a sci-fi, action-adventure, rom-com or a low-budget drama? You need to know the conventions of your chosen genre and the audience expectations that go along with the commercial use of these labels.

Generic story worlds have their own possibilities and limitations that you need to study in order to deliver on audience expectation. If you are writing a thriller, you need to thrill, and a comedy has to be funny. Even if you choose to write against genre, subvert or satirize, you need to be aware of its demands and deliver on its promise without being formulaic.

Telling the Story

At every stage you will be refining your story by telling it to friends and strangers. As you tell the story, watch their response and your own. Where do you get lost or bored? What's not clear? Do they want to know how it ends? Listen to the feedback, then rework and build your story.

To be a good screenwriter you have to be a good storyteller and telling the story leads to the outline. Before discussing the story outline in more detail, we need first to look again at the heart of your story – character.

Character Biography and Networks

For Michael Haneke, the individual psychologies of his protagonists and what happens between them is central to his storytelling. He needs to know his characters and their key relationships before he can fully outline his story.

In mainstream cinema, plot springs from character action and desire: what characters want and need, what they hope and fear, drives the story. How they respond to failure and frustration of their desires and how they interact with others reveals their true character.

Because characters are not static or isolated, they can only be understood in relation to others and to themselves. Characters illuminate each other in conflict and contrast. Strength of will, persistence, determination are important in characters, but so is insight. How well a character understands their failings is important to the possibility of character change. A screenplay needs to be felt as well as understood and the best way to achieve that is through a character we care about, who is working out how to solve her problem and recognizes the need for change.

In this sense, the essential character journey is internal and the drama a movement between the external events of the plot and the internal journey of the protagonist. For the story to be dramatically interesting, we need to enter their life at a point of crisis or internal pressure: a conflict in the protagonist's outer life that demands change or transformation, established near the beginning, for example Jo in *Midnight Cowboy*, Michael in *The Godfather* and Cynthia in *Secrets and Lies.*

The foundation of character may lie in their physical qualities, their personality and the social context of their life. But a dramatic narrative is driven by character progression, by the revelations and recognitions and the impact on their inner life.

The writer's task is to take a character that initially feels coherent and move them into the unknown, and design the trials and tribulations, the incidents and events of the plot that will test and transform them. At the same time, the writer needs to leave a space for mystery around their character; not knowing everything about them allows you to be surprised, to find your characters taking the story in unexpected directions. It is good to keep possibilities open, since character and plot are intertwined, and understanding the possibilities in your characters opens up options for the plot. Just as the more you work on the plot, the more you will understand your characters.

Drawing a map of the key relationships and character networks, how each character is connected to each other and why, is a useful exercise as part of the preparation, along with a developed premise and story world, for outlining the plot of your story.

Plotting (Outline, Step Outline and Treatment)

You can outline the plot and character developments in a series of stages that are useful ways of both exploring your idea in more depth and finding the dramatic shape for your screenplay. These are different stages of interrogation and presentation, diagnostic tools to help you locate the gaps in the dramatic narrative and to discuss with collaborators the direction you intend to go with the story.

Synopses, outlines and treatments can also be used as the basis for professional relationships, in which case you would write and present your idea with a specific audience in mind and ensure they were a clear, lively and engaging read. But for personal use as working documents, outlines can be more open and subject to note-taking and constant revision as your ideas develop.

1. *One-page synopsis*: this establishes the story idea or story concept in three paragraphs written in the third person and present tense, and including the one-sentence logline. The synopsis should focus on the heart of the story and show characters and interactions developing over three acts from the set-up to the final crisis and climax. The style and genre of the film idea should be implied through the turns and twists and rising action of the plot. This gives you a deeper understanding of the basic shape of the story but should not to be confused with the synopsis of the screenplay, which is written after the first draft has been written.

2. *Outline*: a more developed outline of the story and usually produced as part of the development process. It can be anywhere from five to fifteen pages, depending on the writer and the purpose. The outline can detail the whole story or be more abstract, though usually it contains the central dramatic progressions, character objectives and turning points of the plot. The purpose is to give the reader the arc of the plot, a sense of the writer's intention and make them want to read more – leaving room for surprising further developments. For the writer, it is a way of building the story and finding out what elements need further exploration.

3. *Treatment*: this is the most complete and detailed account of the film idea, written in prose and the third person, like a short story, and can be anywhere from fifteen to thirty pages. Detailed treatments have every scene and story beat clarified in short, sharp and visually driven paragraphs, bringing the characters to vivid life but also implying the mood and atmosphere and defining the story world of the film – how the story will be 'treated' cinematically. It can be a writer's tool to help organize their thoughts but, more often, it is required by the producer as a selling document for the project, when it may also include a synopsis and statements on theme and tone. Some writers find them harder to write than the screenplay, requiring months of work and a different skillset; but sometimes it is an essential requirement. Shorter forms of treatment can be used as pitch documents. A producer or script reader will want to know:

- What the story and theme is.
- Who the protagonist and antagonists are.
- Where and when it takes place.
- The dramatic hook.
- The key dramatic moments.
- The shape of the story.
- An idea of the intended market.

It may also be a document that involves input from a producer or director if the treatment is part of a package. This will be discussed in more detail shortly.

4. *Step outline*: a system involving 100+ index cards, where each card has a brief description of a step in the narrative, a simple description of the substance and action of each scene. These can be pinned on a notice board or transferred to a computer (e.g. the formatting program Final Draft has this facility) and then moved around as a way of organizing the plot into sequences and acts, as well as giving a clear overall view and the gaps in plot and character development. It can be used as the basis for a detailed treatment or a first-draft screenplay.

THE OUTLINE

David Mamet suggests that by asking three basic questions, the writer will arrive at a logical structure from which he can outline the drama:

- What does my protagonist want?
- What hinders them from getting it?
- What happens if they don't get it?[32]

While Mamet emphasizes character desire and objective, Aristotle points to the importance of plot and the kind of dramatic devices that heighten the emotional impact on an audience such as reversal of fortune and recognition. An audience takes pleasure in surprising revelations and new understandings especially if they are an integral part of the plot. In the *Poetics*, Aristotle argues that there is an intimate connection between cohesion of the plot and the impact at which the drama aims.

In other words, what is being outlined is the protagonist's pursuit of their objective, the turns and twists, and the rising action of incidents and events of the plot that reveal their internal conflict. Every character, line and action is selected for a reason and related to plot or theme. The more skilful you are in bringing the different elements and levels of the plot into alignment, the more likely you are to connect with the audience's emotions. A good outline demands craft skill, as well as personal vision, and this is a technique that can be practised.

Whatever stage you are at in outlining your story, it is a process of constant revision and re-writing, an exercise in exploration and discovery, each draft offering you clues about what requires further thought and development. This will require moving scenes around or cutting away what is not relevant. The focus is on the story, the central conflict and the through-line of action. There may be leaps and gaps but you are searching for the dramatic shape of your story that will create tension in the mind of the audience. Continuing to work on your character backstories and networks, as well as clarifying the details of your story world, will enrich your preparation.

As a tool in the development of your story, an outline is never fixed but fluid and open to fresh thinking and new ideas. It is an ordered account of what you know about your story so far: what happens and what needs to happen. Your understanding of the story will change and deepen as you write and reflect on what you have written. Allow the characters to lead you: you will learn more about them through the situations they have to face.

Decide which parts of the story you want to show and which parts to hide, and from which point of view the story is being told: is it the narrator's or the protagonist's or are there multiple points of view? The audience needs to know the rules, so they won't be confused.

The outline is a tool, a dialogue between your original impulse and audience expectation: the aim is to clarify character and plot development, so that you are ready to begin writing scenes and the first draft. Concentrate on structure but also don't forget that your film is not composed of words but images and thoughts that lie between and behind the words.

THE FIRST-DRAFT SCREENPLAY

Before writing a first draft, you will know your genre, protagonist and objective, obstacles and stakes; you will have prepared character biographies and networks, have a detailed knowledge of your story world and plot outline. It is also worth checking back through some of the earlier chapters on character and structure, as well as reading a variety of feature screenplays, to remind yourself of layout and pacing.

There are only three kinds of word on the page:

• Description of setting and character.
• Action or gesture.
• Dialogue.

The words on the page, the description of character, setting and action should imply where the cuts or edits might take place, but the final decision will depend on the director and editor. Description, action and dialogue are the three kinds of words that are used to give us this feeling that we are not reading a short story, and can best be understood by reading several screenplays of films that you have previously viewed.

She half-smi...   Cla...

        Yeh. Sing to me.

                    TONY
        Your request.

                    CLAIRE
        The one you always used to sing.

He clears his throat.

And starts to sing softly.

He takes his daughter's hand.

                    TONY (SINGING)
        Catch a falling star

And gently strokes her hair.

Her eyes begin to flicker closed.

                    TONY (cont'd)
        And put it in your pocket
        Save it for a rainy day,
        Catch a falling star
        And put it in your pocket
        Never let it fade away.

It's having the desired effect.

Tony gets up and moves away slowly.

                    TONY (cont'd)
        For love may come
        And tap you on the shoulder
        Some sunny day
        And you will find
        Before you get much older
        There'll be a pocket full of stardust..

The heavy breathing of sleep.

He slowly closes the door.

                    TONY (cont'd)
        Never let it fade away..

Tony pulls the door quietly behind him.

IN.

Ton

In t
bedro
the c

Tony tur

        M.

        Don
        mat

Tony puts his a

        Shhh!

He starts to tip-

        Dad.

        Yeh?

            C.
        Do you think

He stops. And turns bac
puzzlement.

                    TONY
        Vacuous? You're
        person I know.

                    CLAIRE
        But I've not done   been
        anywhere.

When writing the screenplay use white space and short, sharp descriptions to create a flow of image and sound, dialogue and action, that reads and feels like a film. Keep the writing clear and simple – this is not literature but a film; screenwriting is film-making.

Tell the story in the cut like a film editor, deciding what to cut from and to and why. Build the scenes and sequences into the act structure whether three, four or five acts, making sure that every part is a self-contained mini-drama contributing to the development of the conflict or revelation of character. Know your end and judge the most effective places to reveal information with maximum dramatic effect.

Give your audience enough to be curious, but hold back and allow space for their imagination to work out the connections or to wonder about what will happen next. Your aim is to make the audience tense and another way you can do this is by making sure that life gets more and more difficult for your protagonist. You are always one step ahead of your audience, thinking about what they know already and what they might expect and, therefore, what might surprise them. What is the secret of the screenplay, the hidden aspect of the story that creates the underlying tension?

Every scene and sequence is there for a reason: to advance the story, prepare for later developments or reveal character. Make use of interesting settings and contrast the atmosphere and rhythm of scene development by mixing dramatic scenes and short, sharp scenes, day with night, fast with slow, light and serious: accelerate and slow down the pace, juxtaposing moments of excitement with moments of reflection and intimacy.

Dialogue is a device with a purpose: defining character, moving the story along, expanding theme, providing information or entertaining us. To be most effective, it should always be used for more than one purpose and combined with action or gesture. It may sound natural but good film dialogue is shaped and edited. Look for the sub-text of thoughts and feelings between the lines and the ambiguity between what is said and what characters actually do. The film should not depend on dialogue. Always search for visual solutions.

Write fast and keep going to the end. You should know your ending, even if it changes through the writing – it will keep you on track. You don't need to stick to a rigid plan or slavishly follow your outline or treatment. Feel free to follow your instinct or characters. Self-doubt and days when the writing seems lost in a swamp are part of the process, but so are the moments when everything seems to come together and the characters take on a life of their own.

When you have finished a rough draft, put it away and look at it fresh the following day. Get a sense of the overall flow and meaning, the patterns and development of narrative lines, the visual and aural motifs that add depth and texture. Read once to get a feel for the overall balance and pacing, then read again, this time making notes and asking questions about what you think needs changing; then rewrite. After this you might want to show the screenplay to one or two friends to get feedback.

REWRITING

Most writing is rewriting but also rethinking, re-conceptualizing and looking at your material anew. Momentum is critical to the first draft, driving your vision through from beginning to end, skipping over problem areas, resisting the impulse to constantly revise what has already been written. Subsequent drafts will return to the energy and motivation of this first draft.

A screenplay is a complex creation requiring craft as well as vision and you will rarely get it right first time. It usually takes several drafts to integrate character, theme and structure, and to produce a screenplay that is ready to send to a producer or production company; or to become the basis for a film. The ability to evaluate, judge and, therefore, to revise your work, is itself an essential skill for your development as a screenwriter.

Being able to identify and find solutions to the inevitable problems of your exploratory and succeeding drafts will not only improve your screenplay, but also make you a better writer and inform your approach to new projects. Rewriting involves approaching the script in a more analytical way; it is where you apply the technical skills discussed in the earlier chapters of this book. Combining technique with the energy and urgency of your original vision is the hoped for outcome.

Diagnosis

First drafts are often problematic; it is easy for the writer to get lost or lose perspective. The process of clarifying requires time, patience and honest feedback and an ability to diagnose where the problems lie.

There are several questions you can ask of the first and succeeding drafts that will help guide your analysis of what needs fixing:

• What are you trying to say?
• What is the central dramatic question?
• What is the spine of your story?
• What is the central conflict?
• Where are the major turning points?
• Is the problem of the set-up resolved in the climax?
• Are the protagonist's objective and stakes clear?
• Is the protagonist faced with difficult obstacles, choices and decisions?
• Is the protagonist changing as the journey intensifies?
• What is the audience's experience of the story? Do they have enough information? What are they paying attention to?
• Is the story told visually?

Writing screenplays is essentially about solving recurring problems. For example:

• One-dimensional characters.
• Too many characters.

• Rambling sub-plots.
• Momentum – too slow a build-up or development.
• Ending not linked to beginning.
• An idea that has not been properly developed.
• Exposition – too much or not enough or in the wrong place.
• Dramatic unity – no clear through line of action.

Feedback and Script Notes

In a professional development context you can expect feedback from a script editor or development executive or, later, a producer. The feedback they will give you is referred to as script notes – they give you notes and you write down their comments to reflect on afterwards.

The notes should be diagnostic rather than prescriptive, pointing out the weak points rather than telling you what you need to do. A good script editor, whether a working professional or a tutor, is there to help you write the best version of your script – not theirs. They will approach this task as you would if you were the one giving feedback, in the spirit of collaboration and support for the project.

As the writer, at some point you will have to relinquish control of the screenplay and shift from creating a story for yourself to creating a story for, and with, others. Mostly, the notes that you pay attention to are the ones that excite you about rewriting.

You have to protect yourself, but be careful of becoming too defensive or inflexible. The script editor should be asking questions or making suggestions that provokes a rethink that excites you about rewriting and reconnecting with your original impulse – not telling you what to do.

Stages of Rewriting

You can't revise all the elements of your screenplay at once, so the rewriting usually takes place in stages, with each stage focusing on a key aspect of the script. You and your collaborators have to agree on priorities for each stage

Early drafts usually focus on the fundamentals of the story and the protagonist's journey: the through-line of action and meaning and how it is organized for an audience, how it opens and ends, the place of act climaxes and sequence structures. As the shape of the story and the interaction of character and plot are clarified, then the focus can shift onto sub-plots, secondary characters, sub-text, the juxtaposition of image and sound, the pattern of visual and aural motifs.

At every stage you are also looking to cut and compress, to build momentum and maximize dramatic revelations and reversals. Later drafts will tighten every scene and sequence, sharpen dialogue and descriptions, re-work transitions, check the plants and pay-offs and polish the text – without losing sight of your initial inspiration.

CONCLUSION

In this chapter, we have discussed the development process and the stages of planning, research, writing and rewriting involved in the shaping of a feature screenplay.

In the next chapter, we will consider the place of the screenplay in the collaborative practice of film-making and the next steps you might take after the writing of your screenplay and the various options that you now have for personal and or professional development.

EXERCISES

1. If you have not already done so, this is a good time to start a notebook or work-book for collecting visual ideas, character notes, plot details, story worlds, historical background and research. What kind of locations and characters do you want to write about and why? Are there particular kinds of stories or human problems you want to explore? What is motivating you as a writer?

2. Start sifting through your ideas and images, looking for new combinations and synergies.

3. Make a list of people, events and locations that interest you. Make a list of stories that involve these characters, themes, events.

4. Identify a moment in your life when you made a mistake or were guilty of some shameful or misguided behaviour. Explore the insight that resulted from the experience and how that changed (or not) how you behaved. Now provide a similar insight to one of your characters. What decision results from the insight and how does this character change her behaviour and if her behaviour doesn't change, why not?

5. Select three ideas from your work-book to develop. Write down what interests you about these ideas and why you want to write about them. What do you hope to explore and understand as part of your research for the project? Write down the protagonist and objective for each of the ideas. Write a one-page biography for each of the main characters and five adjectives to describe them.

6. For each of the three ideas prepare:
    • The premise of the idea in three sentences.
    • A logline of twenty-five words or less.
    • A brief description of the ideal audience.
    • A personal statement of your interest in the characters, theme and story world.
    Use your notes as a basis for a practice pitch, telling each of the three stories to friends or colleagues. Listen to their feedback and re-write each of the three ideas. Which one is the strongest? Why?

7. With each idea add the following:
    • A paragraph on the world of the story.
    • Brief character outlines.
    • Visual references/images.
    • A story outline focusing on the initial conflict and its development to crisis/climax.

8. Select one of the ideas and create a portfolio of preparatory work:
    • Logline in twenty-five words or less.

- Genre.
- Story world (two to three pages).
- Character profiles (one page).
- Character networks/relationships (one page sketch).
- Story outline (three to five pages).
- Visual references.
- Sample scenes.
- Opening sequence.
- Context (a page on why you are writing this particular story).

9. As preparation, read two or three feature screenplays and Chapter 10 of this book. Either write a detailed treatment or step outline of your selected idea.
10. Write a first-draft screenplay.

ANALYSIS

1. Select a film that you admire and watch the DVD. Write down a brief description of what happens in every scene.
2. Do the same exercise with the sound off and this time focus on the images, actions and gestures. How is the story conveyed visually?

Read *Adaptation* by Charlie Kaufman and write the logline and a brief synopsis.

1. Who is protagonist? How does his character connect to the plot and theme of the story?

2. What is the central dramatic question?
3. Give a brief account of the protagonist's journey – both (a) external and (b) internal.
4. What is his objective and what's at stake for him?
5. Who is the antagonist?
6. List the key storylines/relationships involved in Charlie's journey. How do each of them contribute to the development of character, plot and theme?
7. What is the theme?
8. List the different timescales of the screenplay. How are they integrated into the overall story?
9. Outline the main story beats of Charlie's journey. How do they build through crisis to climax?
10. What is the outcome – the revelation/meaning – of the journey for both Charlie and the audience?

Rewriting

Apply the above questions to your own feature project and give an account of the main focus for the second draft rewrite. What are three aspects you will most concentrate on in the second draft? How will you approach this task? What aspects of your screenplay still excite you? What would you not change? What is your central dramatic question? What is your central theme?

10
THE COLLABORATIVE PROCESS

In a sense, a screenplay is always being rewritten until the final edit of the completed film – but not just by the screenwriter. The screenwriter is not the sole author of a film but a collaborator along with many other creative people in the process of film-making: the director and producer, the editor, actors and photographer who will all add significantly to the final image. So the screenwriter's job also changes as the screenplay evolves in creative dialogue with the team making the film. Screenwriting is film-making.

The screenplay, rather than a text to be photographed, becomes the basis of a conversation that all can share, a narrative structure that is open and flexible to change, a shifting set of suggestions that will inspire the creative team involved in turning the screenplay into a film. For the producer, the screenplay is a working document for pulling a team together and a tool of business for raising money and attracting talent.

As the producer Tony Garnett emphasizes, film is a social creation and the writing of a screenplay is a social act, with the producer, director and writer forming a creative triangle working together to nurture the overall vision.

In this respect, the screenwriter is a film-maker.

Film-Making Skills

The screenwriter ought, therefore, to acquire a technical knowledge of how film gets made, the contributions and impact of sound, image, editing and performance as the film is rewritten. Editing is a great tool for refocusing and rearranging, playing with different rhythms, while a good actor will know more about their character than the writer or director.

The writer should also know something about the practicalities of time and budget. Budget decisions are artistic decisions that impact on the script and vice versa.

Screenwriter's Role

The best way to learn about film-making, of course, is to become part of a group of people making a film and experience directly how a script is transformed into a film and the place of the screenwriter in that process.

The screenwriter's role in the film-making team is to offer ideas, solutions and alternatives as the screenplay is interrogated and modified, but from within their own deep knowledge of the characters and story world. They need to know the screenplay from the inside, to know what they are writing and why.

Working with the Director

One of the key collaborators and potential allies in this endeavour will be the person at the centre of the decision-making process – the director.

When American director Sydney Lumet first meets with the writer, he always asks the same questions that you might ask of your project:

- What is this story about?
- What was your intention?
- What do you hope the audience will feel or think?
- In what mood do you want them to leave the cinema?
- Is the storyline moving in an increasing arc of tension?
- Is the storyline being driven by the characters?[33]

He then moves on to discuss with the writer the details of the screenplay, including an examination of each scene and how it contributes to character and storyline, as well as the overall theme. For Lumet, the director and writer combine their talents and agree an intention for the film, to the point where they are working on the same film. From this interchange, sometimes a third intention emerges, which neither of them saw at the beginning.

Collaboration may take different forms from occasional conversations to sitting down and writing together. Directors and producers are often after something different than the writer, but these different points of view can be invigorating and productive for the final film.

The French screenwriter Jean-Claude Carrière always seeks to work closely with the director, checking scenes and lines of dialogue, discussing ideas for research and script changes, as well as talking obsessively about the film itself. For he is clear from the beginning that what he is working on is not a screenplay, but a film and, therefore, ideally he wants to work with the one making the film. He believes that a good screenplay gives birth to a good film and that a developed script is not the end of a literary adventure, but the beginning of a film adventure.

Digital Film-Making

In our digital world, the professional boundaries between writing, directing and editing are becoming blurred. With computer software it is easier to cut, shape and reshape ideas and images from development through to post-production.

Film-makers on low budgets collaborate with each other or often write, direct, shoot and edit themselves.

In effect they set-up their own film school, where they learn by making short films or trailers for features or even feature-length films, experimenting and improvising; sometimes working with actors and developing a script through a mix of writing, improvisation and rewriting, and creating film stories that don't conform to the classical model, as outlined in this book.

There have always been film-makers like Anges Varda operating outside of the Hollywood system, making films with friends and family, experimenting with film style and form beyond industrial norms. Another reason for working outside the system is that raising money to make commercial films is complicated and time-consuming, with most scripts failing to find funding.

New screenwriters can use networks like Shooting People to find possible collaborators or set up small groups of their own with the aim of not only writing, but directing and distributing their films online and building up a body of work. Explore the listed websites at the end of the book to find collaborators and sources of funding and development money.

Writing for Digital Media

In the same way that directors trained as film-makers can build careers in commercials or corporate videos, writers can take their storytelling skills into writing for digital media across a range of online platforms (websites, blogs, social media), which might include short narrative films. While you may develop your creative writing and editing abilities, your talents will usually be at the service of a corporate organization's marketing and communication department.

In this arena, screenwriting is not so much film-making as a form of journalism and design, a glimpse into the future of storytelling in the digital age that can be also be found in games and virtual reality scenarios: interactivity, hyperlinking, spatial orientation and non-linear narratives.

THE NEXT STEP

If you are concentrating on writing a feature screenplay and have now developed your premise from outline to a revised first draft, what is the next step for your screenplay and for you personally?

If this is your first feature screenplay and you have not already done so, you will want to show it to friends and colleagues to get some feedback or, if you think it good enough, you might want to send it to an agent, a producer or a production company to see if there is any commercial interest in you or your idea.

More likely, you may feel the screenplay still needs work and you would benefit from further practice or professional support. You can, of course, pursue all three approaches simultaneously, as well as using the Internet to research a wide range of useful websites to help clarify your thinking. You will find a list of further resources and websites at the back of the book.

Writing for Television

As a new screenwriter, you should also consider writing for television. In the UK, and in many other territories, television is the medium where you can develop your storytelling skills, find regular work and build a career. Formats include the half-hour sit-com, long-running soap, closed serials and the one-hour drama series. They all require the basic skills of character, plot and dialogue developed in the writing of a feature script, but differ in tone, length and complexity.

SERIALS

A serial is a drama told in two to six parts, sometimes over successive evenings or weekly. Each episode is usually one hour, organized around a main storyline with sub-plots.

SOAPS

The most popular serials are the long-running dramas of everyday life, usually half an hour in length, screened three nights a week, with two or three interweaving storylines in each episode and a regular cast of characters in a set location, such as *EastEnders*, *Casualty*, *Coronation Street*.

Soaps are the entry-level for many writers in television and a place where they can learn and practise their craft.

SERIES

A series is a drama that has a self-contained one-hour story or storyline each week and unresolved story strands that develop through the series. In other words, they are a combination of closed and serialized storytelling, for example *Game of Thrones*, *Sopranos*, *Breaking Bad*.

TV SERIES VS FEATURE

TV series writing is distinguished from other forms of screenwriting by its long narratives and slowly developing character arcs. You get to write and know the characters in depth and shape the internal conflicts that create tension and lead to incremental change. There is a new event each week, but you are also building parallel storylines around other key characters and their relationships.

Some writers love the time and freedom to develop character and plot that TV series allow, as well as the collaborative nature of the work, often involving a writers' room where a group of writers will work out the story beats and character arcs together. The work is intense and the deadlines tight and you need to really understand craft skills involving act breaks, dramatic hooks and the interweaving or juxtaposition of parallel storylines.

The basic building block of both forms of storytelling remains the ability to develop intriguing characters and the ability to structure the key moments and dramatic scenes of a story.

Despite the obvious attractions of long-form storytelling, many screenwriters and film-makers still find the feature-film format the most exciting and demanding, with its focus on a single complete story in a limited time-frame, a unique discipline and experience – like haiku or twelve-bar blues.

APPROACHING TV PRODUCTION COMPANIES

If you want to write for television, you need to study your chosen format and research the producers and production companies behind your favourite shows. Find out what writing samples they would like to see, including whether they would be interested in reading a spec script based on the show.

You may have an idea for a TV series of your own, in which case you need to prepare a proposal or pitch document, which would include the premise, logline, story outline, character sketches and a pilot episode. A good screenwriting course would help you to prepare and package a TV series idea, as well as develop a feature.

The best approach, however, would be through an agent, and we discuss this later in this chapter.

Festivals

Film Festivals, such as Edinburgh, Glasgow and London, and specialist forums like the Screenwriter's Festival and Raindance Film Festival are also good places to network, attend industry seminars and make contacts.

Screenwriting Competitions

Screenwriting competitions are worth researching; they are mainly run out of the USA and, if you make the shortlist, your screenplay will get read and be given feedback by a production company, or they might also be interested in buying it.

Development Schemes

As well as the BBC Writers' Room and Film London, there are several regional initiatives aimed at supporting new writers. There are also a number of European-wide development schemes, which is funded by the EU Media programme. Explore the websites listed at the end.

Radio/Web Series

As a writer, you will, of course, be continuing to write short stories or plays, and researching a variety of platforms for your work, including radio and web series.

The Trades

You should read the trades – *Variety*, *Screen International* and the *Hollywood Reporter* to see what films are being financed, as well as what is selling and finding audiences.

Further Training or Study

At the same time as developing your understanding of the business and practice of screenwriting, you need to build up a portfolio of work and get regular feedback on current projects.

Joining a writers' group or attending a short course is a good way to meet like-minded people and build your confidence, skillset and portfolio of script ideas. Script workshops will give you deadlines and regular feedback on your developing work.

The Script Factory, City Lit, Euroscript and Raindance are amongst the independent organizations that run short courses in the UK.

If you feel you are ready, this may also be the time to apply for a place on one the specialist MA Screenwriting courses in the UK or USA.

ScreenSkills have a list of the accredited MA courses in the UK, including the screenwriting programmes run by the London Film School and the National Film and Television School, where screenwriters are able to work in the context of a practical film-making community.

A good course will accelerate both your personal and professional development.

It should provide:

- A space to write and explore ideas and working practices.
- A space to develop critical and analytical thinking.
- A place to explore the boundaries between writing and directing.
- A place to discuss and experiment with alternative approaches to screenwriting.
- The opportunity to master technical and craft skills of screenwriting.
- The opportunity to develop skills in script editing and script reading.
- A group of professional writing tutors to give you regular feedback and guidance on the writing of short and feature screenplays.
- A historical and theoretical context for the practice of screenwriting.
- A group of peers dedicated to writing and making films who will also become the basis of a networking group on graduation.
- The opportunity to have your screenplay read by actors.
- The possibility of working on a film on set or in the cutting room.
- The possibility of having a film made from one of your screenplays and to network with film-makers.
- Guidance on career development and the business context of screenwriting and film-making.

The teachers, tutors, your fellow writers and the visiting professionals will help you become better editors of your own work and push you to go deeper. You will be a much better writer at the end of the course and more realistic about your skills and how to connect with the professional world.

Deadlines will give you the focus and discipline to produce a body of work that you can take out into the professional world and start to build a career.

Agents

Most producers here and in the USA will not accept unsolicited scripts and other written material unless through an agent. An agent is able to get your script read by decision-makers and also help you to decide whether it will sell or whether it is best sent as a 'writing sample' for possible future commissions.

A good agent can help you build a successful career as a writer, but you have to be realistic and patient in your search for representation.

WHAT DO AGENTS DO?
- Promote their clients.
- Set-up meetings.
- Negotiate contracts and give legal advice.
- Offer career guidance and creative feedback.
- Provide a buffer between the writer and producer.
- Share insider knowledge of industry.
- Get your script read by decision-makers.
- Take 10–12% commission on work sold.

Agents are busy and not always looking for clients and the big agencies take on only a few new writers each year – and usually because they have already raised their profile with a commission or through a working relationship with an established producer.

Agents are looking for writers who have the talent and commitment to build and sustain a career – as well as an ability to collaborate. Like many other aspects of the business, it is about relationships.

WHAT YOU CAN DO
- Develop a body of work.
- Find a young agent who is just starting out.
- Write a feature screenplay.
- Get a commission.
- Get a referral from an established producer.
- Check the list of agencies in the *Writers' and Artists' Yearbook* and research the client lists.
- Select the agencies who represent writers or projects close to your interests.

- Cold call and find out if they consider submissions from new writers.
- If so, find out who to send any submission to and what should be included. Some will want to read a feature screenplay, others only a brief letter, including the logline of the script you want them to read. This is known as a query letter.

THE QUERY LETTER

This is a one-page letter that you send to agents or producers, either with an accompanying script or a logline that might entice them to read the script.

- It should be no more than three or four short paragraphs.
- Outline why you are writing and why you think the project is appropriate.
- Pitch your idea in one or two sentences.
- Include a brief CV relevant to your writing experience.
- Add a paragraph on any attachments.

You may have to wait several weeks for a reply but, if your script is read and liked, you may get a meeting at which you may have an opportunity to pitch other ideas.

Pitching

In a meeting with a producer or agent, you want to convey the essence of your screenplay or any new idea, and excite them with its potential. Pitching is simply this skill of selling a film idea with clarity and passion in meetings or encounters at networking events. Many pitches are impromptu in cafés or bars or social events.

It is an important skill because a good pitch can attract interest, development money or creative collaborators who can help realize the project. It is also a test of how well you know and understand your own screenplay and how marketable it might be.

You can pitch an already developed screenplay or a new idea, but either requires preparation and practice. Preparation would include writing a pitch document as a crib sheet for verbally pitching your idea.

Ask yourself:

- What is the essential idea and what is my relationship to it?
- Why do you want to tell this story?
- What is the story about?
- Who is the audience/market for this story?
- What is the story's appeal?
- Who are the central characters?
- What is the world of the story?
- How does the story develop and resolve?

Use these questions as prompts to writing a one-page synopsis of the idea, then reduce to one paragraph and a logline.

Practice a 2 then 10 and 20min verbal pitch and get feedback and questions from friends or colleagues. Rewrite. Work out what are the most effective ways of communicating your story.

Do your research on the producer/broadcaster before the meeting and prepare your approach according to their interests. What have they done? What are they looking for? Be enthusiastic and communicate your passion. Know why you are pitching – usually you are trying to persuade them to read your outline or screenplay.

The key is to know your story so well that you can lead into the material from any angle – genre, theme, setting and central conflict, contemporary relevance. You don't need to cover everything in the pitch. In fact, you want to leave room for questions that get the producer involved in the story. So don't go into too much detail. Give them the story in broad-brush strokes and listen to what they say. Make notes – even if they're not interested, you can get useful feedback on how to revise for the next meeting with a producer who will be interested.

OVERVIEW

In this chapter, we have discussed the place of the screenplay in the collaborative practice of film-making. We have also considered the next steps you might take after the writing of your screenplay and the various options that you now have for personal and or professional development.

In earlier chapters, we have traced the classical narrative tradition from its roots in oral storytelling, ritual and Greek drama through nineteenth-century theatrical forms to the emergence of a distinctive cinematic language. The aim has been to provide you with a historical and theoretical context for screenwriting, as well as some practical insights and examples that you can apply to the writing of a short film script or feature screenplay.

The emphasis throughout has been on the importance of developing your original voice, encouraging you to explore your own life and passions, as well as looking outward to the range of human encounters and experience in the everyday and wider world. Along with a continuing study of classical approaches, there is also a huge variety of world cinema to explore beyond the mainstream that may give you reason for hope and inspiration.

As you progress in your writing, you can take the screenwriting skills that you have studied and practised not only into film and television, but also to the wide range of emerging digital platforms: trans-media, animation, games and interactive fiction. Consider other ways of working with artists or actors in improvisation, where storytelling techniques play their part in new forms of expression.

Screenwriting is film-making, which means it is also researching, improvising, performing and collaborating with others: creating and combining images and words in ways familiar to musical composition. The industrial film-making model is not the only one – you should seek out collaborators and diverse other ways of making films and telling stories.

Screenwriting is an expanding and changing activity but one aspect has not changed: the continued need for exciting, relevant, human stories that engage with our current and recurrent desires and dilemmas. Finding new stories or new forms for old stories is the screenwriter's task. Films and movies are more than commodities: at their best they express the mystery, cruelty and beauty of the world and help define our natures, show us who we are, and who we might become.

The journey has just begun.

ENDNOTES

1   Lyons M (2008) *The Arabian Nights: Tales of 1001 Nights.* Penguin Books.

2   Mamet D (1992) *On Directing Film*. Penguin Books.

3   Newton J *Amazing Grace*, song lyrics.

4   Homer *The Odyssey*.

5   Carter A (1982) *The Bloody Chamber.*

6   Lynch D (2006) *Catching the Big Fish*, p. 1.

7   Lynch D (2006) *Catching the Big Fish*, p. 23.

8   Salt B (2009) *Film Style and Technology*, pp. 120–123.

9   Sontag S (1969) *Styles of Radical Will*, pp. 99–122.

10 Taylor V (2008) *How To Write Plays and Screenplays*, p. 1.

11 Ondaatje M (2008) *The Conversations: Walter Murch and the Art of Editing Film*, p. 23.

12 Ondaatje M (2008) *The Conversations: Walter Murch and the Art of Editing Film*, p. 90.

13 Mamet D (1992) *On Directing Film*, Penguin Books, p. xv.

14 Eisenstein S (1977) *The Film Sense*, Faber and Faber, p. 14.

15 Hass R (ed.) (2013) *The Essential Haiku*, p. 35.

16 Eisenstein S (1977) *The Film Sense*, p. 24.

17 McGrath D and MacDermott F (2003) *Screenwriting*, p. 90.

18 McGrath D and MacDermott F (2003) *Screenwriting*, p. 90.

19 McGrath D and MacDermott F (2003) *Screenwriting*, p. 90.

20 Grisoni T (2012) Keynote speech to graduating students on MA Screenwriting programme at the London Film School.

21 Midgley M (2010) *The Solitary Self*, p. 61.

22 Nussbaum MC (1992) *Love's Knowledge*, p. 365.

23 Brooks P (1992) *Reading for the Plot*, Harvard University Press, pp. 38–39.

24 Belknap RL (2016) *Plots*, p. 38.

25 Parker T and Stone M (2014) New York University writing seminar.

26 Belknap RL (2016) *Plots*, p. 51.

27 Morgan A (2018) *Desert Island Discs*, BBC Radio 4.

28 Goffman E (1990) *The Presentation of Self in Everyday Life.*

29 Cardullo B (ed.) (2011) *World Directors in Dialogue*, p. 109.

30 Cardullo B (ed.) (2011) *World Directors in Dialogue*, p. 109.

31 Grierson T (ed.) (2013) *Screenwriting*, p. 75.

32 Mamet D (1992) *On Directing Film*, p. xv.

33 Lumet S (1996) *Making Movies*, p. 26.

GLOSSARY

Act One of the narrative sections that make up a unit of drama. A screenplay for a feature film can be organized or analysed in terms of three, four or five acts.

Action The efforts and initiatives of the protagonist to achieve her objective.

Action Line The main storyline or plot. Refers to the exterior action of the story, as opposed to the internal journey of the protagonist.

Adaptation The transposition of a prose text or other document into a work of drama.

Antagonist The one who opposes the objective of the protagonist.

Aristotelian Relating to Aristotle's theories about drama, as set out in the *Poetics* with an emphasis on identification, plot causality and unity of action.

Backstory Anything that happens before the film story begins that the audience needs to know in order to understand character and plot developments.

Beat Can refer to a pause within a dialogue speech or the rhythm of conflict within a scene where one character acts and another reacts. These changing behaviours shape the development of a scene beat by beat. It can be also be used in relation to the major developments or beats of the overall storyline.

Catalyst/Inciting Incident An event that starts the story; an incident near the beginning that disturbs the life or routine of one or more characters and sets them in pursuit of an objective. A story begins when a conflict is initiated that has to be resolved.

Catharsis According to Aristotle, the purging of pity or terror experienced through viewing a tragedy. In film it refers to the relieving of emotional tensions and a clarification of plot events for both the protagonist and audience.

Causal Relationship The conflict takes place because something happens or has happened. Each crisis takes place because of an earlier action or decision or failure to act or decide. Action and conflict have a causal relationship that has a powerful emotional effect on the audience.

Character A person or personality in the drama. Major characters are vital to the development and resolution of the conflict. Minor characters complement the major characters and help move plot events forward. A static character is one who does not change over time or whose personality does not transform or evolve. A rounded character has a complex personality and is often portrayed as conflicted and contradictory.

Character Arc The path of a character's emotional or moral journey through the story.

Characterization The art of creating characters and the traits that go to make up character; the presentation of these traits in a dramatic context.

Climax From the Greek for a ladder: the highest point of the action. The culminating moment of action, where the complications are reversed and the conflict resolved.

Complication Sometimes referred to as 'rising action': those parts of the plot that make relationships and conflicts complex; plot developments that affect the overall objective of the protagonist. The way in which the main character handles these unexpected difficulties, reveals their character and determines plot.

Conflict Typically refers to the opposition between two forces, the outcome of which is in doubt. This uncertainty keeps the audience involved: they want to know how the conflict will be resolved. In a mainstream narrative, this clash is usually expressed in the struggle between the protagonist and the antagonist. The opposing force can be internal (within the protagonist's mind), as well as external (a character, a group, the environment).

Crisis From the Greek meaning a crucial or decisive moment. A film narrative can be seen as a series of crises culminating in a final crisis; a moment of discovery where the protagonist is under the greatest pressure and seems likely to fail in her/his objective. At this point, the true nature of the problem s/he must face is revealed and a last attempt is made to find a solution.

Denouement The falling action of the screenplay, where all the problems not resolved in the climax are unravelled and any needed explanation takes place.

Deus ex Machina From the Latin 'god out of the machine'; refers to any character or event brought in arbitrarily to solve a dramatic or script problem.

Discovery The principle of surprise; an unexpected character/plot revelation. Surprise helps keeps the audience involved in the story, never sure what is going to happen next. To be effective, it needs to be linked to an aspect of plot or character planted earlier.

Drama From the Greek meaning 'to do' or 'to act'; in film, a story of human action and conflict involving an objective, obstacles and an uncertain outcome.

Dramatic An intensification of life; a series of absorbing, exciting or tense events involving suspense and surprise.

Dramatic Irony A dramatic device where the audience knows something that one or more characters don't know. This creates suspense and heightens the audience's involvement in the story. Sometimes the writer has to choose between dramatic irony and surprise, i.e. letting the spectators in on the secret or startling them with it later.

Dramatic Need The unresolved issue facing the protagonist presented in the first act and dealt with in the second; related to internal/thematic objective.

Dramatic Question The dramatic question – will the protagonist achieve their objective? – is established in the spectator's mind during the first act and not resolved until the end; it gives rise to suspense.

Ellipsis Gap in the narrative where you deliberately leave out information in order to heighten the sense of mystery and suspense, and draw in the audience: the most important things are left unspoken. It can also speed up the narrative.

Exposition Refers to information (backstory/off-screen) that the writer needs to convey in a subtle way to an audience, so that character action, motivation and relationships are credible.

Flashback A moment, scene or sequence that shows us something from the past that has significance for the present drama; a form of exposition that should be dramatic rather than merely informational.

Foreshadowing/Pay-Off An atmosphere, a clue, an action – that is set-up and paid off later in the story; a form of preparation that adds to the pleasure of the spectator by hinting at future plot developments.

Genre Types of film stories – western, detective, gangster, science fiction – with recognizable characteristics and formal conventions.

Logline A one-line summary or pitch of the main action of a film idea.

Motif A recurring image, rhythm or sound.

Motivation The reasons that underlie a character's behaviour and actions.

Pay-Off The moment when an aspect of the drama acquires a particular meaning as a result of prior planting.

Pitch A term taken from baseball referring to the brief presentation of a film idea to a producer or decision-maker. The one-line pitch is also known as a logline – the summary of the action in a single phrase.

Plant An object, line of dialogue, etc. that is planted earlier to excite audience's expectation and make credible what happens later.

Plot The organized selection of causally related incidents from which the audience has to work out the story. A specific arrangement of events for an intended effect, built around rising action, conflict, reversal, suspense and so on.

Plot Point An event or piece of information that impacts on the protagonist's objective and moves the story forward.

Point of Attack The point at which the writer has chosen to begin the story. This is usually *in media res* (in the middle of things) and hence the need for backstory exposition during the development of the story.

Point of View The perspective from which the writer tells the story, e.g. first person.

Premise The central concept or idea uniting the story elements – usually expressed in terms of the main conflict/dilemma of the protagonist. High-concept refers to a plot-oriented premise; low-concept to a character-centred story.

Preparation A detail or action carried out in the immediate moment that prepares us for later action. It heightens audience involvement by creating an expectation of future outcomes and makes credible a later action that might otherwise appear contrived.

Protagonist From the Greek meaning, literally, 'the one who struggles'. The main character whose story we are following. An audience will be involved in the film to the extent with which they identify with the protagonist's dilemma.

Reversal A plot twist that involves a reversal of fortune. Setbacks build tension and heighten concern. In a conventional narrative, the plot usually builds through a series of minor reversals to the major reversal of crisis and climax. It is often accompanied by the protagonist recognizing or realizing the true meaning of events for the first time.

Scene The basic building-block of the screenplay. A unit of single and continuous dramatic action in which mood is established, character revealed and plot developed. A scene takes place at a given place and time and involves a given set of characters. The scenes in a screenplay are introduced with a brief heading thus: INT. KITCHEN. NIGHT.

Sequence A series of linked scenes, united by a common action or theme, structured around a beginning, a middle and an end.

Setting The environment of the scene or story that creates mood, tone and atmosphere, as well as contributing to the meaning of the film. It is an integral and interactive element of the storytelling.

Stake What a character stands to gain or lose as a result of his actions. What is at stake provides motivation for the characters and may be of a psychological or unconscious nature relating to an internal but unrecognized need.

Story A sequence of events designed to interest, amuse or inform: usually showing what happens to the protagonist and why. Most film stories are developed to a more sophisticated level through plotting. The formalist analysis of narrative distinguishes between story (*fabula*) and plot (*siuzhet*) as a way of highlighting how the plot is designed, so that the audience has to work out the protagonist's story.

Structure The relation of the parts to the whole. As applied to film – the way the story material is selected, organized or plotted. The three-act structure is the most common paradigm used by screenwriting texts and mainstream cinema. This defines the basic structure of a film as built around three acts – beginning, middle, end or set-up, development, resolution. From the point of view of the protagonist, the story is structured around her initial problem and her struggle to solve that problem. Her story builds through crisis and climax to resolution.

The movement from one act to another is sometimes referred to as a turning or plot point.

Sub-Plot A secondary storyline that complements the main narrative. In a feature film there can be several sub-plots, but in a short film screenplay they are kept to a minimum.

Sub-Text The interior struggle of the main character: what characters are really thinking and feeling, the latent meaning of a scene, the undercurrent of emotions and thoughts that truly motivate the characters to behave as they do.

Surprise An unexpected development sprung on the audience: often the pay-off from an earlier plant designed to mislead the spectator.

Suspense Dramatic suspense is one of the writer's most powerful techniques. Creating anticipations in the audience means creating concerns about what will happen next and whether the protagonist will succeed in solving their problem or achieving their goal. The audience must care about the fate of the protagonist and have a sense of what is at stake for suspense to be truly effective.

Theme The idea or underlying meaning of the screenplay uniting the various elements.

Tone Relates to the mood and atmosphere of the story, usually set by the screenwriter's attitude to the characters and theme of the story, e.g. serious or humorous.

Treatment A prose outline of your story written in a way that indicates how the story would be treated cinematically, i.e. through visual action.

Turning Points Also called plot points – the moments in a story when characters are confronted with choices, actions or insights, which significantly affect their character path and turn the plot in a new direction.

Unity of Action The principle according to which all the elements of the screenplay must serve the main action of the plot. Correlates with the importance of a single objective and the human need for order and meaning. Aristotle believed dramatic unity enhanced audience engagement and the emotional impact of the plot.

BIBLIOGRAPHY

Argentini, P., *Elements of Style for Screenwriters* (Lone Eagle, 1998)

Aristotle, *Poetics,* translated and edited by Malcolm Heath (Penguin Classics, 1996)

Armes, R., *Action and Image: Dramatic Structure in Cinema* (MUP, 1994)

Aronson, L., *Screenwriting Updated* (Silman-James Press, 2001)

Aulier, A., *Hitchcock's Secret Notebooks* (Bloomsbury, 1999)

Baxter, C., *The Art of Sub-Text: Beyond Plot* (Graywolf Press, 2007)

Belknap, R.L., *Plots* (Columbia University Press, 2016)

Bergala, A., *The Cinema Hypothesis: Teaching Cinema in the Classroom and Beyond* (Synema, 2016)

Bettleheim, B., *The Uses of Enchantment: the Meaning and Importance of Fairy Tales* (Penguin Books, 1991)

Biro, Y., *To Dress a Nude: Exercises in Imagination* (Kendall/Hunt Publishing, 1998)

Bordwell, D., *Narration in the Fiction Film* (Routledge, 1997)

Bordwell, D., *The Way Hollywood Tells It: Story and Style in Modern Movies* (University of California Press, 2006)

Bordwell, D., Thompson, K. and Smith, J., *Film Art* (McGraw-Hill Education, 2016)

Boyd, B., *On the Origin of Stories: Evolution, Cognition and Fiction* (Belknap Press of Harvard University Press, 2009)

Bresson, R., *Notes on the Cinematographer* (Quartet Books, 1986)

Brook, P., *There Are No Secrets: Thoughts on Acting and Theatre* (Methuen Drama, 1994)

Brooks, C. and Warren, R.P., *Understanding Fiction* (Prentice-Hall, 2003)

Brooks, P., *Reading for the Plot: Design and Intention in Narrative* (Harvard University Press, 1992)

Brooks, P., *The Melodramatic Imagination* (Yale University Press, 1995)

Buchan, D., *The Ballad and the Folk* (Tuckwell Press, 1997)

Bunuel, L., *My Last Breath* (Flamingo, 1985)

Calvino, I., *Six Memos for the Next Millenium* (Vintage, 1996)

Cameron, J., *The Artist's Way: a Course in Discovering and Recovering your Creative Self* (Pan Books, 1995)

Cameron, J., *The Right to Write: an Invitation and Initiation into the Writing Life* (Macmillan, 1998)

Campbell, J., *The Hero with a Thousand Faces*, 2nd edn (New World Library, 2008)

Cardullo, B. (ed.) *World Directors in Dialogue: Conversations on Cinema* (The Scarecrow Press, 2011)

Carter, A., *The Bloody Chamber and Other Stories* (Penguin Books, 1981)

Catmull, E., *Creativity Inc: Overcoming the Unseen Forces that Stand in the Way of True Inspiration* (Bantam Press, 2014)

Cavell, S., *The World Viewed: Reflections on the Ontology of Film* (Harvard University Press, 1979)

Cole, H.R. and Haag, J.H., *The Complete Guide to Standard Script Formats* (CMC Publishing, 1991)

Conway, C., *Agnes Varda* (University of Illinois Press, 2015)

Cook, D.A., *A History of Narrative Film* (W. W. Norton, 1990)

Cooper, P. and Dancyger, K., *Writing the Short Film* (Focal Press, 2004)

Corbett, D., *The Art of Character: Creating Memorable Characters for Fiction, Film and TV* (Penguin Books, 2013)

Cowgill, L., *Writing Short Films* (Lone Eagle Publishing Co., 2005)

Crowe, C., *Conversations with Wilder* (Faber and Faber 1996)

Dancyger, K. and Rush, J., *Alternative Scriptwriting* (Focal Press, 2006)

Dethridge, L., *Writing Your Screenplay* (Allen and Unwin, 2003)

Douglas, P., *Writing the TV Drama Series* (Michael Wiese Productions, 2011)

Edgar, D., *How Plays Work* (Nick Hern Books, 2009)

Egri, L., *The Art of Dramatic Writing* (Simon & Schuster, 2004)

Eisenstein, S., *The Film Sense* (Faber and Faber, 1977)

Eisenstein, S., *The Short Film Scenario* (Seagull Books, 1984)

Elena, A., *The Cinema of Abbas Kiarostami* (Saqi, 2005)

Engel, J., *Screenwriters on Screenwriting: The Best in the Business Discuss Their Craft* (MJF Books, 2000)

Field, S., *Screenplay* (Delta, 2005)

Finney, A., *The International Film Business: A Market Guide beyond Hollywood* (Routledge, 2010)

Fleischer, F., *An Approach to Screenwriting for the Feature Film: Four Lectures* (Sources, 1995)

French, R. and Simpson, P., *Attention, Cooperation, Purpose: An Approach to Working with Groups Using Insights from Wilfred Bion* (Karnac Books, 2015)

Frensham, R., *Teach Yourself Screenwriting* (Hodder and McGraw-Hill Companies, 2003)

Ganz, A., Time, Space and Movement: Screenplay as Oral Narrative, *Journal of Screenwriting* Vol. 1.2, 2010, pp. 225–36.

Goffman, G., *The Presentation of Self in Everyday Life* (Penguin Books, 1990)

Goldberg, N., *Writing Down to the Bones: Freeing the Writer Within* (Shambhala Publications, 1986)

Goldman, W., *Adventures in the Screen Trade: A Personal View of Hollywood* (Abacus, 1996)

Grierson, T., *Filmcraft: Screenwriting* (Ilex Press, 2013)

Grimm, J. and W., *Selected Tales* (Penguin Books, 1982)

Hass, R., *The Essential Haiku: Versions of Bashō, Buson and Issa* (Bloodaxe Books, 2013)

Highsmith, P., *Plotting and Writing Suspense Fiction* (St. Martin's Griffin, 1990)

Hills, R., *Writing in General and the Short Story in Particular* (Mariner Books, 2000)

Homer, *The Odyssey*, translated by Robert Fagles (Penguin Books, 1997)

Homer, *The Iliad*, translated by Robert Fagles (Penguin Classics, 1998)

Howard, D. and Mabley, E., *The Tools of Screenwriting* (St. Martin's Griffin, 1993)

Hyde, L., *Trickster Makes This World: How Disruptive Imagination Makes This World* (Canongate, 2017)

Iglesias, K., *The 101 Habits of Highly Successful Screenwriters* (Adams Media, 2001)

Johnson, C.H., *Crafting Short Screenplays that Connect* (Focal Press, 2005)

Johnstone, K., *Impro: Improvisation and the Theatre* (Eyre Methuen, 1994)

Johnstone, K., *Impro for Storytellers: Theatresports and the Art of Making things Happen* (Faber and Faber, 1999)

Jung, C.G., *Four Archetypes: Mother, Rebirth, Spirit, Trickster* (Routledge, 1972)

Karetnikova, I., *How Scripts are Made* (Southern Illinois University Press, 1990)

King, S., *On Writing: a Memoir of the Craft* (Hodder and Stoughton, 2012)

Lavandier, Y., *Writing Drama* (La Dramaturgie) (Le Clown and L'Enfant, 2004)

Leech, C., *Tragedy* (Routledge, 1994)

Lodge, D., *The Art of Fiction* (Vintage, 2011)

Lumet, S., *Making Movies* (Bloomsbury, 1996)

Lynch, D., *Catching the Big Fish: Meditation, Consciousness, and Creativity* (Tarcher Penguin, 2006)

Lyons, M.C. (ed.), *The Arabian Nights: Tales of 1001 Nights* (Penguin Classics, 2010)

Mackendrick, A. and Cronin, P. (eds), *On Film-Making* (Faber and Faber, 2005)

Mamet, D., *On Directing Film* (Penguin, 1992)

Mamet, D., *Three Uses of the Knife: On the Nature and Purpose of Drama* (Methuen Drama, 2007)

Martin, B., *Difficult Men: Behind the Scenes of a Creative Revolution* (Faber and Faber, 2013)

May, R., *The Courage to Create* (Bantam Books, 1990)

McGilligan, P. (ed.), *Backstory 3. Interviews with Screenwriters of the 1960s* (UCP, 1997)

McGowan, T., *Spike Lee* (University of Illinois, 2014)

McGrath, D. and MacDermott, F., *Screenwriting* (Rotovision, 2003)

McKee, R., *Story* (Methuen, 1999)

Midgley, M., *The Solitary Self: Darwin and the Selfish Gene* (Acumen Publishing, 2010)

Millard, K., *Screenwriting in a Digital Era* (Palgrave Macmillan, 2014)

Murch, W., *In the Blink of an Eye: A Perspective on Film Editing* (Silman-James Press, 2001)

Murdock, M., *The Heroine's Journey: Woman's Quest for Wholeness* (Shambhala Publications, 1990)

Nussbaum, M.C., *Love's Knowledge: Essays on Philosophy and Literature* (Oxford University Press, 1992)

Nussbaum, M.C., *The Fragility of Goodness: Luck and Ethics in Greek Tragedy and Philosophy* (Cambridge University Press, 2001)

Ondaatje, M., *The Conversations: Walter Murch and the Art of Editing Film* (Bloomsbury Publishing, 2008)

Owen, A., *Story and Character: Interviews with British Screenwriters* (Bloomsbury Publishing, 2004)

Perez, G., *The Material Ghost: Films and their Medium* (John Hopkins University Press, 1998)

Potolsky, M., *Mimesis* (Routledge, 2006)

Potter, C., *Screen Language* (Methuen, 2001)

Raskin, R., *The Art of the Short Fiction Film* (Macfarland, 2003)

Rilke, R.M., *Letters to a Young Poet* (BN Publishing, 2008)

Salt, B., *Film Style and Technology: History and Analysis* (Starword, 2009)

Sayles, J., *Thinking In Pictures: The Making of the Movie Matewan* (Houghton Mifflin Company, 1987)

Schön, D.A., *Educating the Reflective Practitioner: Toward a New Design for Teaching and Learning in the Professions* (Jossey-Bass, 1987)

Scott, K.C., *Screenwriters' Masterclass* (Faber and Faber, 2005)

Segar, L., *The Art of Adaptation* (Henry Holt, 1992)

Selbo, J., *Film Genre for the Screenwriter* (Routledge, 2014)

Sennet, R., *Respect: the Formation of Character in a World of Inequality* (Allen Lane, 2003)

Sennet, R., *The Craftsman* (Penguin Books, 2008)

Shakespeare, W., *Henry IV Parts 1 and 2* (Penguin Books, 2017)

Shakespeare, W., *King Lear* (Penguin Books, 2017)

Smith, A., *The Theory of Moral Sentiments* (Penguin Classics, 2009)

Snyder, B., *Save the Cat* (Michael Wiese Productions, 2005)

Solnit, R., *The Faraway Nearby* (Granta Publications, 2013)

Sontag, S., *Styles of Radical Will* (Farrar, Straus and Giroux, 1969)

Stanislavski, C., *An Actor Prepares* (Eyre Metheun, 1980)

Stepheson, B., *Ritual: a very Short Introduction* (OUP, 2015)

Tarkovsky, A., *Sculpting in Time: Reflections on the Cinema* (University of Texas Press, 2014)

Taylor, C., *The Ethics of Authenticity* (Harvard University Press, 2003)

Taylor, V., *How to Write Plays and Screenplays* (Guardian News and Media, 2008)

Tharp, T., *The Creative Habit* (Simon and Schuster, 2006)

Truffaut, F., *Hitchcock* (Paladin, 1986)

Turner, V., *Dramas, Fields and Metaphors: Symbolic Action in Human Society* (Cornell University Press, 1975)

Venis, L. (ed.), *Inside the Room: Writing Television with the Pros at UCLA Extension Writers' Program* (Gotham Books, 2013)

Vernant, J.-P. and Vidal-Naquet, P., *Myth and Tragedy in Ancient Greece* (Zone Books, 2006)

Vogler, C., *The Writer's Journey* (Michael Wiese Production, 2007)

Warner, M., *From the Beast to the Blonde: On Fairytales and their Tellers* (Chatto and Windus, 1994)

Wilkinson, D.N. and Price, E. (eds), *Ronald Harwood's Adaptations: from Other Works into Films* (Guerilla Books, 2007)

Yorke, J., *Into the Woods: A Five-Act Journey into Story* (Penguin Books, 2013)

Zipes, J., *Creative Storytelling: Building Community, Changing Lives* (Routledge, 1995)

Zipes, J. (ed.), *The Oxford Companion to Fairy Tales: the Western Fairy Tale Tradition from Medieval to Modern* (Oxford University Press, 2002)

FILMOGRAPHY

Adaptation (US: 2002) screenplay by Charlie Kaufman, based on the book by Susan Orlean.

Assault On Precinct 13 (US: 1976) written by John Carpenter.

Bicycle Thieves (Italy: 1948) Suso D'Amico & Vittorio de Sica, based on the novel by Luigi Bartolini.

The Big Chill (US: 1983) written by Lawrence Kasdan and Barbara Benedek.

Blue Velvet (US: 1986) screenplay by David Lynch.

Boudu Saved From Drowning (France: 1932) screenplay written by Jean Renoir and Albert Valentin, based on the play by René Fauchois.

Cave of Forgotten Dreams (Canada/France/Germany/US/UK: 2010) written by Werner Herzog.

The Child (Belgium: 2005) written by Jean-Pierre Dardenne and Luc Dardenne.

Chinatown (US: 1974) written by Robert Towne.

Chocolat (France: 1988) written by Clair Denis and Jean-Pol Fargeau.

Chungking Express (Hong Kong: 1994) written by Kar-Wai Wong.

Code Unknown (France/Germany/Romania: 2000) written by Michael Haneke.

Cold War (Poland: 2018) screenplay by Pawel Pawlikowski and Janusz Glowacki.

Decalog (Poland: 1989) written by Krzysztof Kieslowski and Krzysztof Piesiewicz.

The Diving Bell and The Butterfly (France/US: 2007) written by Ronald Harwood, based on the book by Jean-Dominique Bauby.

Do the Right Thing (US: 1989) written by Spike Lee.

Don't Look Now (UK/Italy: 1973) screenplay by Allan Scott and Chris Bryant, based on the short story by Daphne du Maurier.

L'Eclisse (Italy: 1962) scenario and dialogue by Michelangelo Antonioni and Tonino Guerro.

A Fantastic Woman (Chile: 2017) screenplay by Sebastian Lelio and Gonzalo Maza.

Fear Eats the Soul (Germany: 1974) written by Rainer Werner Fassbinder.

Fish Tank (UK: 2009) written by Andrea Arnold.

Force Majeure (France/Norway/Sweden: 2014) written by Ruben Ostlund.

A Girl Walks Home Alone at Night (US: 2014) written by Ana Lily Amirpour.

The Girl With a Pearl Earing (UK/Luxembourg/Netherlands: 2003) screenplay by Olivia Hetreed, based on the novel by Tracy Chevalier.

The Godfather (US: 1972) screenplay by Mario Puzo and by Francis Ford Coppola, based on the novel by Mario Puzo.

Kes (UK: 1969) written by Barry Hines and Ken Loach and Tony Garnett, based on the novel by Barry Hines.

In This World (UK: 2002) written by Tony Grisoni.

Little Miss Sunshine (US: 2006) written by Michael Arndt.

Lourdes (Austria/France/Germany: 2009) Geraldine Bajard and Jessica Hausner.

Midnight Cowboy (US: 1969) screenplay by Waldo Salt, based on the novel by James Leo Herlihy.

Moonlight (US: 2016) story by Tarell Alvin McCraney, screenplay by Barry Jenkins.

Mulholland Drive (US: 2001) written by David Lynch.

The Music Room (India: 1958) script by Satyajit Ray.

Night Of The Hunter (US: 1955) screenplay by James Agee, based on the novel by Davis Grubb.

Night of the Living Dead (US: 1968) screenplay by John Russo and George A. Romero.

No Country for Old Men (US: 2007) screenplay by Joel Cohen and Ethan Cohen, based on the novel by Cormac McCarthy.

Nosferatu (1922) screenplay by Henrik Galeem, based on the novel by Bram Stoker.

Performance (UK:1970) written by Donald Cammell.

Pickpocket (France: 1959) written by Robert Bresson.

Poetry (South Korea: 2010) written by Lee Chang-Dong.

Precious (US: 2009) screenplay by Geoffrey Fletcher, based on the novel by Sapphire.

Secrets and Lies (UK: 1996) written by Mike Leigh.

A Separation (Iran: 2011) written by Asghar Farhadi.

The Servant (UK: 1963) screenplay by Harold Pinter, based on the novel by Robin Maugham.

Seven Samurai (Japan: 1954) screenplay by Akira Kurosawa, Shinobu Hashimoto and Hideo Oguni.

A Short Film About Killing (Poland: 1988) written by Krzysztof Kieslowski and Krzysztof Piesiewicz.

A Short Film About Love (Poland: 1988) written by Krzysztof Kieslowski and Krzysztof Piesiewicz.

Sideways (US: 2004) screenplay by Alexander Payne and Jim Taylor, based on the novel by Rex Picket.

Silence of the Lambs (US: 1991) screenplay by Ted Talley, based on the novel by Thomas Harris.

Simple Men (US: 1992) written by Hal Hartley.

The Son (Belgium/France: 2002) written by Jean-Pierre Dardenne and Luc Dardenne.

Thelma and Louise (US: 1991) written by Callie Khouri.

The Third Man (UK: 1949) screenplay by Graham Greene.

Timbuktu (France/Mauritania: 2014) written by Abderrahmane Sissako and Kessen Tall.

Tokyo Story (Japan: 1953) scenario by Koga Noda and Jasujiro Ozu.

Toni Erdman (Germany: 2016) screenplay by Maren Ade.

Toy Story (US: 1995) screenplay by Joss Wheedon, Andrew Stanton, Joel Cohen and Alex Sokolow.

Up In the Air (US: 2009) screenplay by Jason Reitman and Sheldon Turner, based on the novel by Walter Kirn.

Vagabond (France: 1985) written by Agnes Varda.

Vertigo (US: 1958) screenplay by Alec Coppel and Samuel A. Taylor, based on the novel by Pierre Boileau and Thomas Narcejac.

Vivre Sa Vie (France: 1962) story by Jean-Luc Godard, based on the book by Marcel Sacotte.

What Richard Did (Ireland: 2012) written by Malcolm Campbell, based on the book by Kevin Power.

Where Is My Friend's House (Iran: 1987) written by Abbas Kiarostami.

Winter's Bone (US: 2010) screenplay by Debra Granik and Anne Rosellini, based on the novel by Daniel Woodrell.

SHORT FILMS

L'Age D'Or (France: 1930) written by Luis Bunuel and Salvador Dali.

Alice (UK: 2010) written by Abi Morgan.

Alumbramiento (Spain: 2007) written by Eduardo Chapero-Jackson.

The Bread and Alley (Iran: 1970) written by Abbas Kiarostami.

L'Ecole Des Facteurs (France: 1947) written by Jacques Tati.

Gasman (UK: 1998) written by Lynne Ramsay.

La Jetée (France: 1962) screenplay by Chris Marker.

Natan (Sweden: 2003) written by Jonas Bergergard and Jonas Holmstrom.

Shark (UK: 1998) screenplay by David Watson.

Stutterer (UK: 2015) screenplay by Ben Cleary.

The War Begins (UK: 1984) written by Brian Dunnigan.

The War Is Over (Italy: 1997) written by Nina Mimica.

ANTHOLOGY FILMS

Amacord (Italy: 1973) screenplay by Federico Fellini and Tonino Guerra.

Coffee and Cigarettes (US: 2003) screenplay by Jim Jarmusch.

Paisa (Italy: 1946) screenplay by Sergio Amidei, Federico Fellini, Roberto Rossellini and Rod E. Geiger.

Paris Vu Par (France: 1965) written by Claude Chabrol, Jean Douchet, Jean-Luc Godard, Georges Keller, Jean Daniel Pollet, Eric Rhomer, Jean Rouch.

The Ballad of Buster Scruggs (US: 2018) written by Joel Cohen and Ethel Cohen.

FURTHER RESOURCES

Arvon Creative Writing courses: https://www.arvon.org/

BAFTA: http://www.bafta.org/

BBC Academy: https://www.bbc.co.uk/academy/en/

BBC Film Network: https://www.bbc.co.uk/programmes/

BBC Writers' Room: https://www.bbc.co.uk/writersroom/

BFI: https://www.bfi.org.uk/

Britflicks: https://britflicks.com/

Creative England: http://www.creativeengland.co.uk/

Creative Scotland: https://www.creativescotland.com/

Edinburgh International Film Festival: https://www.edfilmfest.org.uk/edinburgh-international-film-festival/

Encounters Film Festival: https://encounters-festival.org.uk/

Film London: http://filmlondon.org.uk/

4Talent Screenwriting: https://careers.channel4.com/4talent/industry-talent-schemes/4screenwriting/

Go Into The Story: https://gointothestory.blcklst.com/

Industrial Scripts: https://industrialscripts.com/

London Film School: https://lfs.org.uk/

London Screenwriters Festival: https://www.londonscreenwritersfestival.com/

My First Job in Film: https://www.myfirstjobinfilm.co.uk/

National Film and Television School: https://nfts.co.uk/

Rocliffe New Writing Forum: http://www.rocliffe.com/index.php/

Salford Media Festival: http://salfordmediafestival.co.uk/

ScreenSkills: https://www.screenskills.com/

Script Factory: https://scriptfactory.co.uk/

The Script Lab: https://thescriptlab.com/

Script Tank writing group: https://scripttank.info/

Shooting People: https://shootingpeople.org/

Women in Film and Television: https://wftv.org.uk/

Writers Guild UK: https://writersguild.org.uk/

Writers Guild of America: https://www.wga.org/

SCREENPLAYS ON-LINE

BBC Writers' Room Scripts: https://www.bbc.co.uk/writersroom/scripts

Daily Script: https://www.dailyscript.com

Drew's Script O Rama: http://www.script-o-rama.com/

Simply Scripts: https://www.simplyscripts.com/

SOFTWARE

Final Draft: https://www.finaldraft.com/

INDEX